IMAGES
of America

GLENDORA
CALIFORNIA

IMAGES of America

GLENDORA CALIFORNIA

John David Landers

ARCADIA PUBLISHING

ISBN 978-0-7385-0826-9

Published by Arcadia Publishing,
Charleston, South Carolina

Printed in the United States of America

Library of Congress Catalog Card Number: 2001087305

For all general information contact Arcadia Publishing at:
Telephone 843-853-2070
Fax 843-853-0044
E-Mail sales@arcadiapublishing.com
For customer service and orders:
Toll-Free 1-888-313-2665

Visit us on the Internet at www.arcadiapublishing.com

Contents

ACKNOWLEDGMENTS

Researching and compiling the photographs for a book like this is not a one-person job. It takes many individuals' help and stories about those pictures to help make them come to life. This was the case for me as I started researching this project.

I would like to thank the Glendora Historical Society for the generous donation of many of the images used throughout this book. The photo archivist, Georgia Hawthorne, was very helpful in digging through the archives and explaining the background on each picture. Many Sunday afternoons were spent in the museum sifting through piles of pictures.

It's not enough to find the picture and have the image explained. What makes a photo come alive is the story behind the picture. I have to thank Bobbie Battler for the hours she spent telling me the stories of the people of Glendora, taking me to various historical spots, and allowing me to comb through her personal collection of photos for use in this project.

Many of the historic buildings in Glendora are still around and in use, but trying to find out a building's exact use today after many face-lifts is challenging. I couldn't have done it without the many phone conversations with the City of Glendora Public Relations Office and Catherine Starkey.

I have learned more about the impact sprinkler than I ever thought possible. I have to thank the Rain Bird Corporation for all of their help with finding out about this unique invention and the history it played here in Glendora.

Scanning these pictures and documents into the computer took many tedious hours, but the help of one of my former students, Nick Robles, made the task go faster. Thanks.

--I must thank my mother for many evenings of typing allowing me to do my "teacher thing": grading. You have shown the pioneer spirit this past year with your fight to defeat cancer.

I also must thank my wife for putting up with the messy office at home with pictures and papers littering the floor. You are the best proofreader anyone could marry. Thanks!

INTRODUCTION

The City of Glendora has been part of the colorful and exciting history of the San Gabriel Valley in southern California. It has taken part in many different growth and expansion cycles like many of the cities around it. It has swallowed up some of the smaller, less-profitable towns such as Alosta. It has kept many of the values of midwestern America but has benefitted from close proximity to large metropolises like Pasadena and Los Angeles which offer the industry and cultural experiences not found in small town America.

The earliest Native-American inhabitants of the valley found their needs supplied by the resources in the area. These people were called Gabrielinos and were probably an offshoot of the Soshone tribe. They lived in small brush homes called *jacales* and lived together in small family groups called *rancerias*. One can still find evidence of these early Native-American inhabitants in the form of arrowheads and cooking items in the hills around Glendora.

The San Gabriel Valley area grew up under the influence of the Spanish mission system with the location of the San Gabriel Mission just 15 miles east of present-day Glendora. Most of the land from present-day Los Angeles to San Bernadineo was considered mission land. The Spanish explorer Juan Bautista de Anza passed through the area in 1774 on his way to the San Gabriel Mission, watering his sheep, cattle, and horses at a place called Mud Springs—the present-day city of San Dimas.

Many of the small farms and rancheros in the area were once owned by Spanish settlers who had obtained large land grants from the Spanish Government. As the mission period faded into history and American influence dawned in the mid-1800s, the landscape became dotted with the small farms of settlers from the east. One cycle of change was completed.

One easterner who had a large influence on the area of Glendora and Azusa was Henry Dalton. He came to the area in 1843, and in three amazing years he established commercial accounts with practically every leading citizen in the area. His goal was to build a large ranch somewhere in the area. Dalton was able to take advantage of the revolutionary troubles that California was embroiled in with Mexico at the time and purchased his ranch, Rancho Azusa, from one of the early Spanish settlers, Luis Arenas, for $1,000 which Arenas owed the Mexican Government. Dalton's new ranch was some 3 leagues in size.

Dalton developed vineyards, tanneries, various crops, and cattle herds and engaged in many of the other activities that one would find on large hacendados in southern California. With the growth of his ranch, he employed many *vaqueros*, carpenters, tanners, and farm laborers.

He built one of the first small communities in the area. Dalton's fortunes didn't last, however. The Mexican American War of 1846–48 brought California into the United States. It destroyed Dalton's trading empire, and various bad business dealings in the gold fields and a crooked land survey by the United States in 1858 helped to end his empire along the San Gabriel River. The foundation was laid for another change in the Glendora area.

In the 1870s the San Gabriel Valley area saw many new settlements spring up. Pasadena, 15 miles west of Glendora, was launched by an organization called the California Colony of Indiana. The city of Pomona to the southeast and other small cities began to appear.

The early settlers of the Glendora area wanted to create civilization in this new community. Many businesses started; stores, blacksmith shops, and a few churches appeared among the scattered houses and roads that began dotting the area. They also started a one-room schoolhouse at the site of the Dalton homestead, the present-day location of Barranca and Dalton Ave. It was named La Fetra School because of its location near the La Fetra residence. Its enrollment grew to 30 pupils, "some of them grown men with mustaches and beards" (Jackson,13).

The 1870s brought many new settlers, including some of the future leaders of the city that would be called Glendora: William Bryant Cullen, John Bender, John P. Engelhardt, La Fetra, Wamsley, Kamphefner, Suydam, and Warren. All of these people played important roles in the development of Glendora, which is testified to by their names being used for many of the buildings and streets in the city. But it took a person with a vision to promote and organize the development of a town. George D. Whitcomb, a Chicago industrialist, came west in 1884 for his health and settled in the San Gabriel Valley. He purchased his first property at the north end of present-day Glendora Avenue. He purchased more property until he eventually owned 200 acres which would become the city of Glendora.

One thing that helped to make the city of Glendora possible was the development of the railroad. Whitcomb persuaded C.M. Smith—a friend and the president of the Atlantic and Pacific Railroad (The Santa Fe)—to run a line along the foothills and right through Glendora. This played an important part in the development of the citrus industry that would dominate the area from the late 1890s until the 1940s.

In 1923 the Glendora Citrus Association and the Glendora Heights Orange and Lemon Growers Association joined to establish the Glendora Fruit Exchange and built their own packing house. The local newspaper, *The Glendora Gleaner*, claimed that "this packing house is the largest citrus fruit packing house in the world with equipment and facilitates good for a pack each season of from 1,500 to 2,000 carloads of 400 packed boxes each" (*Glendora Gleaner*, Aug. 10, 1921).

With the production of over a million boxes of fruit annually and its numerous packing houses, Glendora could be considered one of the citrus capitals in the state of California. Glendora had the distinct honor of having the White House in Washington D.C. place an order for oranges to be shipped to President Taft once a month.

By 1950 the Glendora citrus industry was struck by a tree disease called "quick decline." First noticed in 1940, this malady caused the fruit to shrivel up and dry out and the tree to slowly die. This, along with the rising costs of labor and water, helped to draw a close the the citrus industry in the area.

Even though the citrus industry is gone and only a few reminders can be seen in buildings or antique farm equipment, Glendora's heritage has survived and helped to develop a strong and vibrant city that today is an important part of the Los Angeles basin.

One

The Beginning

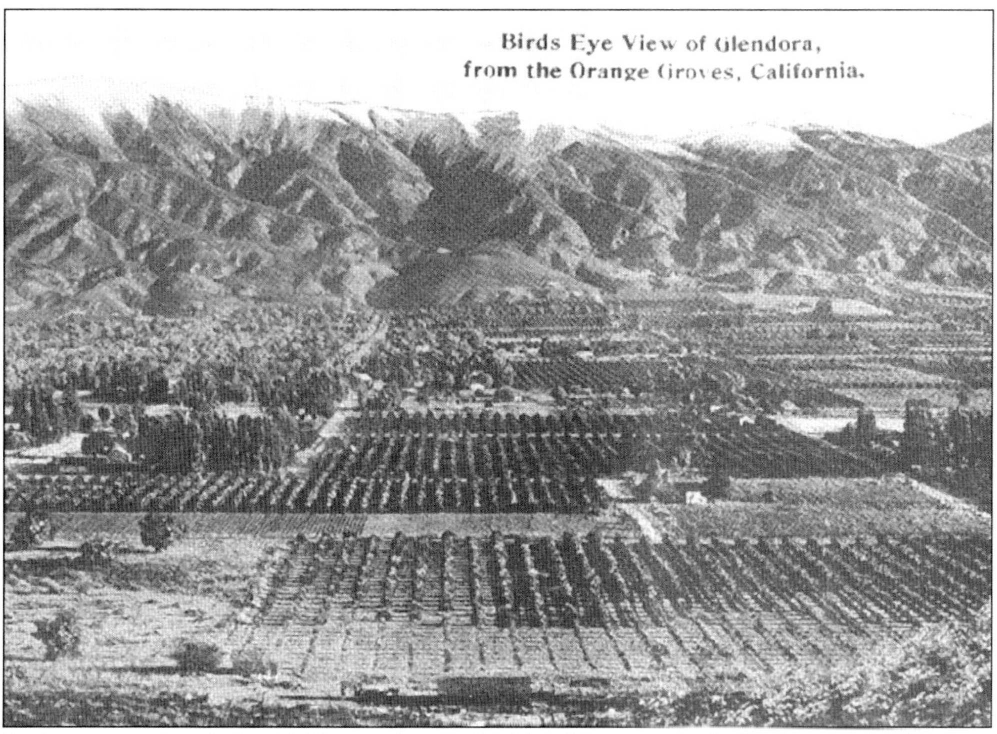

Early postcards of the 1900s tried to sell Glendora to people back east by showing sunshine, citrus groves, and space, as seen in this birds-eye view of Glendora. (Glendora Historical Society.)

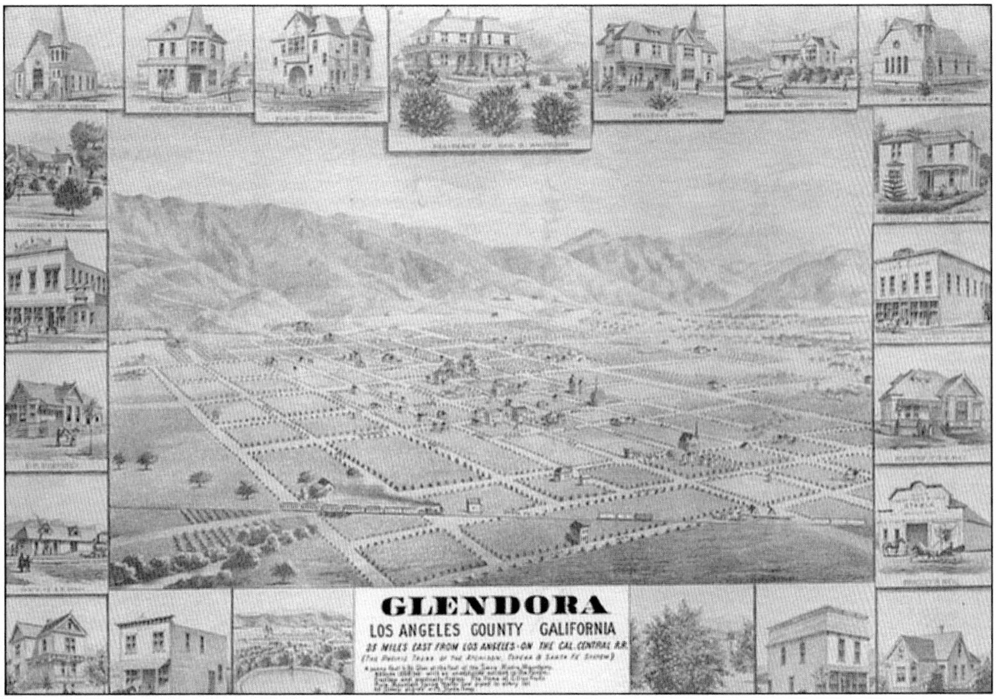

To sell the land and an image, an early map from the land office showing Glendora and the prominent families. (Glendora Historical Society.)

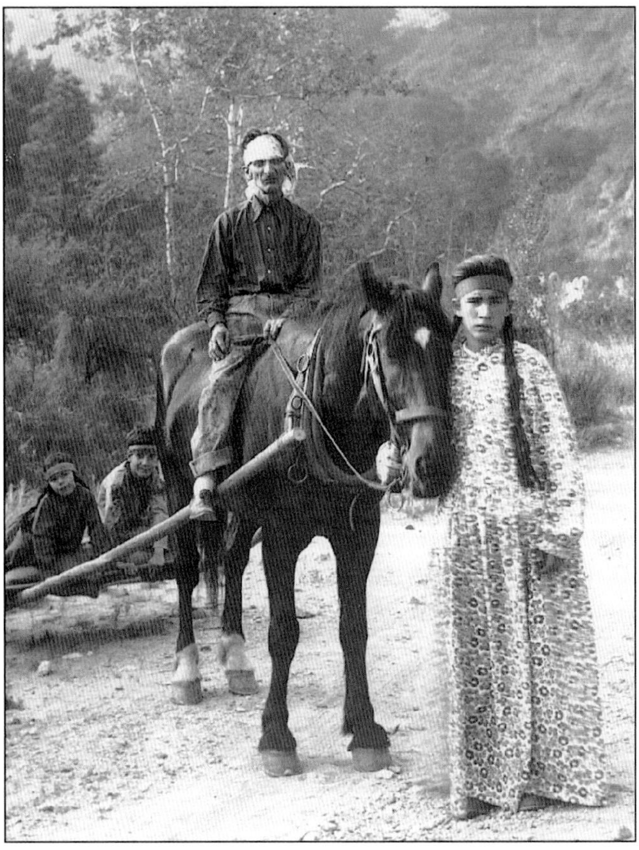

The early settlers of the Glendora area were Gabrialeno Indians—an offshoot of the Shoshone tribe. One can still find arrowheads and cooking objects in the hills around the city. (B. Battler.)

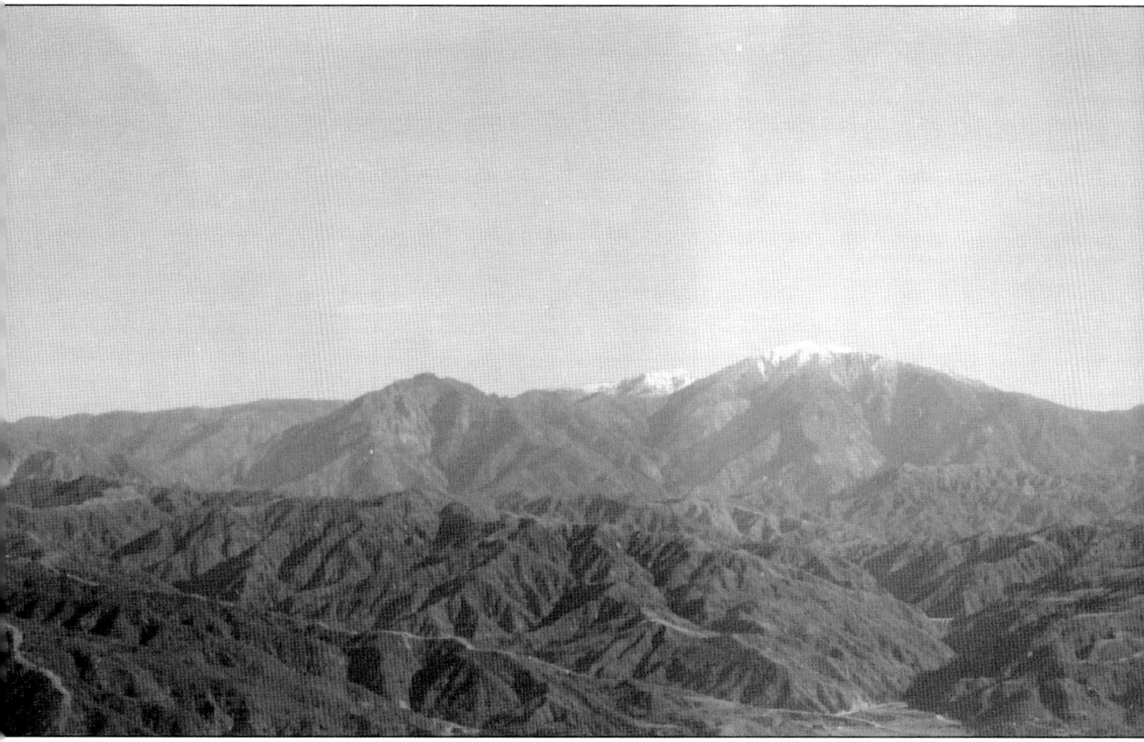

One of the selling points and prominent land features that was used to entice people to come to the Glendora area was the scenic views of the San Gabriel Mountains in winter: a little snow and a lot of sunshine. (B. Battler)

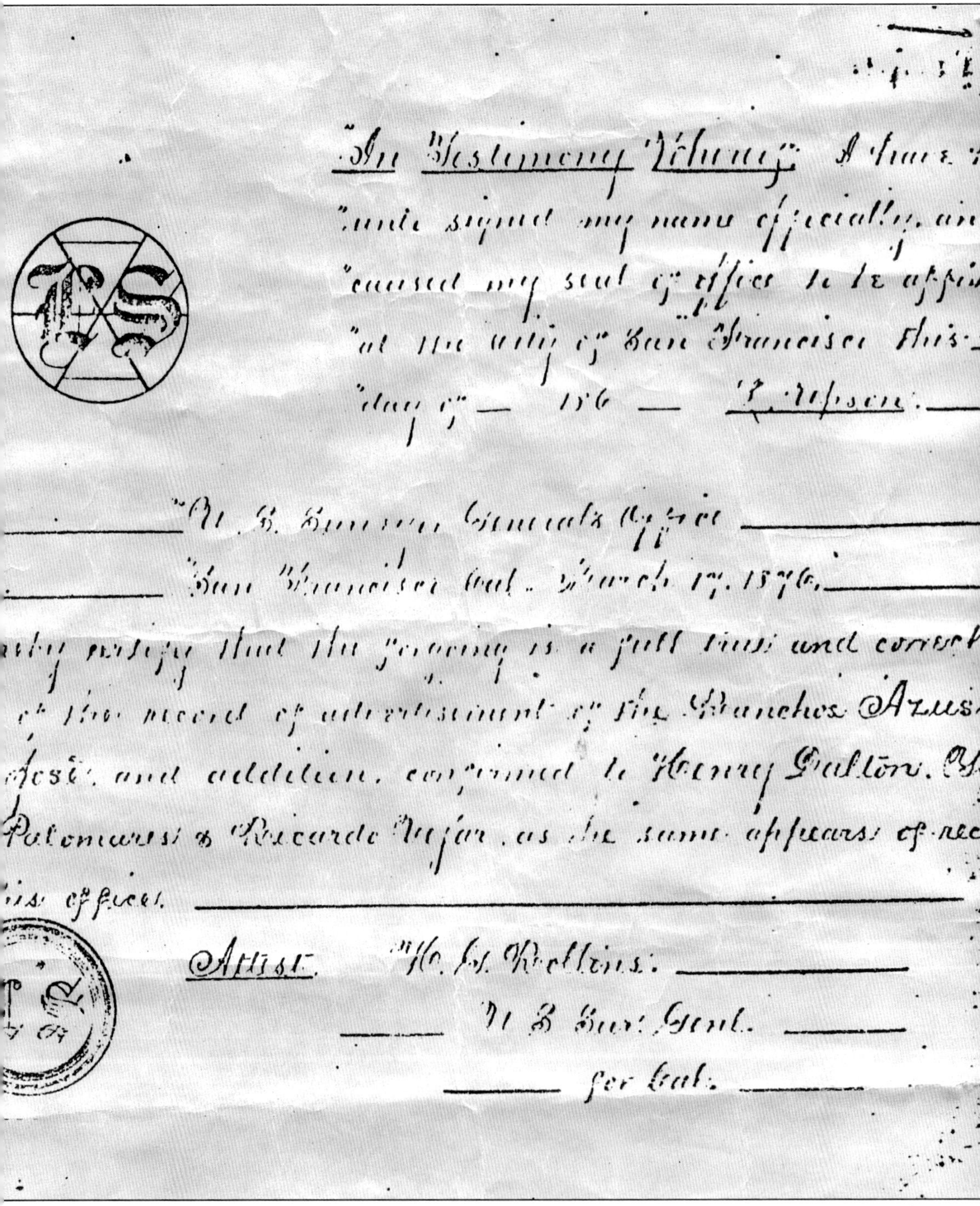

"In Testimony Whereof" I have hereunto signed my name officially and caused my seal of office to be affixed at the City of San Francisco this day of — 186 — [illegible]

"U.S. Surveyor General's Office
San Francisco Cal. March 17. 1876.

[illegible] certify that the foregoing is a full true and correct [illegible] of the record of advertisement of the Ranchos Azusa, [illegible] and addition, confirmed to Henry Dalton. [illegible] Palomares & Ricardo Vejar as the same appears of record [in th]is office.

Attest. H. G. Rollins:
U.S. Sur: Genl.
for Cal.

Pictured is the deed that was given to Henry Dalton by the United States Government after the Mexican-American War. (B. Battler.)

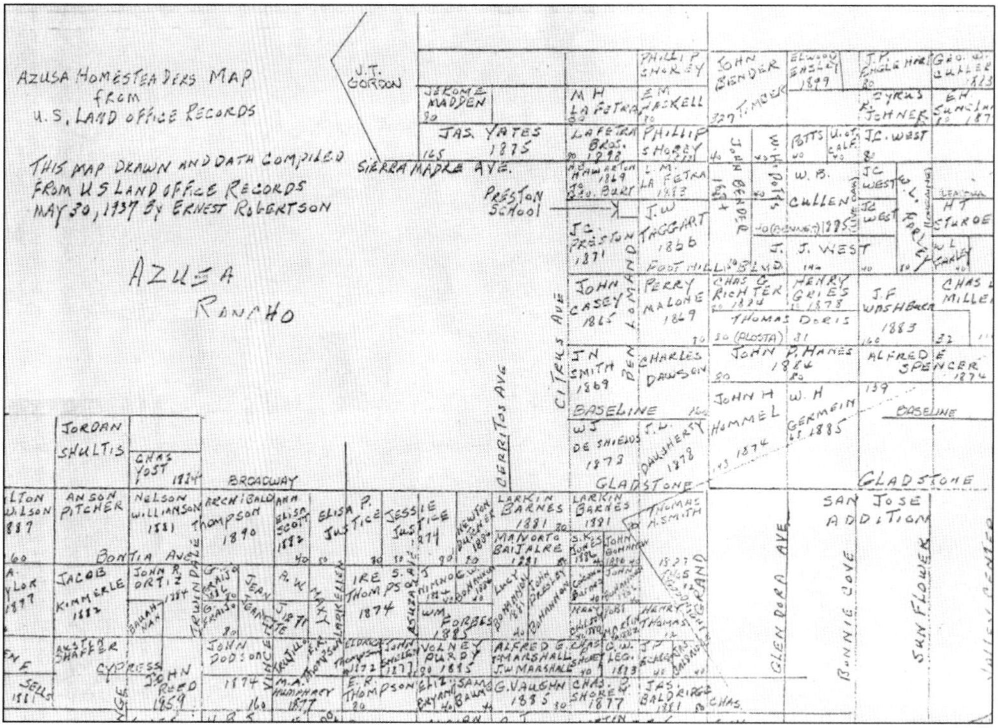

This is a parcel map of the Glendora/Azusa area showing the division of Henry Dalton's land after he lost most of it because of taxes owed to the U.S. Government. (B. Battler.)

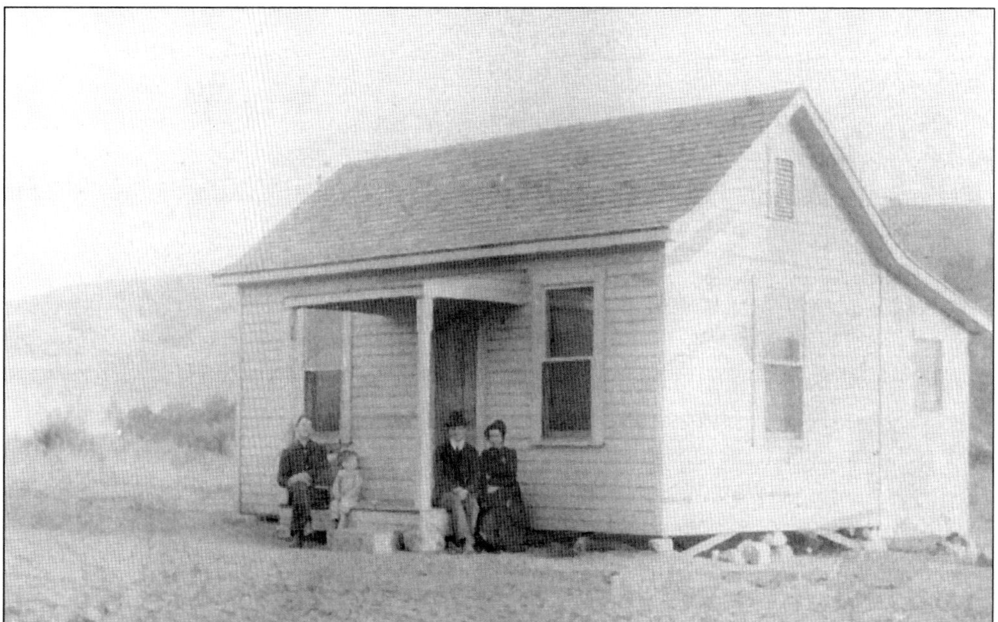
The Dietler House was owned by one of the original homesteaders in the Glendora area. It was located at what is now the site of Citrus Community College on Citrus Ave. (Glendora Historical Society.)

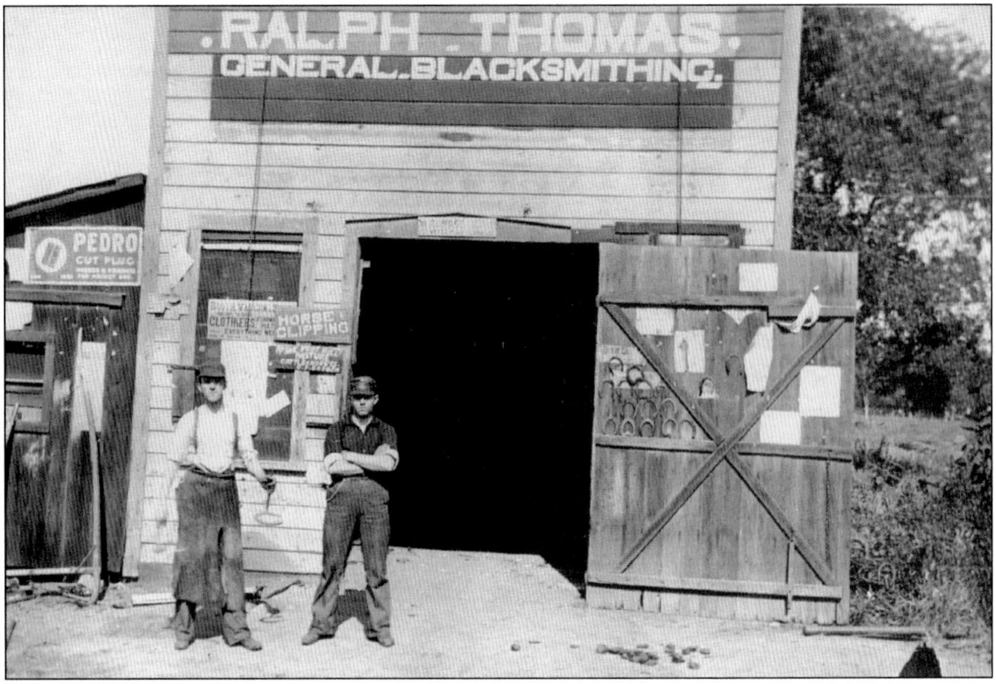

Ralph Thomas's blacksmith shop served the needs of the community that would later grow into the towns of Glendora, Alosta, and Azusa. The early businesses of the area were established to meet the needs of the area farmers. Many of these would later become the founding businesses of these towns. (Glendora Historical Society.)

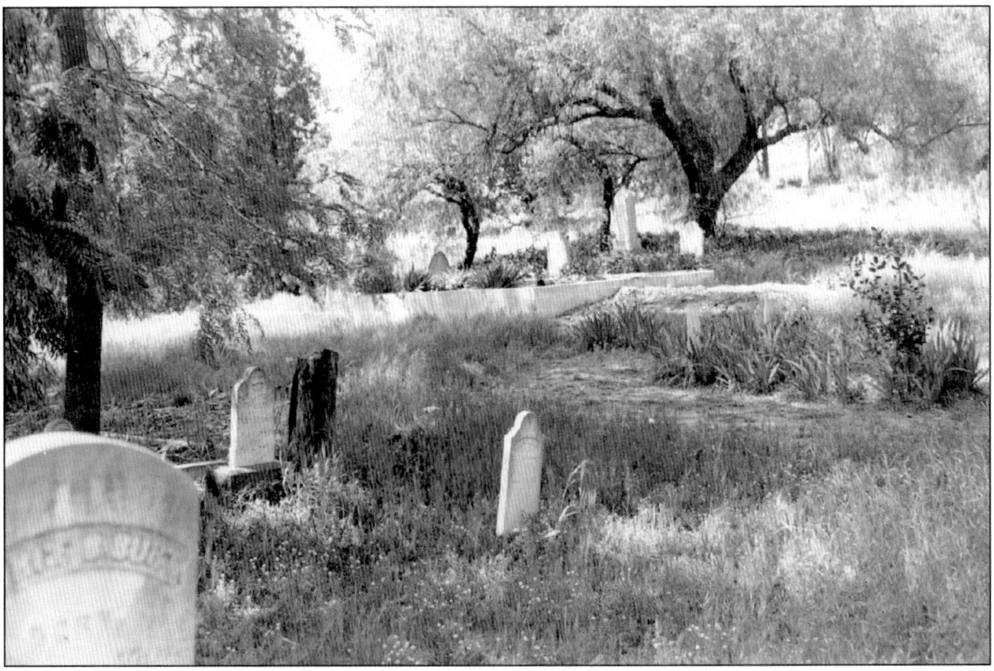

Used by the local communities of Azusa, Alosta, and Glendora, the Fairmont Cemetery became the resting place of many of the early settlers. (Glendora Historical Society.)

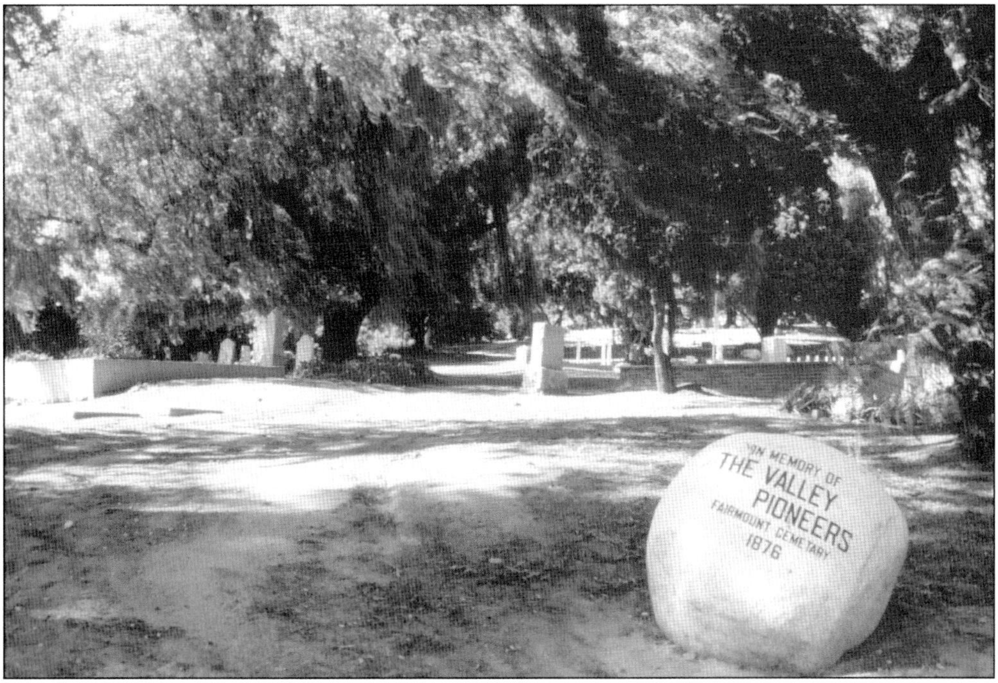

Pictured is the dedication marker for the Valley Pioneers at the Fairmont Cemetery. (Glendora Historical Society.)

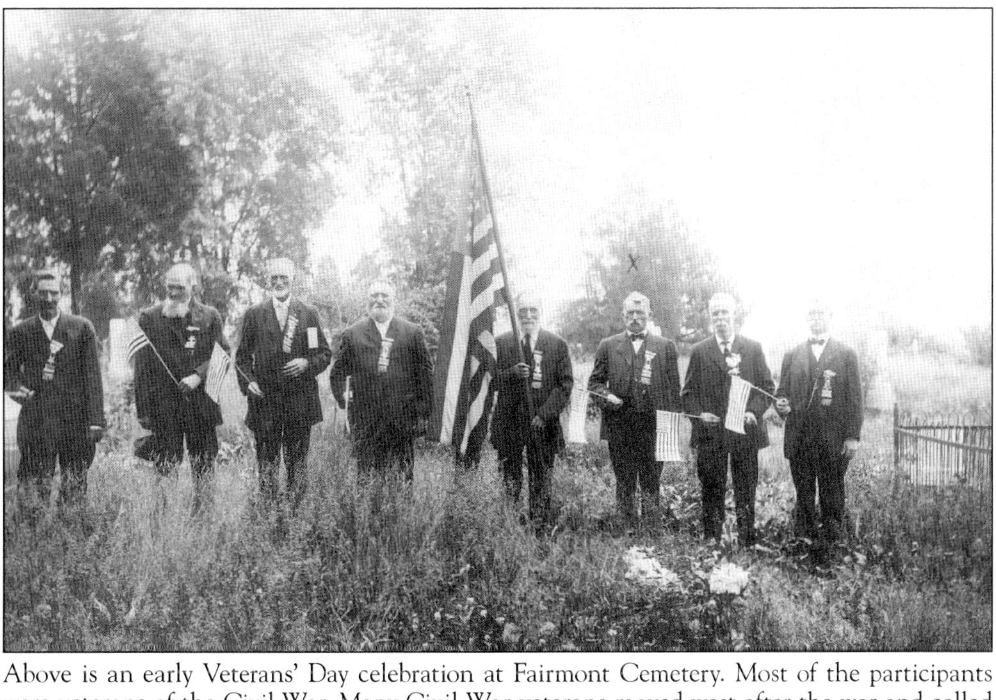

Above is an early Veterans' Day celebration at Fairmont Cemetery. Most of the participants were veterans of the Civil War. Many Civil War veterans moved west after the war and called the San Gabriel Valley area home. (Glendora Historical Society.)

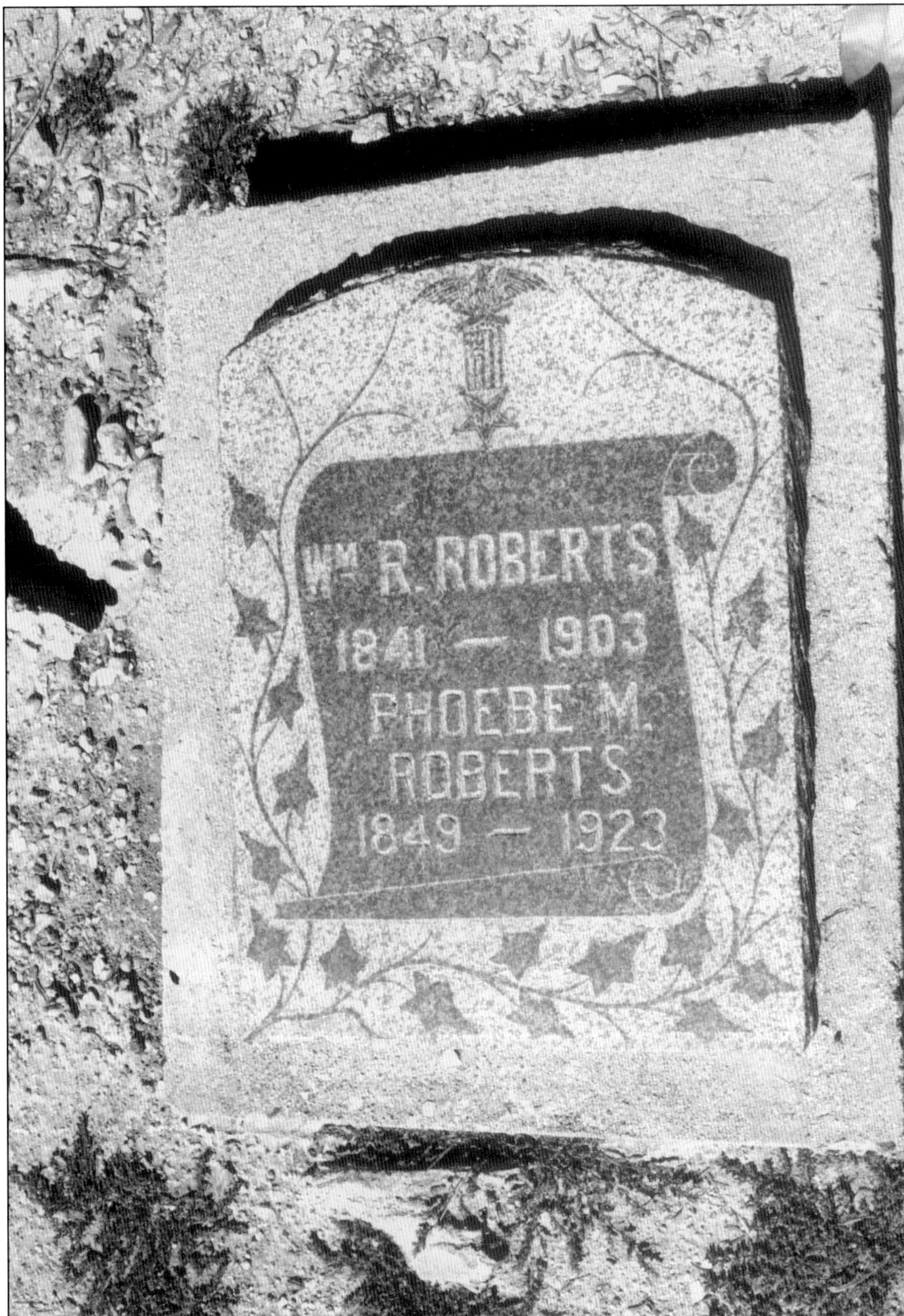

Pictured here is the grave marker of William Roberts and his wife Phoebe. Roberts was a veteran of the Civil War and an early settler of the Glendora area. Many other brave veterans started a new life here in the Glendora area, far from the war-torn East, after the war. (J. Landers.)

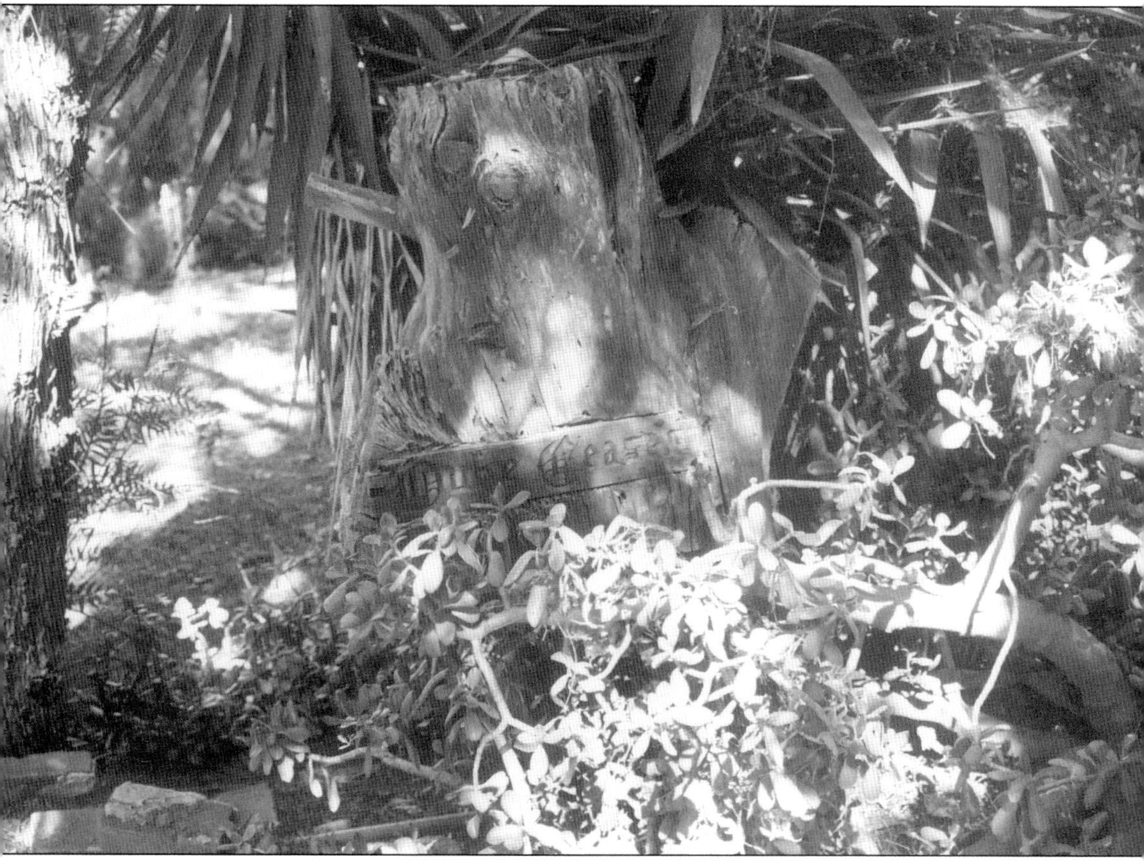

Throughout America, there are strange stories about local cemeteries. Fairmont Cemetery is not without its own. Mike Ceaser, "the man buried in the tree," is one of Fairmont's stories. When asked where he wanted to be buried when he died, he said "In a tree." His wife placed his urn in a small tree at the cemetery, and it eventually grew up around the urn, completely encasing it inside. It is said that he is still inside the tree today. (J. Landers.)

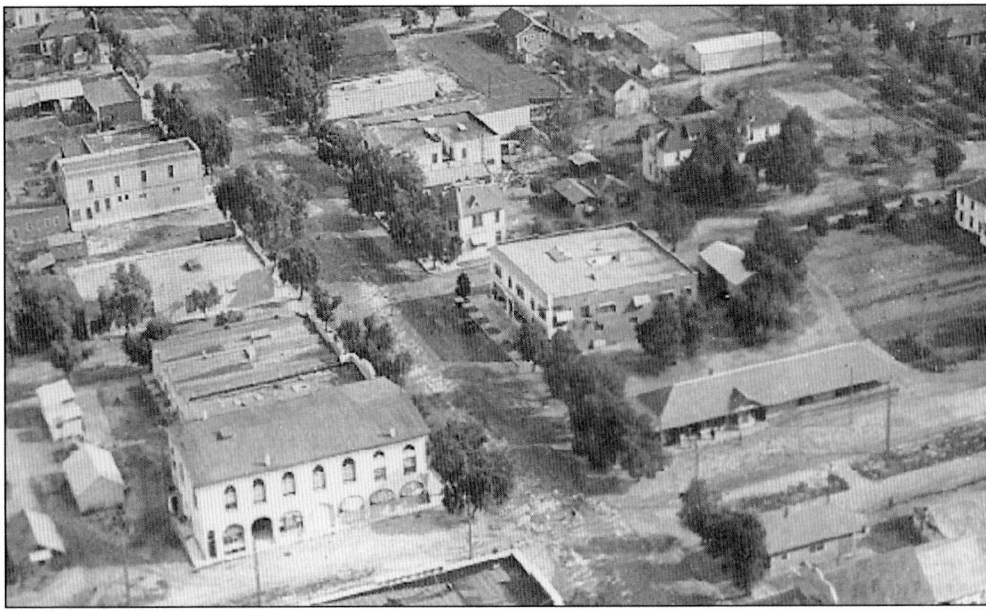

Here is a birds-eye view of the business district of the growing city. (Glendora Historical Society.)

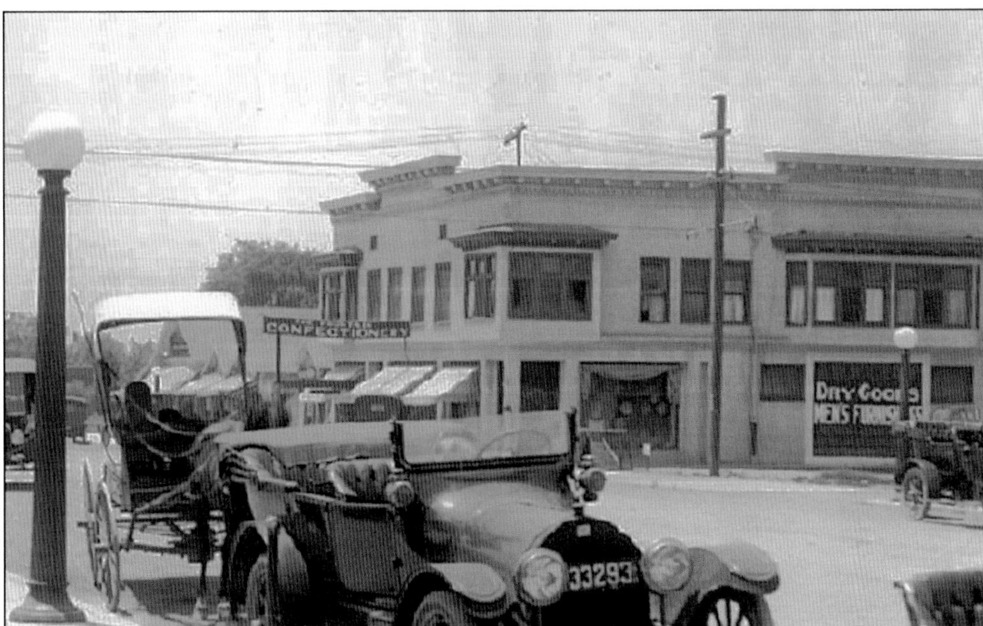

As the business district grew, the city fathers saw the need for electric lights on the streets. (Glendora Historical Society.)

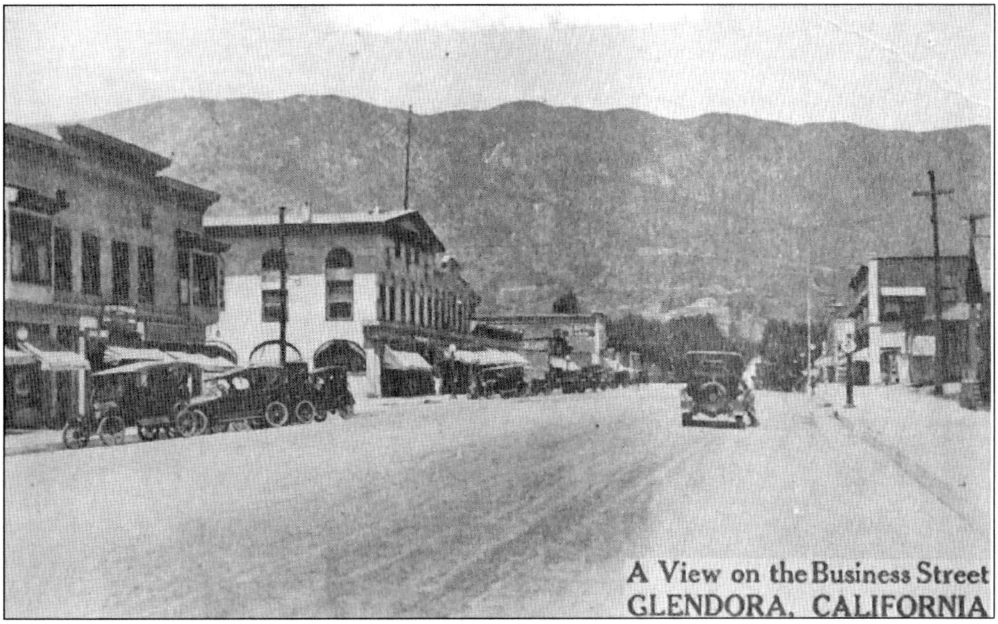

A postcard *c.* 1918 shows the business district of Glendora facing north on Glendora Ave. (Glendora Historical Society.)

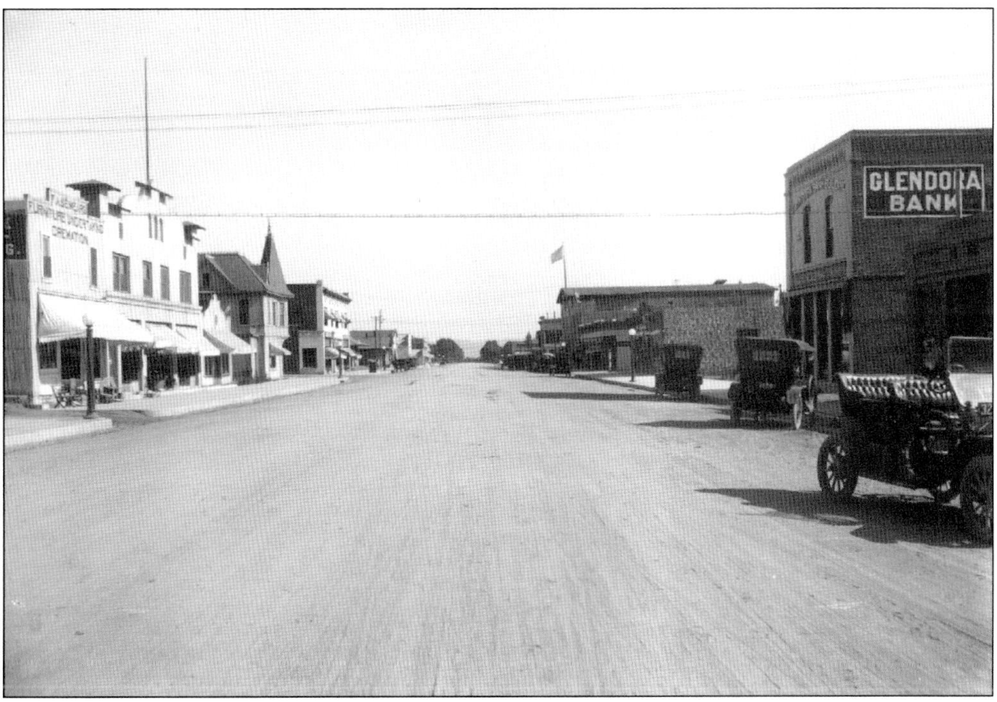

This picture of the business district in 1918 shows the bank of Glendora and the new horse-less carriages.

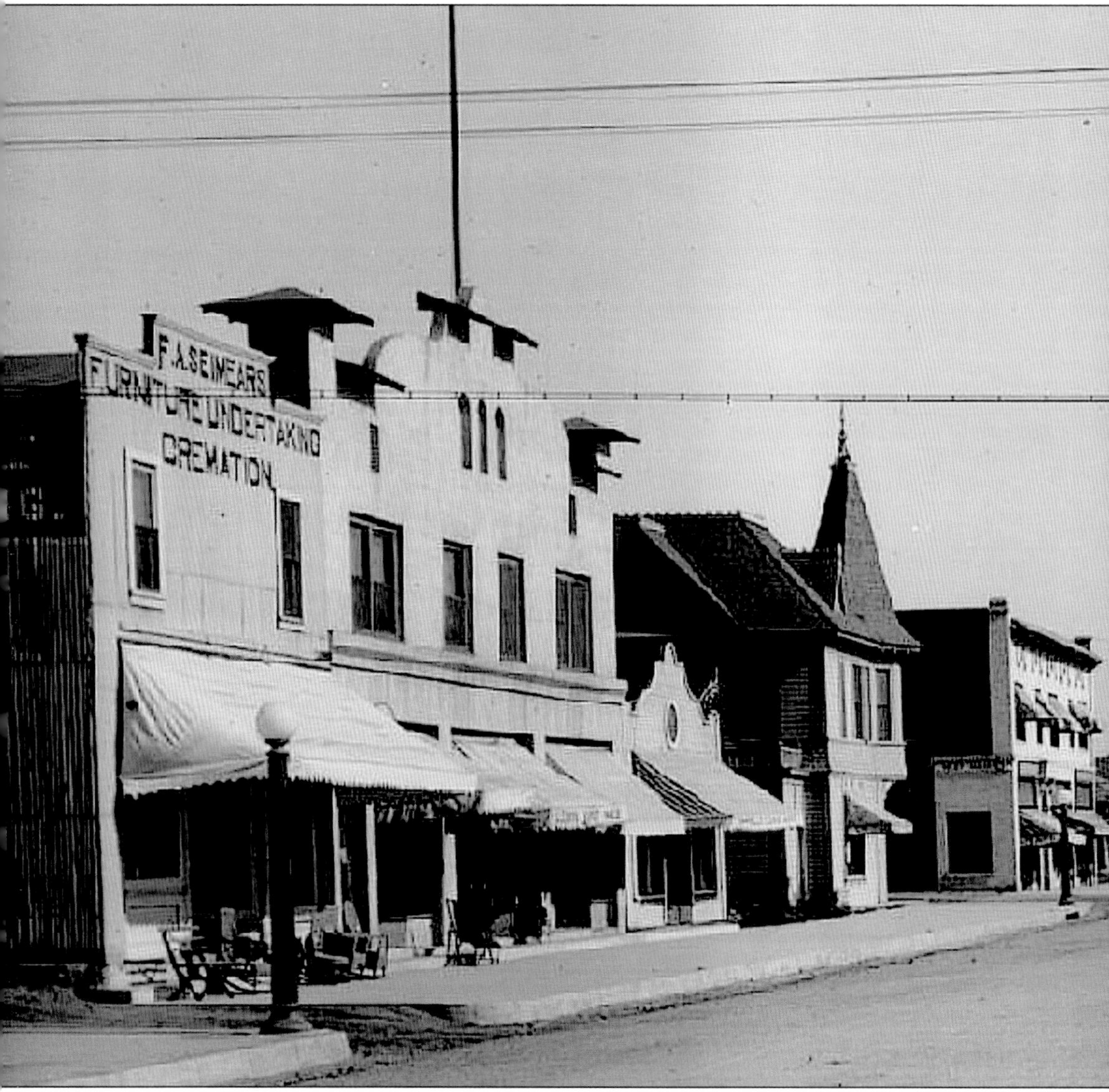

Like many undertakers throughout the west, as F.A. Seimers was also a furniture maker. (Glendora Historical Society.)

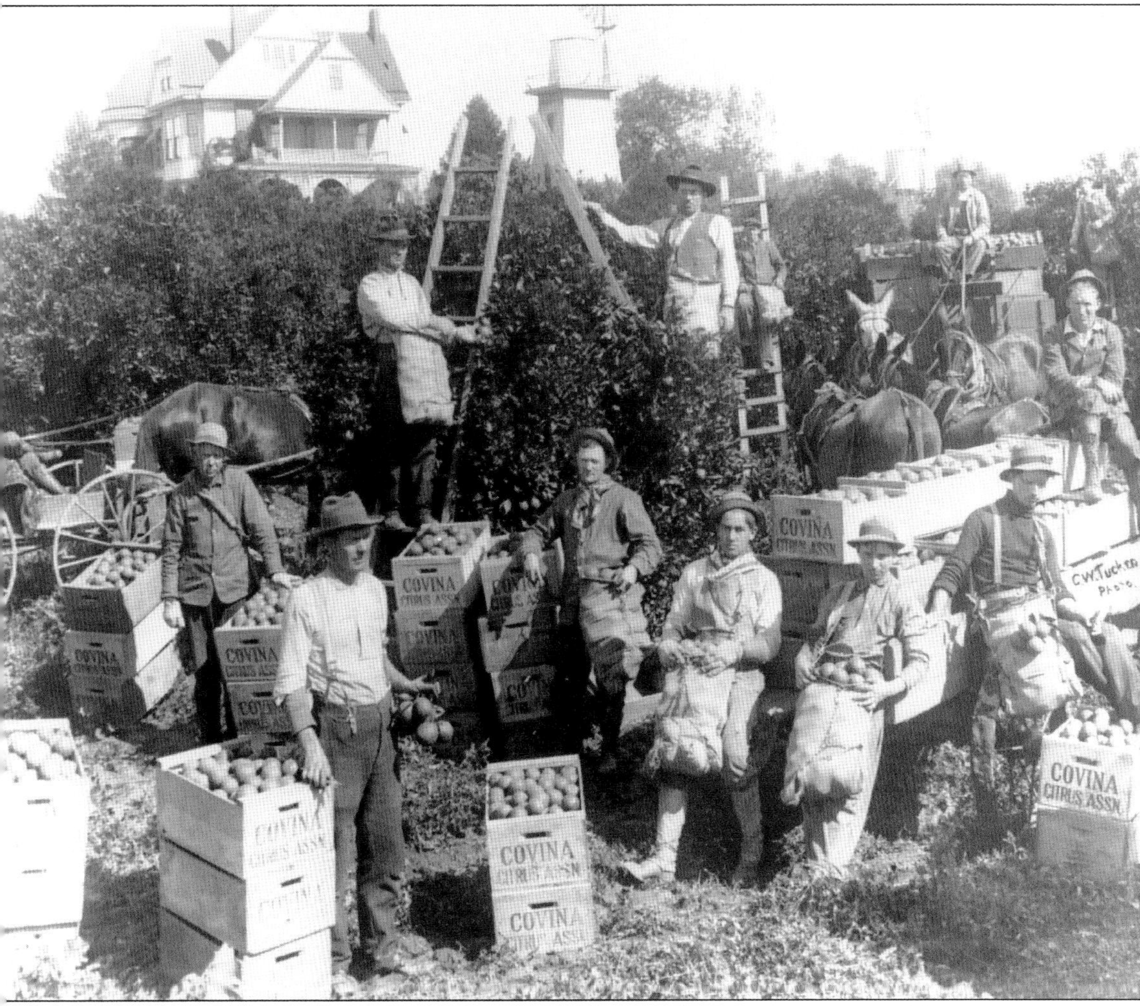

In the early 1900s, if one drove down nearly any road in the Glendora area one would have noticed many scenes like this one of laborers picking the citrus crop. (Glendora Historical Society.)

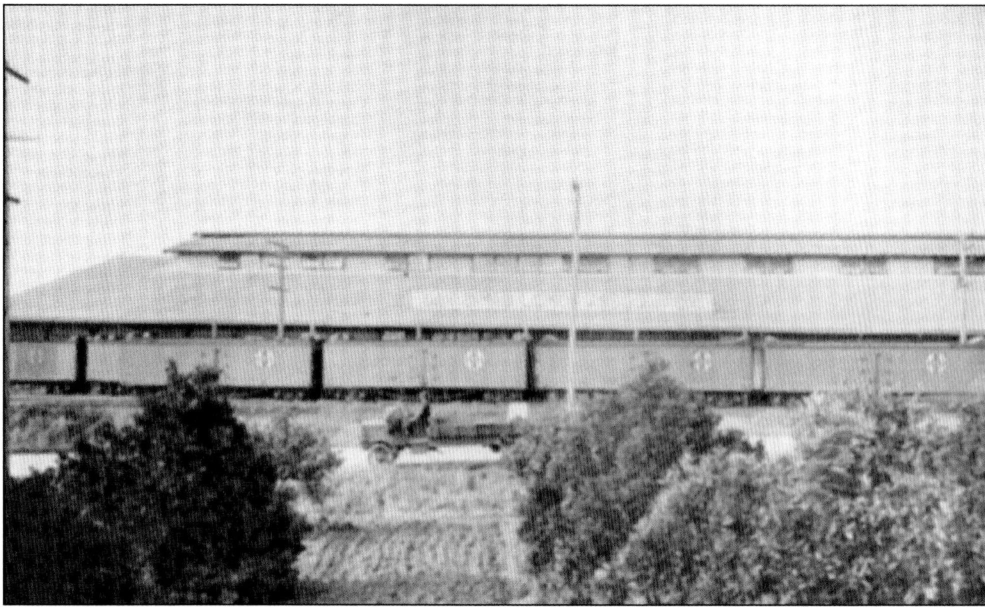

Citrus is being transported by rail from one of the many packing houses in Glendora in this c. 1920s image. (B. Battler.)

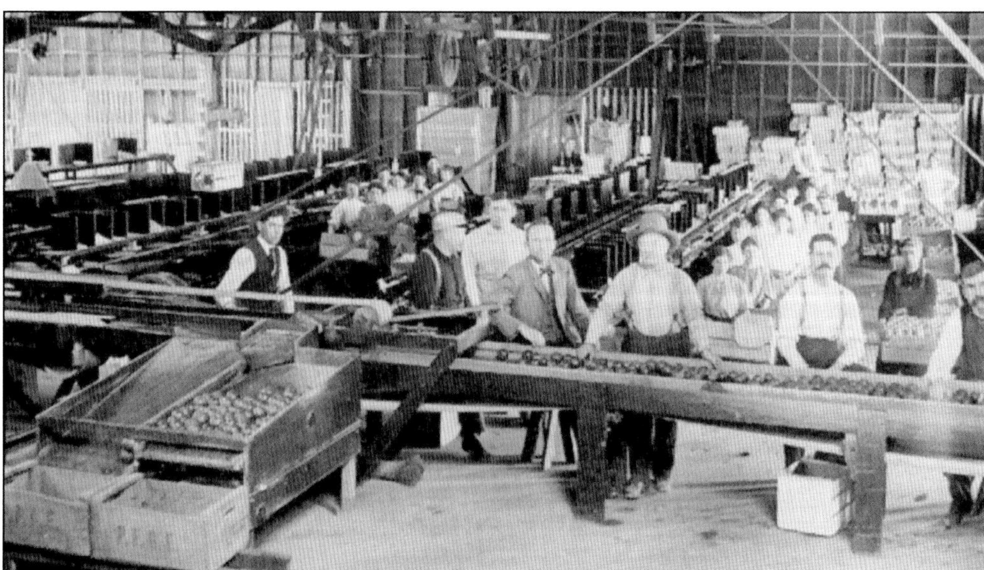

Pictured is a citrus packing plant in Glendora, 1910. (B. Battler.)

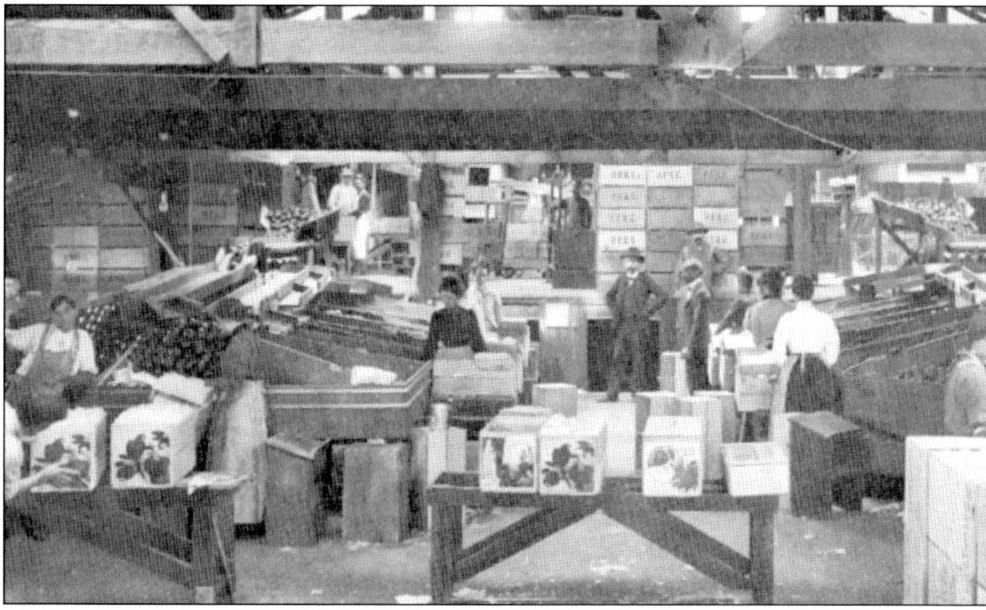

Jobs outside of the home for women included packing citrus into shipping crates in one of the many packing houses in the area. (Glendora Historical Society.)

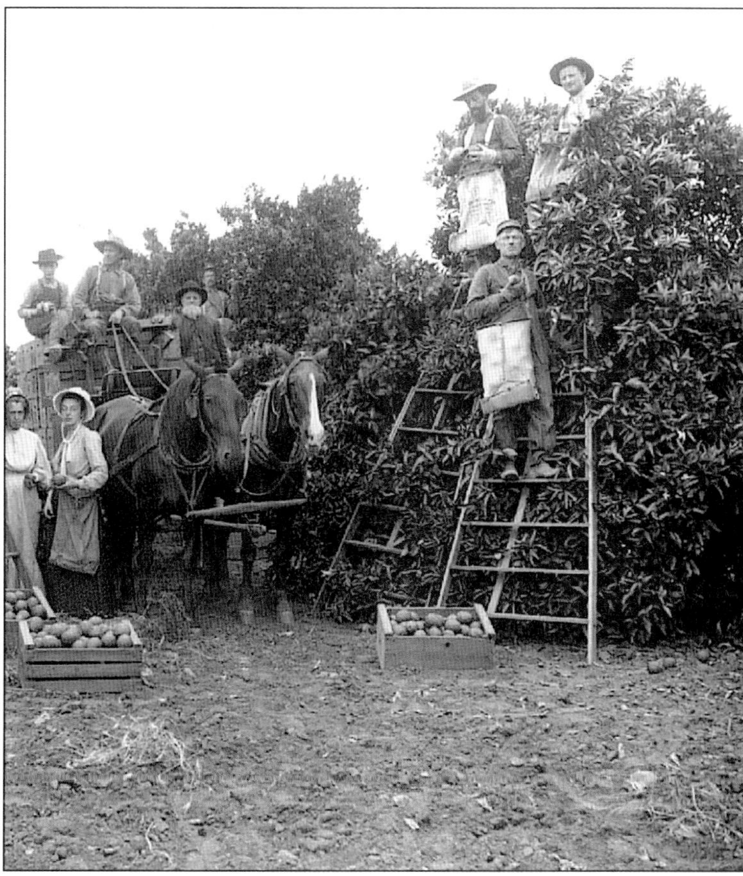

In addition to the large citrus ranches in and around Glendora, there were many small, family-run orchards. The entire family worked during the harvest season, c. 1900. (Glendora Historical Society.)

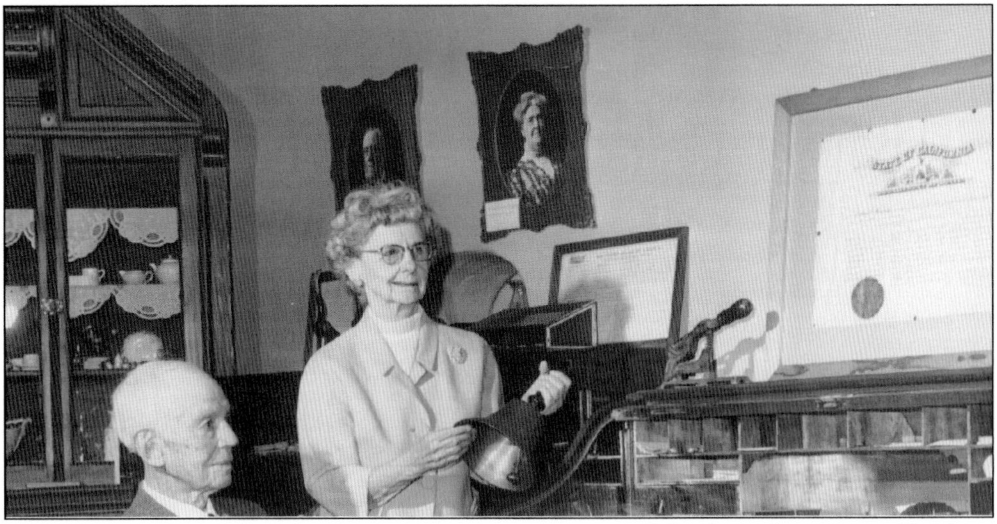

At the dedication of the Glendora Historical Society, one of the first educators in Glendora, Grace Sutherland, donates one of the original "teachers bells" to the museum in 1982. (Glendora Historical Society.)

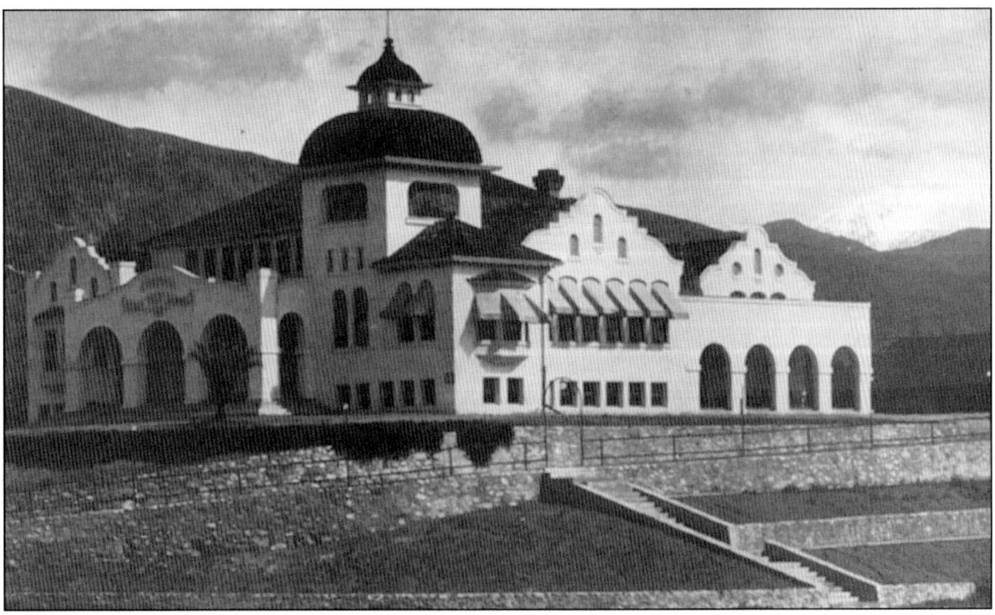

In 1901 Citrus Union High School was the only school for the surrounding areas of Covina, Glendora, Azusa, and Charter Oak. (Glendora Historical Society.)

William B. Cullen—one of the original settlers of Glendora—moved from Memphis, Tennessee, to the L.A. area after the Civil War. He found and purchased a small, dirt-floored shack a short distance north of the future town of Glendora and made it his homestead. He would later buy 160 acres and build his permanent home. (Glendora Historical Society.)

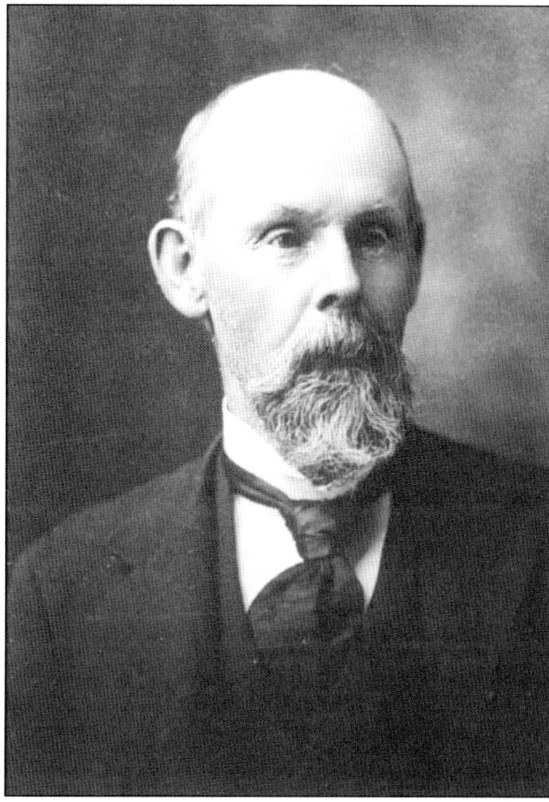

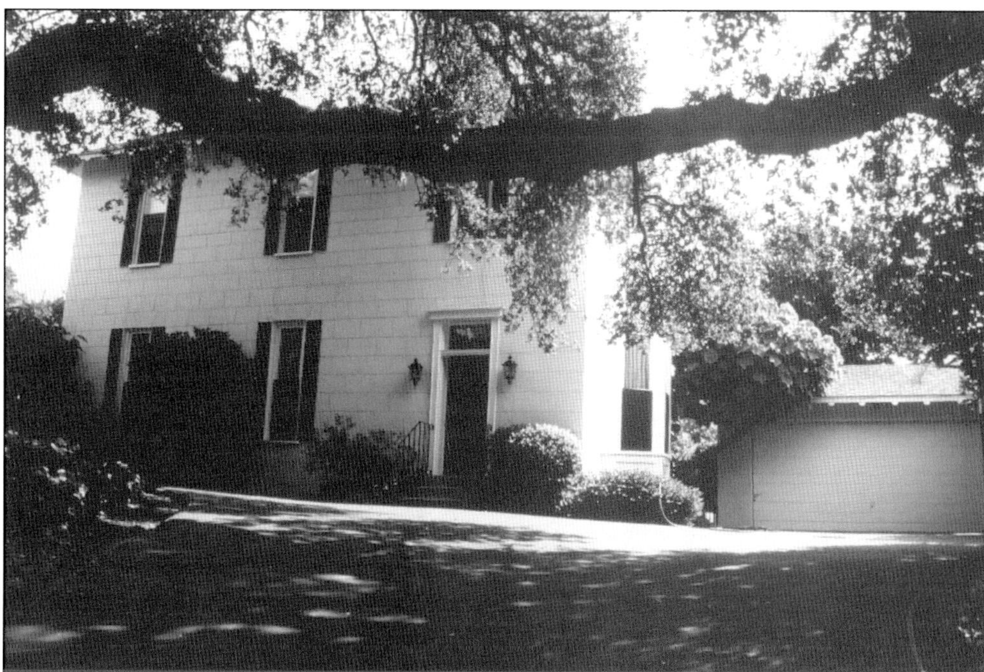

The Bender home can still be seen today and shows how prosperous John Bender's dream was. (Glendora Historical Society.)

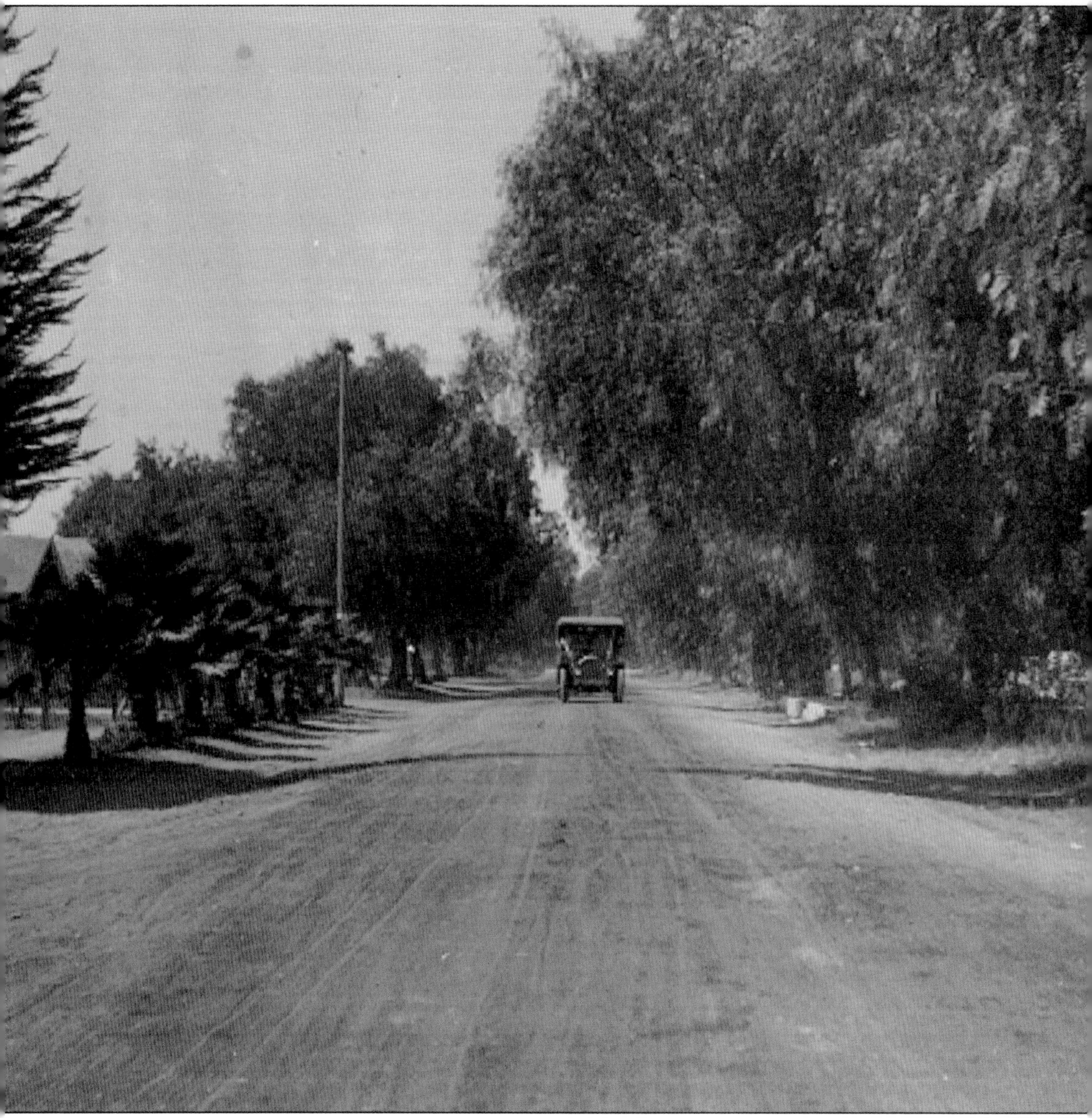

As Glendora moved out of the 19th century and into the 20th century, changes could be seen in the forms of transportation used by the local citizenry. A Model-T is driven down a dirt road in a citrus orchard. (Glendora Historical Society.)

Two

BUILDING A DREAM

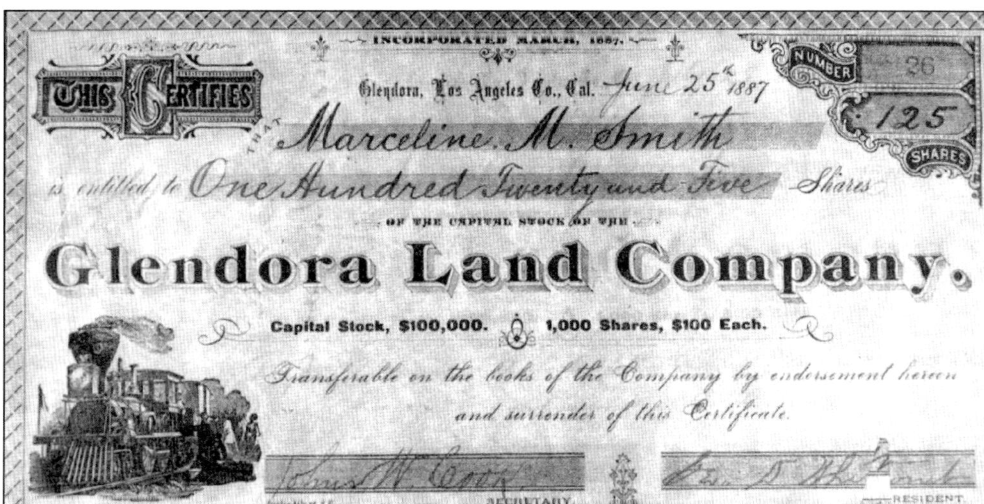
INCORPORATED MARCH, 1887.

NUMBER 26

THIS CERTIFIES

Glendora, Los Angeles Co., Cal. June 25th 1887

THAT Marceline M. Smith

is entitled to One Hundred Twenty and Five Shares

125 SHARES

OF THE CAPITAL STOCK OF THE

Glendora Land Company.

Capital Stock, $100,000. 1,000 Shares, $100 Each.

Transferable on the books of the Company by endorsement hereon and surrender of this Certificate.

SECRETARY.

PRESIDENT.

As land parcels/shares were sold to buyers, they received a certificate like this one from the Glendora Land Office issuing them their shares. (B. Battler.)

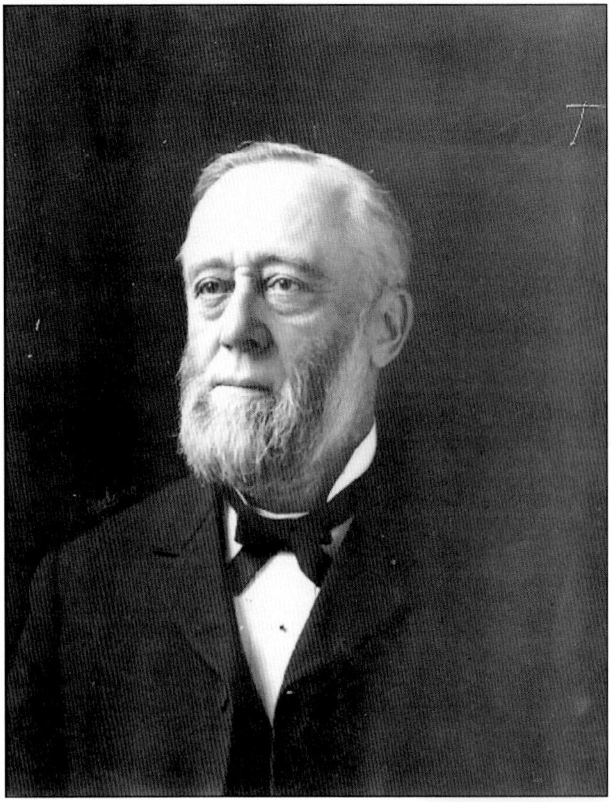

The founder of the city of Glendora was George Whitcomb. He designed his town around Christian principals and morals. He had written into each sale that the owner would not drink "hard liquor." This was an unusual prerequisite since the town just to the south, Alosta, had more saloons than any other business. Whitcomb also designed the streets of Glendora so that they would not line up with any street from Alosta. (Glendora Historical Society.)

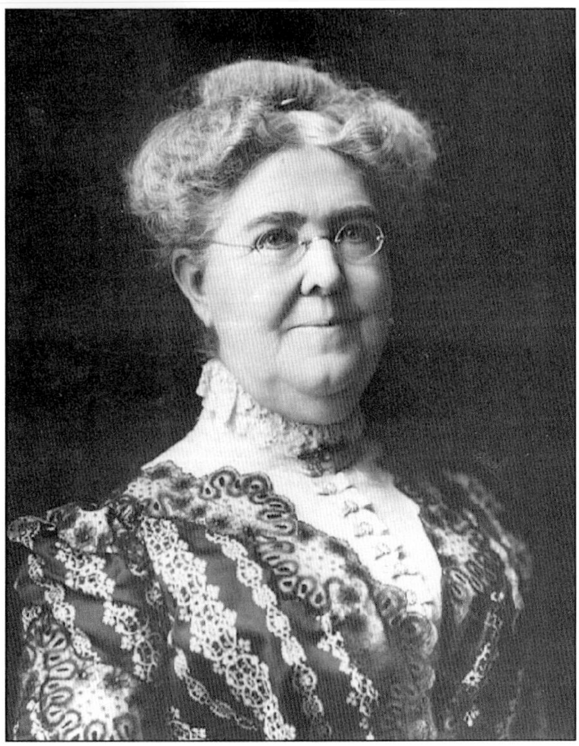

Leadora Whitcomb was the wife of George Whitcomb and her name was incorporated into the name of the city. (Glendora Historical Society.)

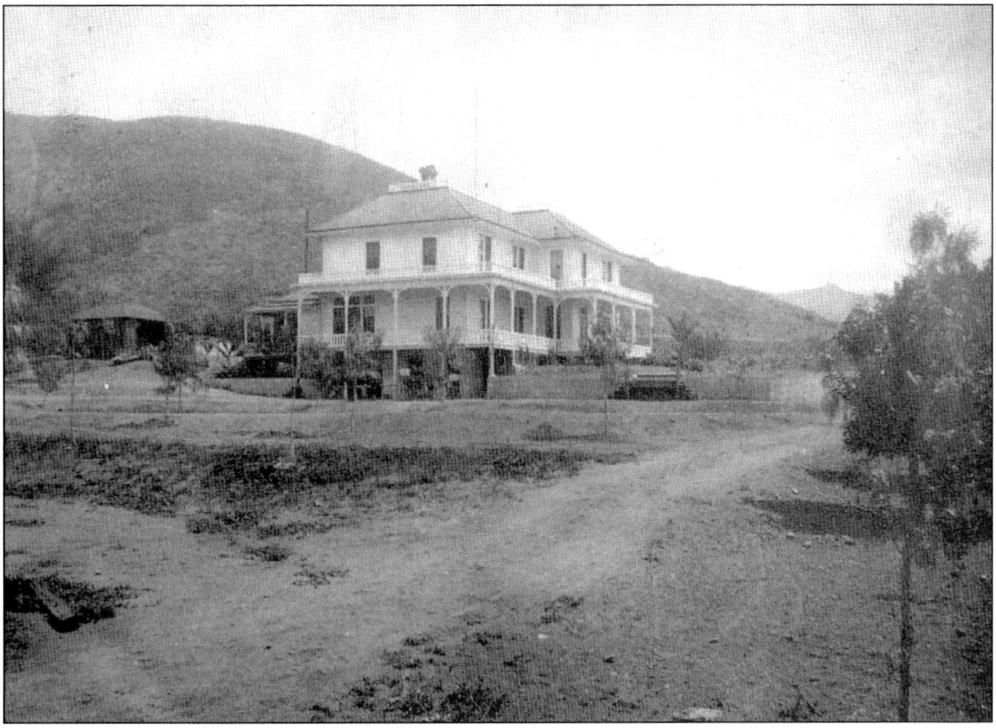

George Whitcomb built his house at the top of Minnesota Ave. (now Glendora Ave.). He also bought more of the land to the south, land which would eventually become the town of Glendora. (Glendora Historical Society.)

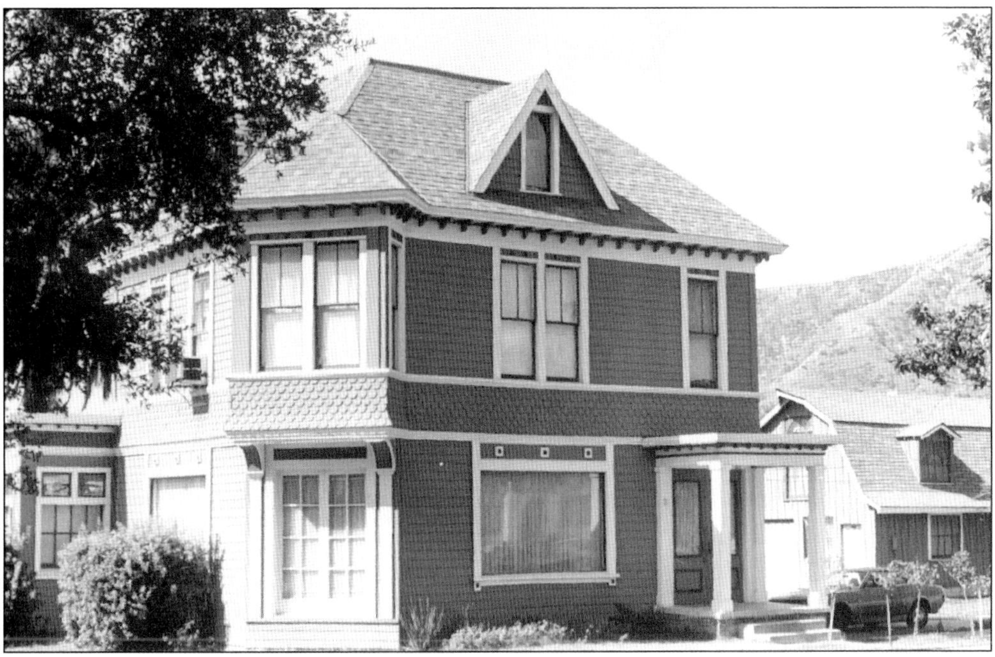

As people started purchasing parcels of land for the new town of Glendora, a Land Office was created to handle all of the sales. (Glendora Historical Society.)

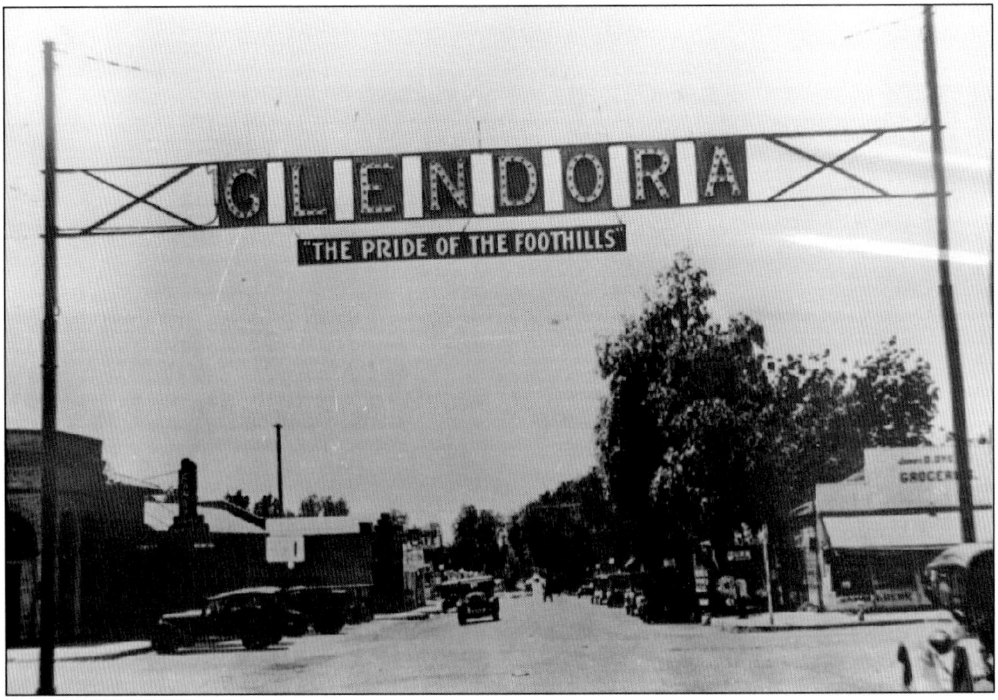

This sign hung across Michigan Ave., welcoming people into the business district of Glendora. (Glendora Historical Society.)

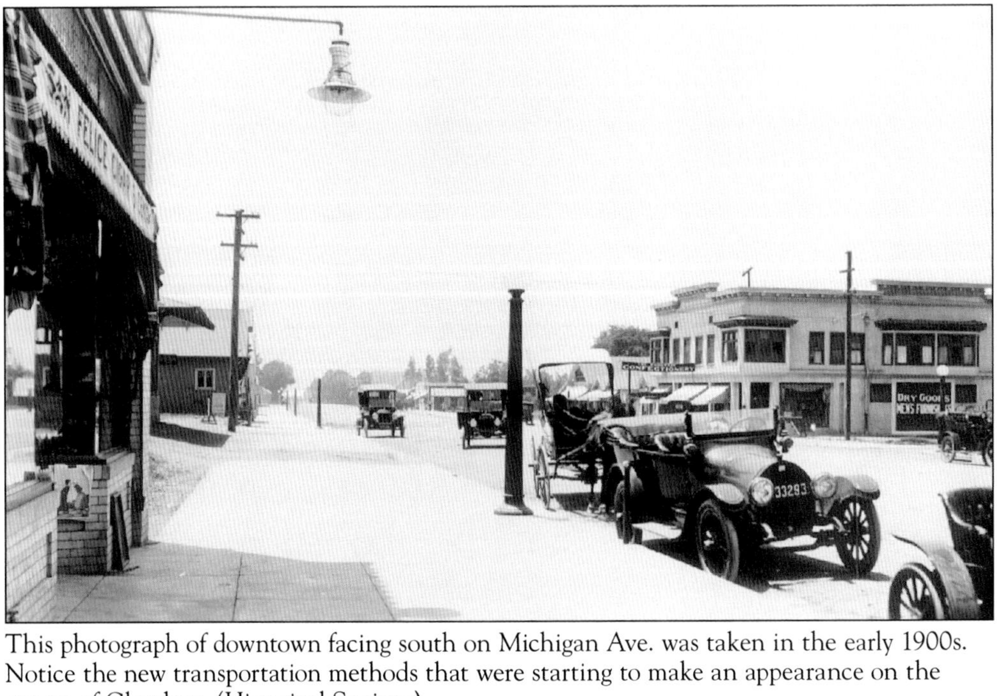

This photograph of downtown facing south on Michigan Ave. was taken in the early 1900s. Notice the new transportation methods that were starting to make an appearance on the streets of Glendora. (Historical Society.)

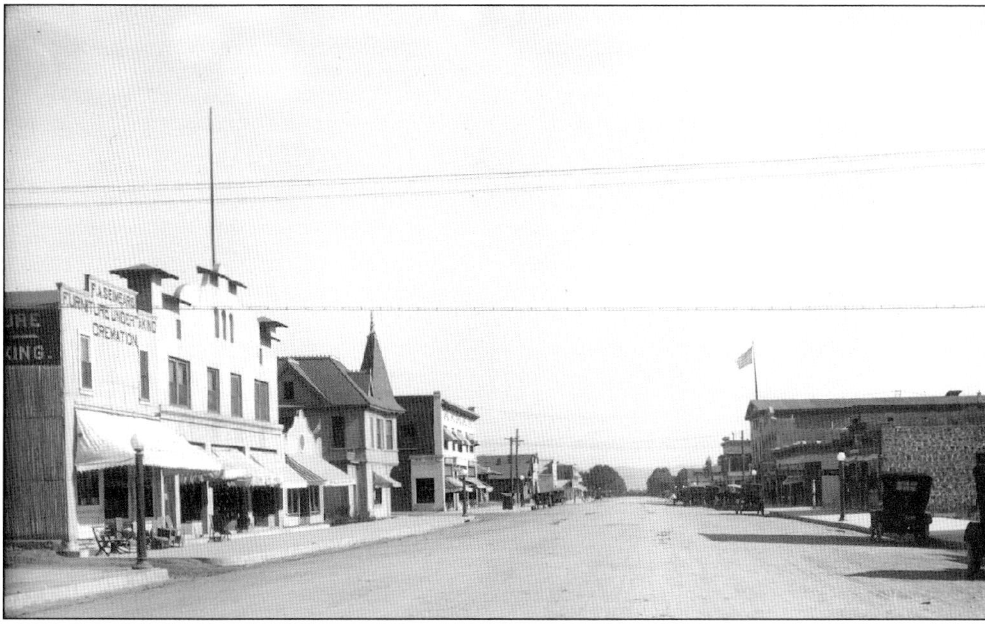

This view facing north on Michigan Ave. shows the opera house and the business district. (Glendora Historical Society.)

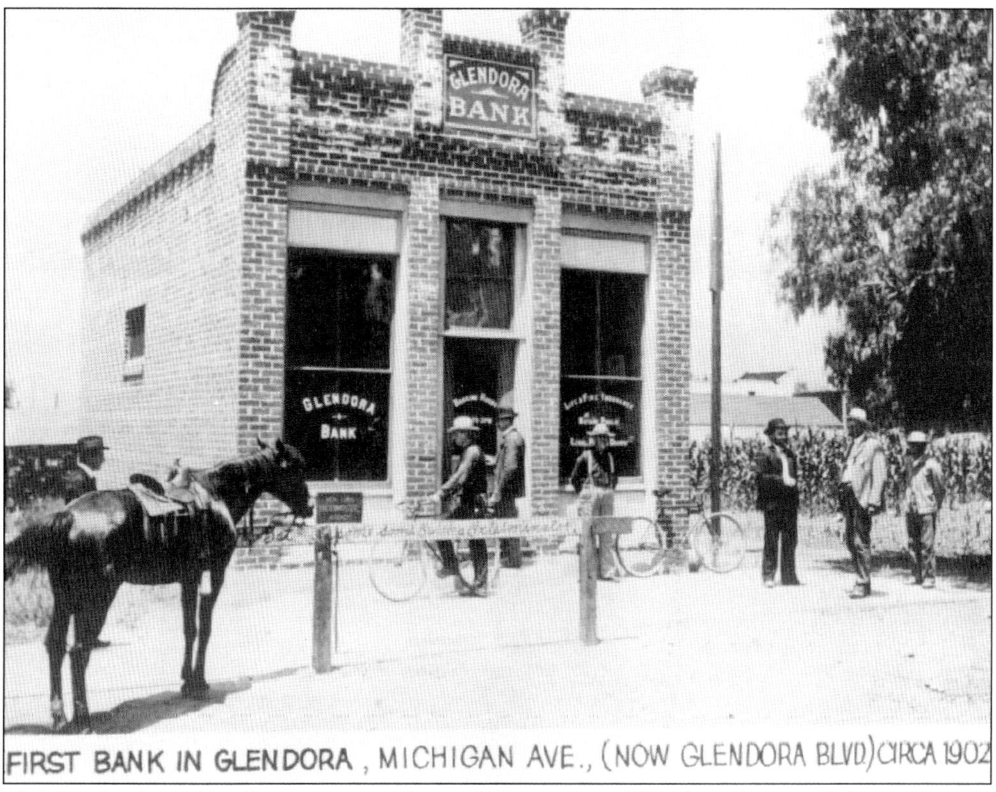

The first bank in Glendora is seen in this c. 1890s image. (Glendora Historical Society.)

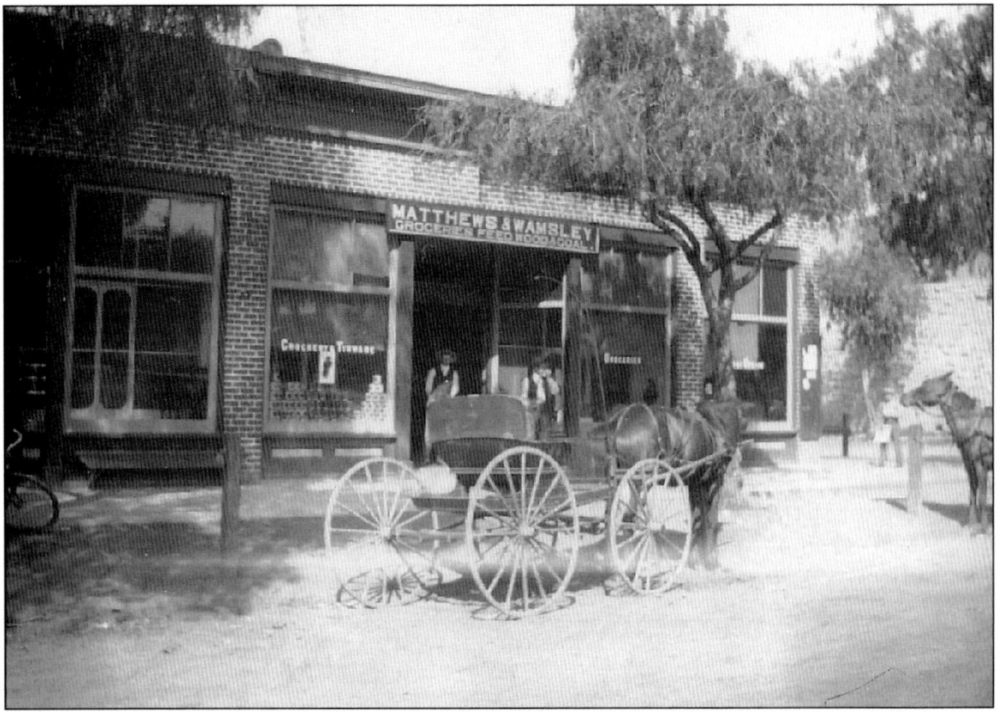

Lewis and Waslmsley General Store on Michigan Ave. provided everything from farm equipment to dry goods. (Glendora Historical Society.)

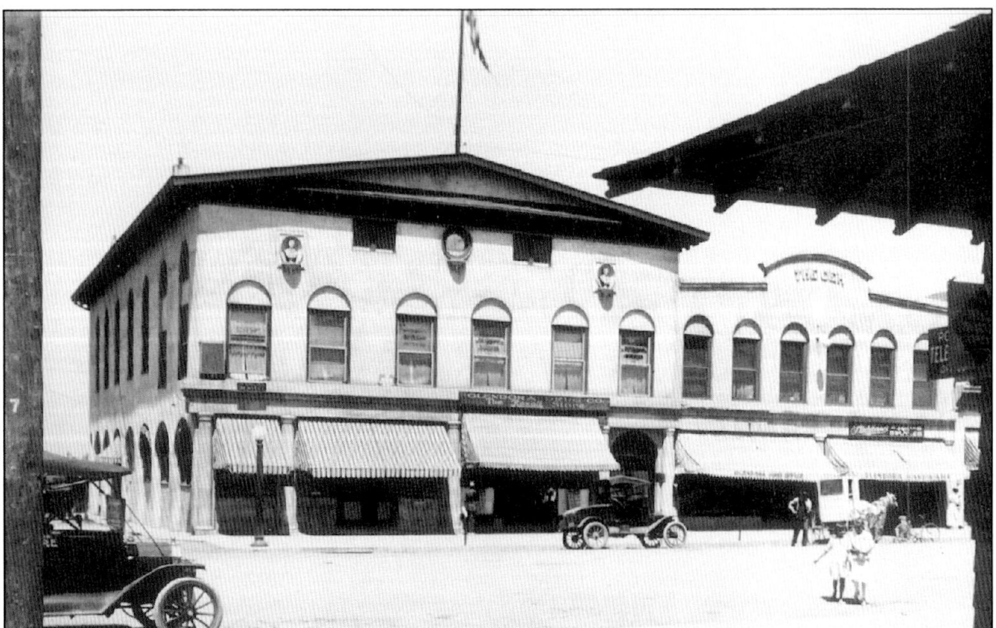

The Glendora Opera House grew out of a desire to allow the citizens of Glendora to experience classical music and theater. It was built on Michigan Ave. in the middle of town. (Glendora Historical Society.

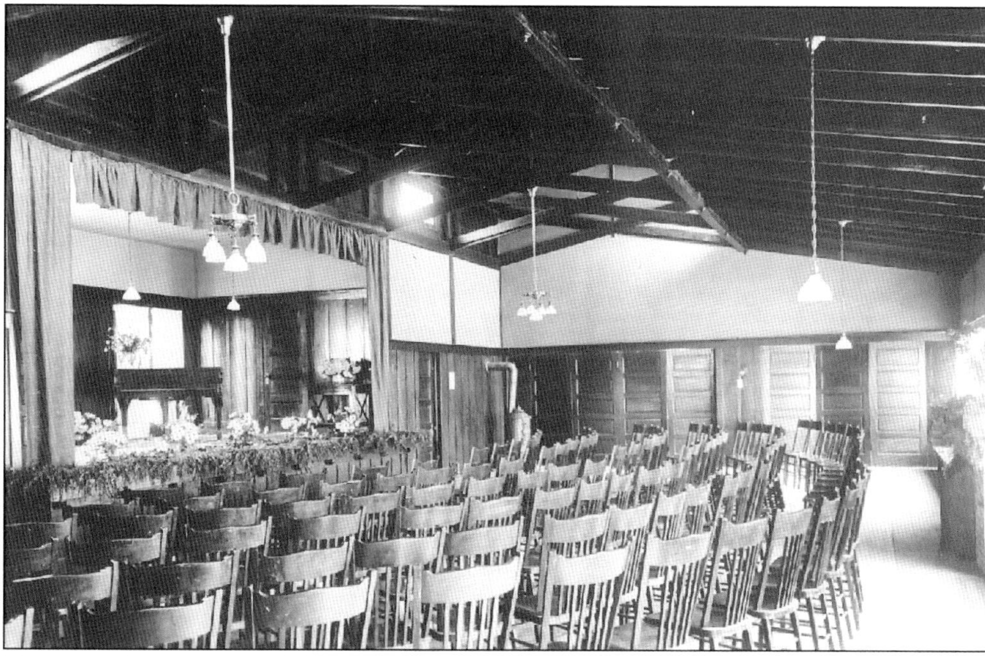

The opera house was used for musical performances as well as lectures and civic functions. (Glendora Historical Society.)

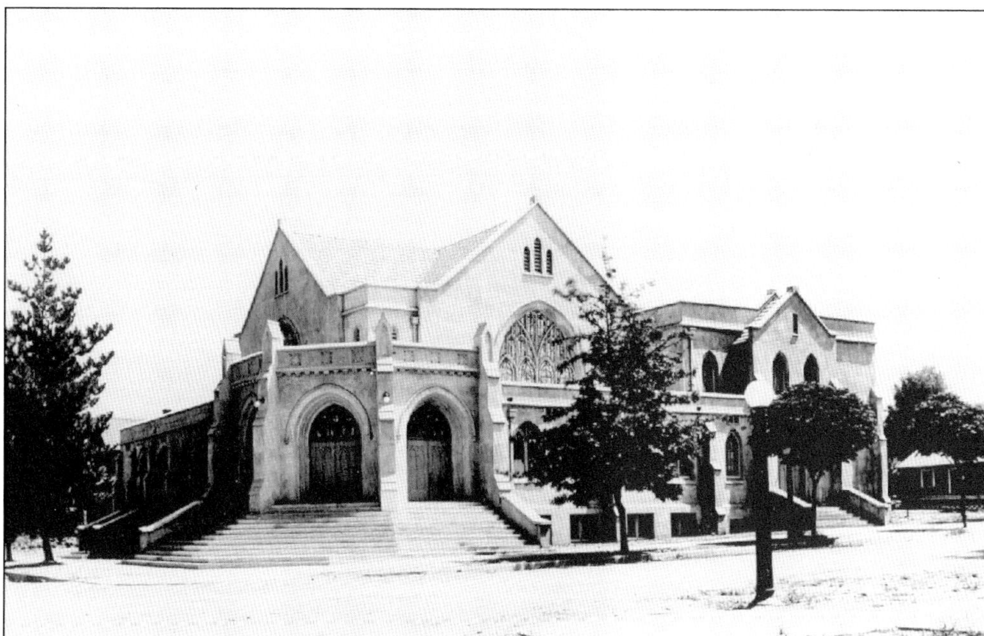

One of the first churches built in Glendora, the Methodist Church, was modeled like many of the eastern churches of the time. (Glendora Historical Society.)

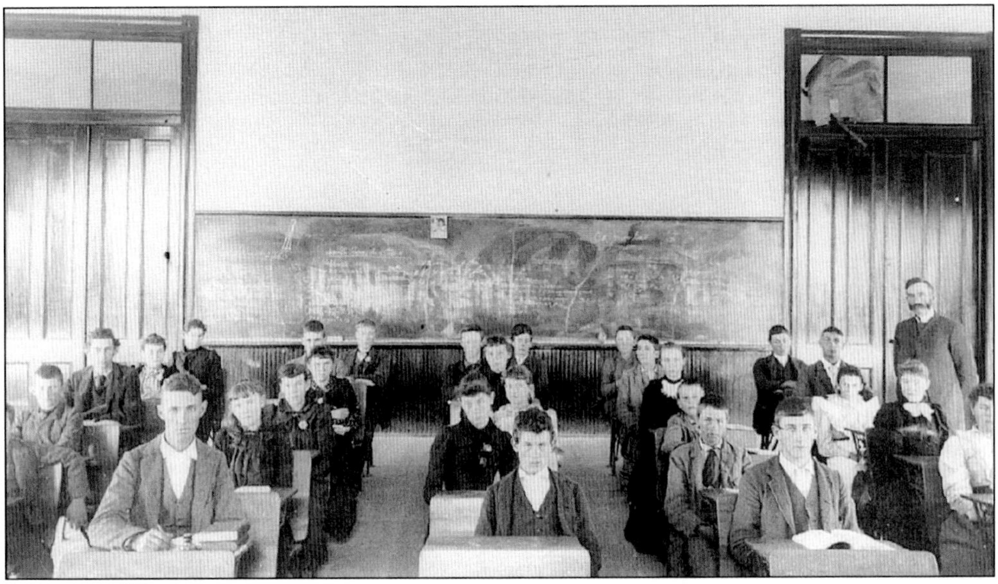

The citrus communities of Azusa, Glendora, Charter Oak, and San Dimas saw the need to educate their youth. No town could afford a school of its own, so these communities combined their resources and sent their children to a one-room schoolhouse on the La Fetra property. (Glendora Historical Society.)

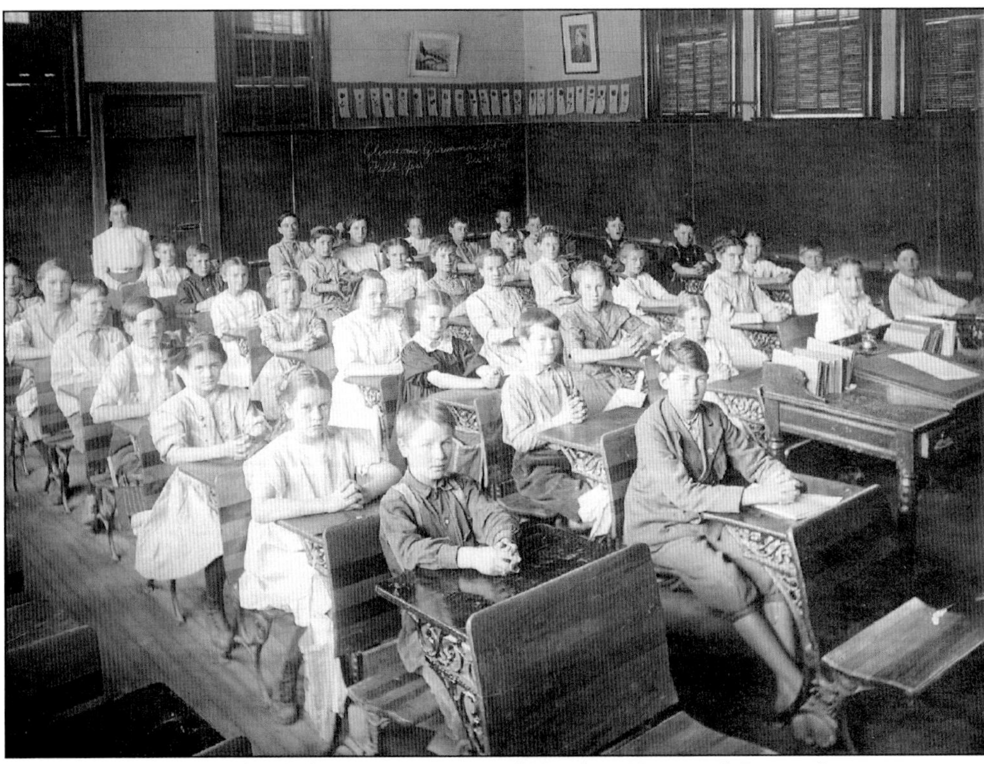

Glendora Grammar School class picture c. 1911. (Glendora Historical Society.)

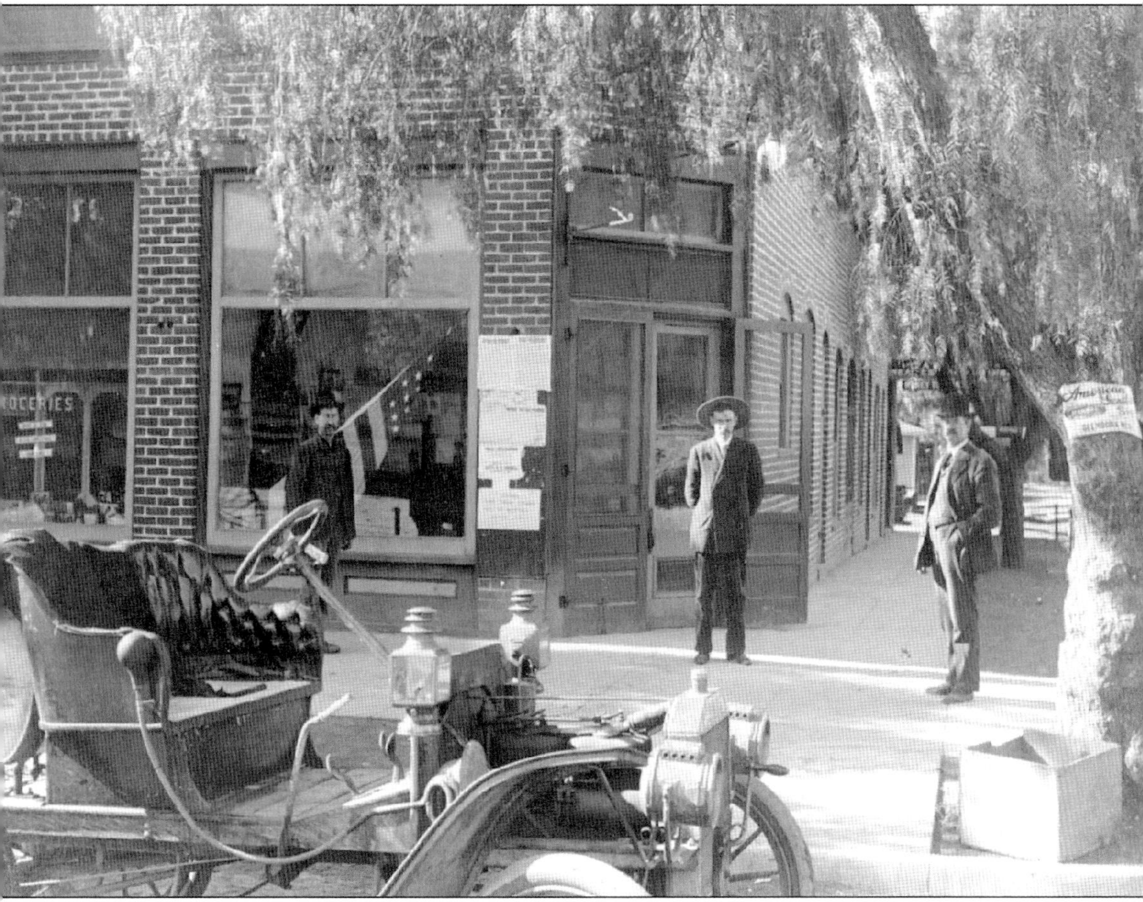

As the town began to grow and more people settled in Glendora, the town took on the feel and look of many other towns, with tree-lined sidewalks and corner grocery stores. (Glendora Historical Society.)

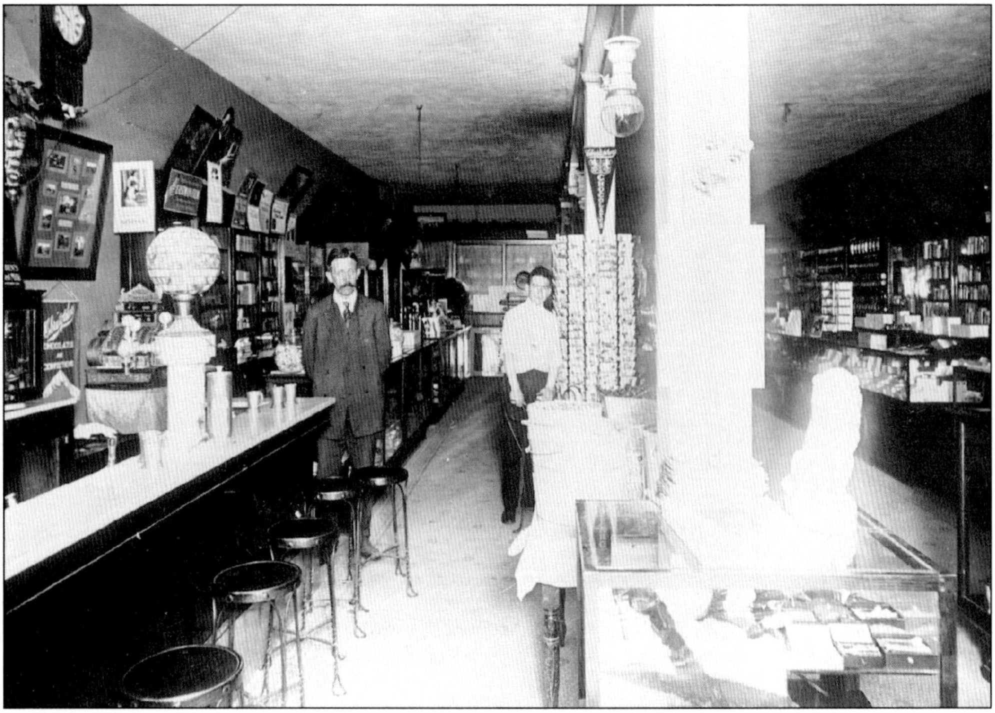

The Kamphefner Market offered all of the dry goods anyone would need, as well as a soda fountain which many Glendora youth visited on hot afternoons. (Glendora Historical Society.)

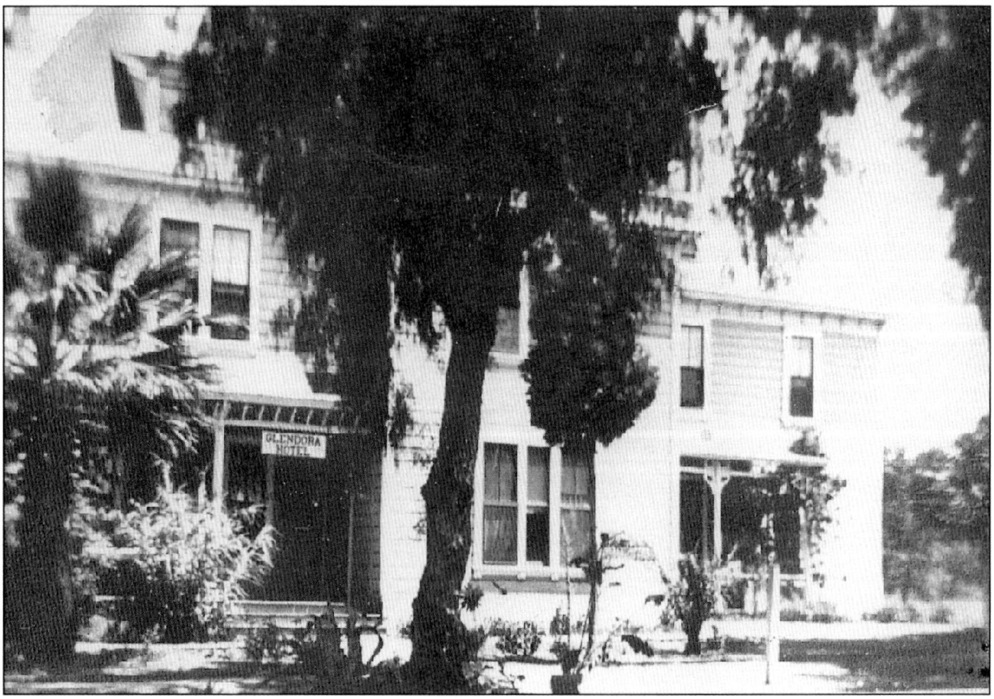

One of the first hotels in Glendora was the Hotel Belview located on Minnesota Ave. (Glendora Historical Society.)

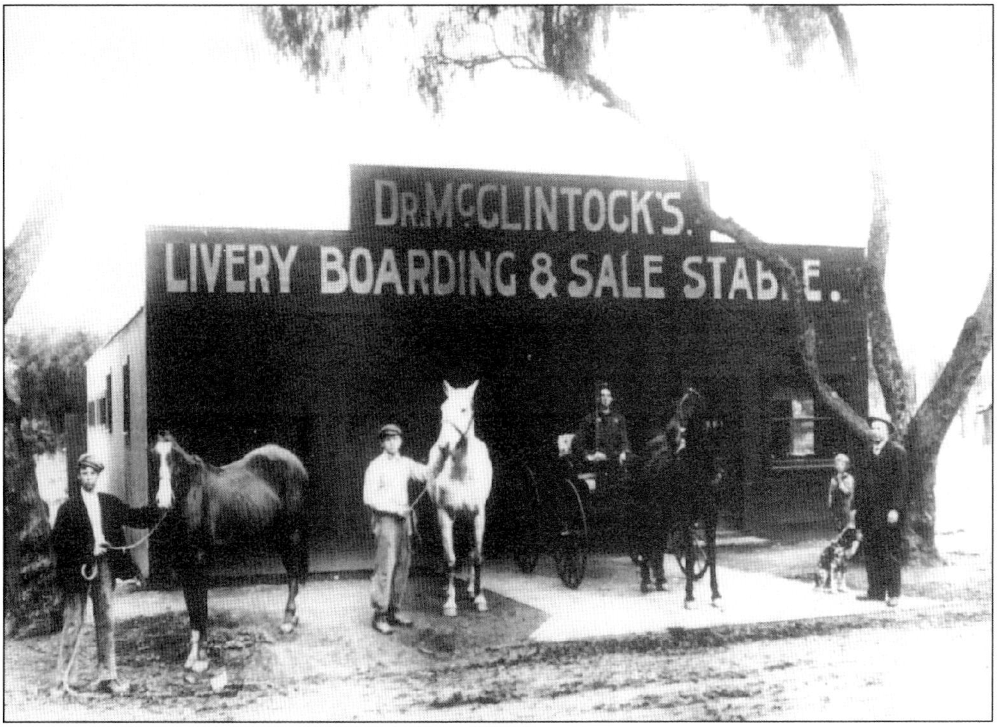

Even at the turn of the 20th century, transportation required a competent blacksmith. McClintock's Livery offered the farming community all of the services needed to keep and board horses. (Glendora Historical Society.)

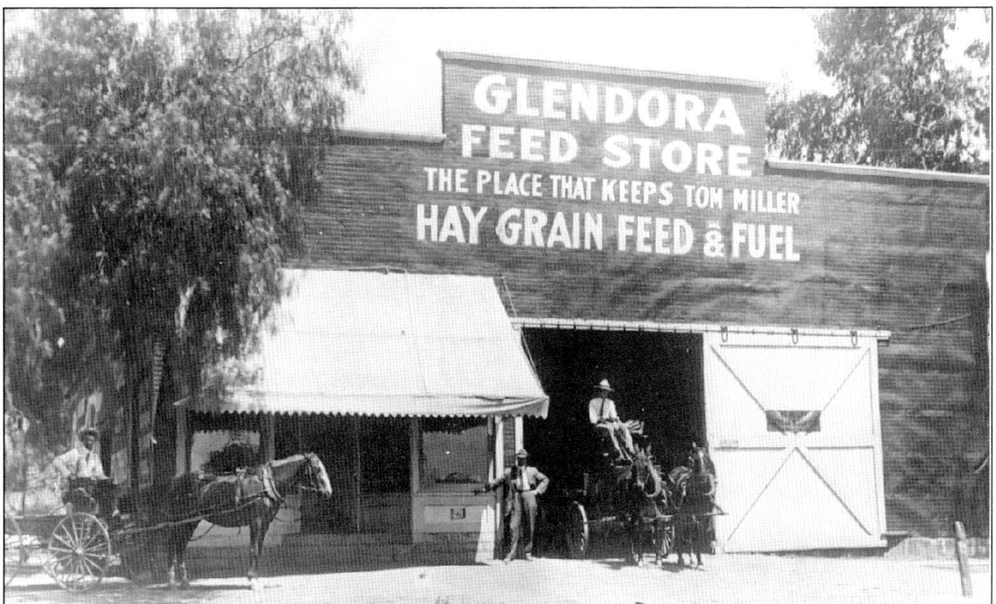

One of the most important businesses any rural community could have was the feed and grain store. Glendora Feed kept the local farms supplied with all the different feeds needed for horses, pigs, and cattle. (Glendora Historical Society.)

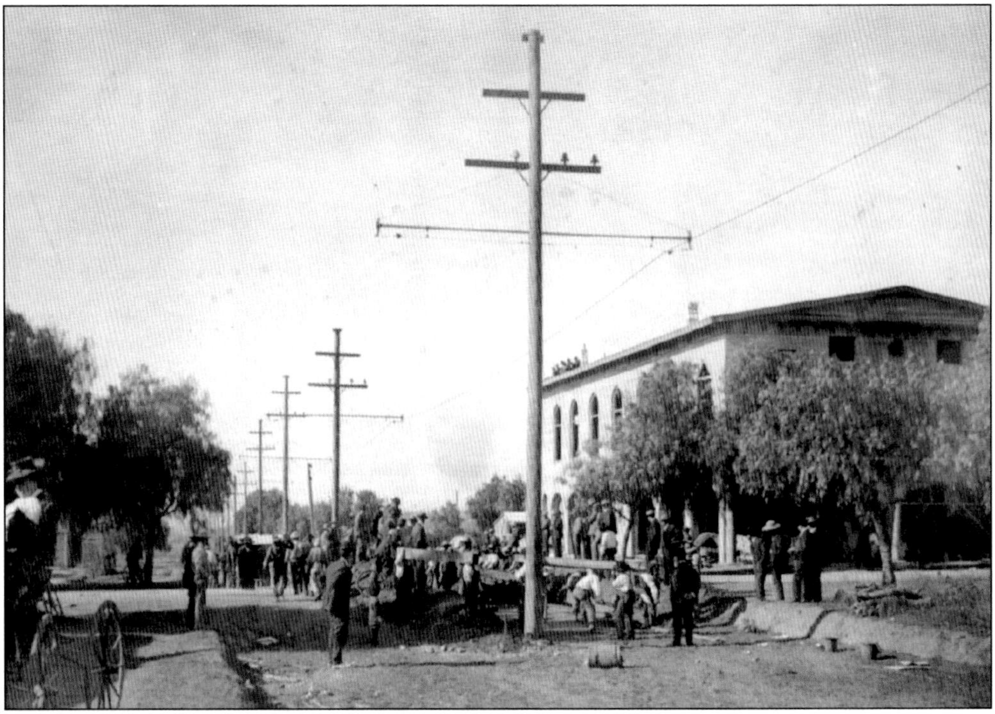

In town, many of the buildings served double duty. The Glendora Market on the first floor met the dry good needs of the townspeople and the office of Dr. Odell was housed upstairs. (Glendora Historical Society.)

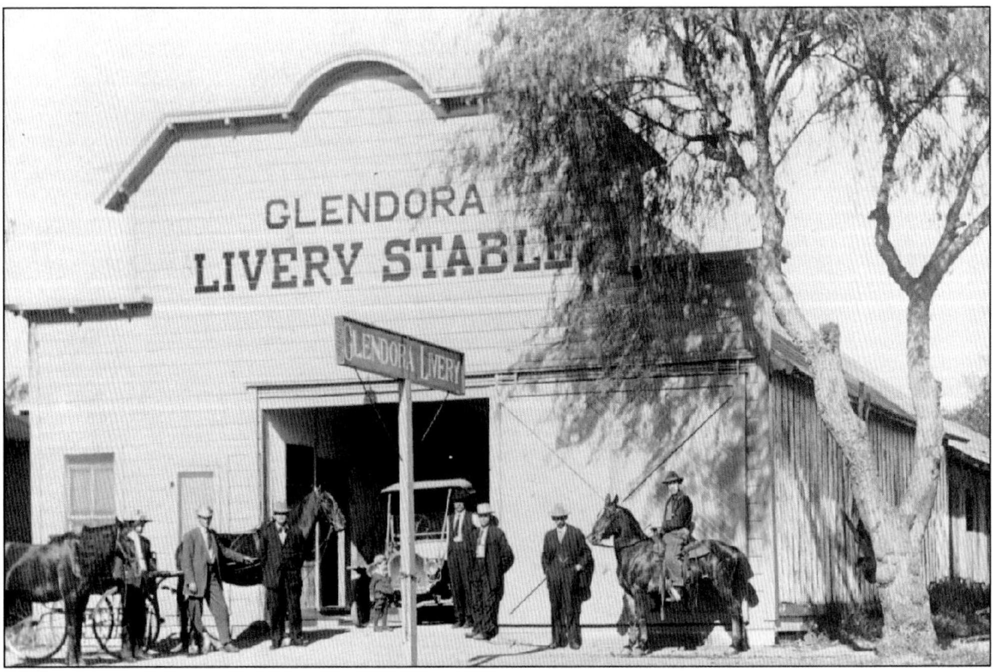

One of the most prominent livery stables in early Glendora was the Glendora Livery located at what is now Glendora Ave. and Foothill Blvd. (Glendora Historical Society.)

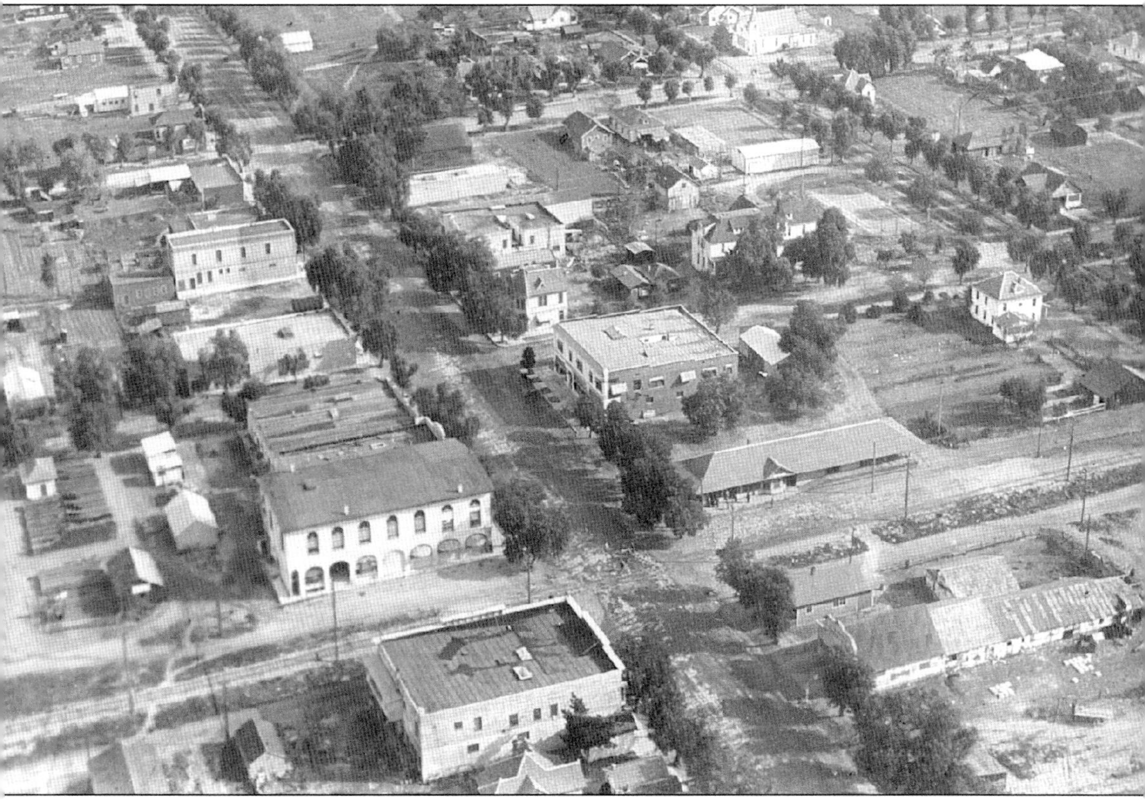

As the 20th century began, one of the new wonders was the airplane. One of the special uses of a plane was the aerial photograph. This one shows the growth of Glendora and the spread of the railroad east from Los Angeles. (Glendora Historical Society.)

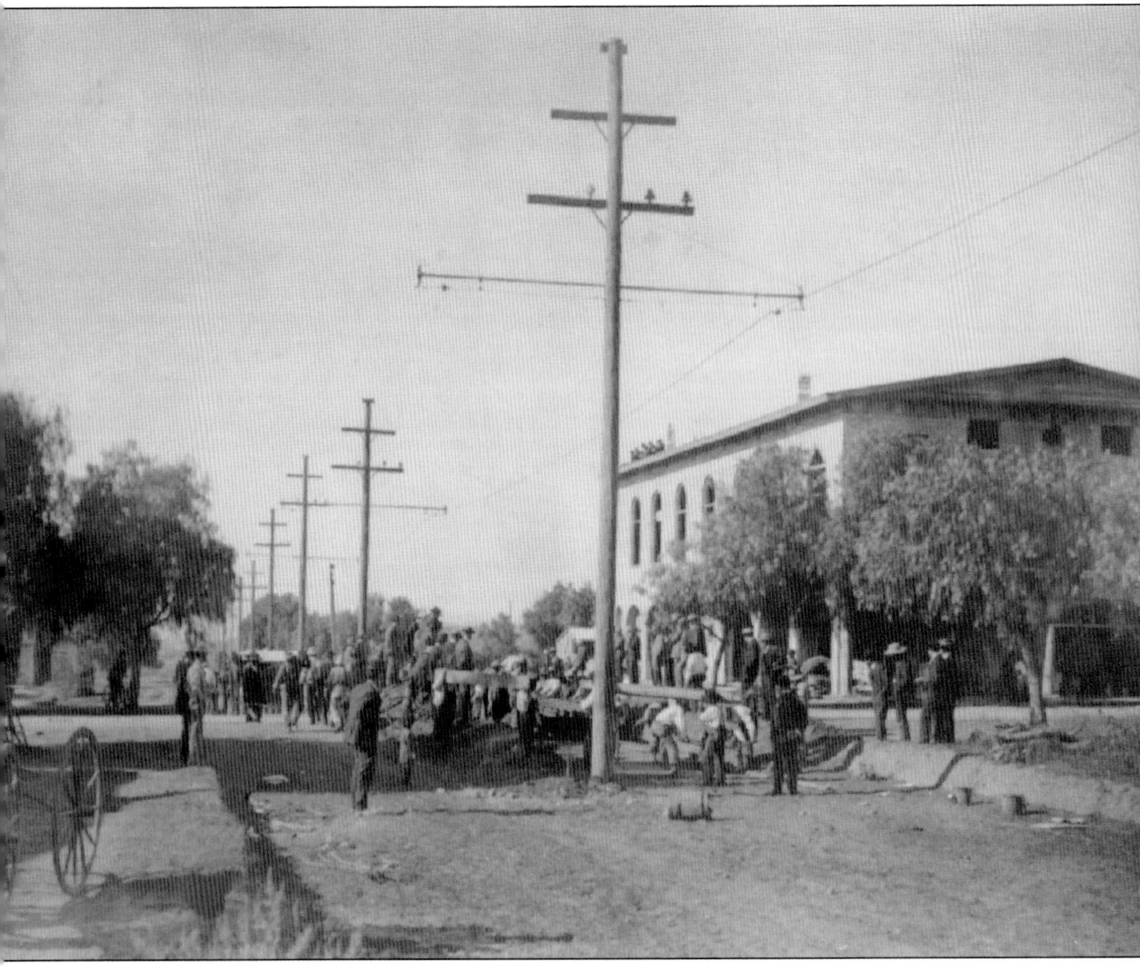

One of the most important features of any town in the Los Angeles basin was the link by rail to the rest of the world. Glendora was able to gain a rail line that ran through the southern part of town next to the opera house. Here they are clearing the land for the rails to be laid.(Glendora Historical Society.)

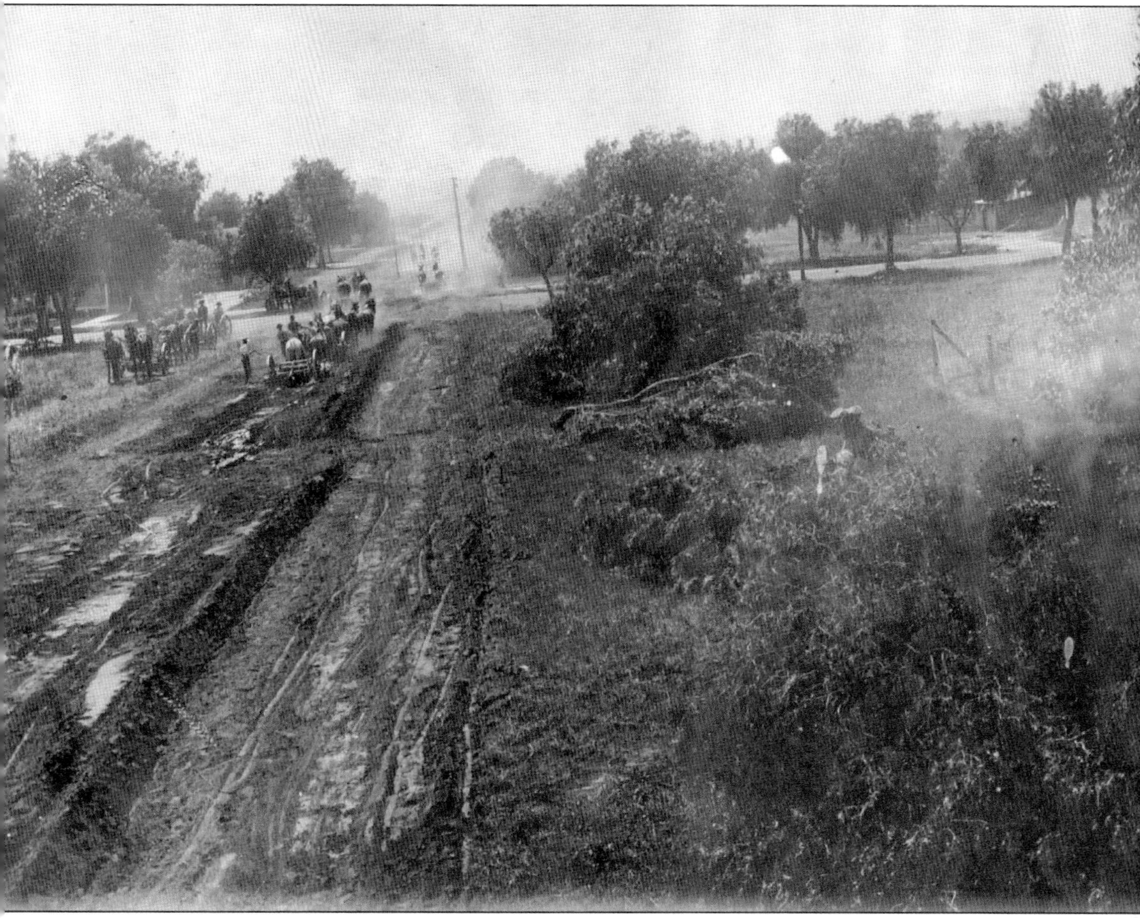

Clearing the land and laying the tracks for the Huntington Red Cars can be seen in this c. early-1900s image. (Glendora historical Society.)

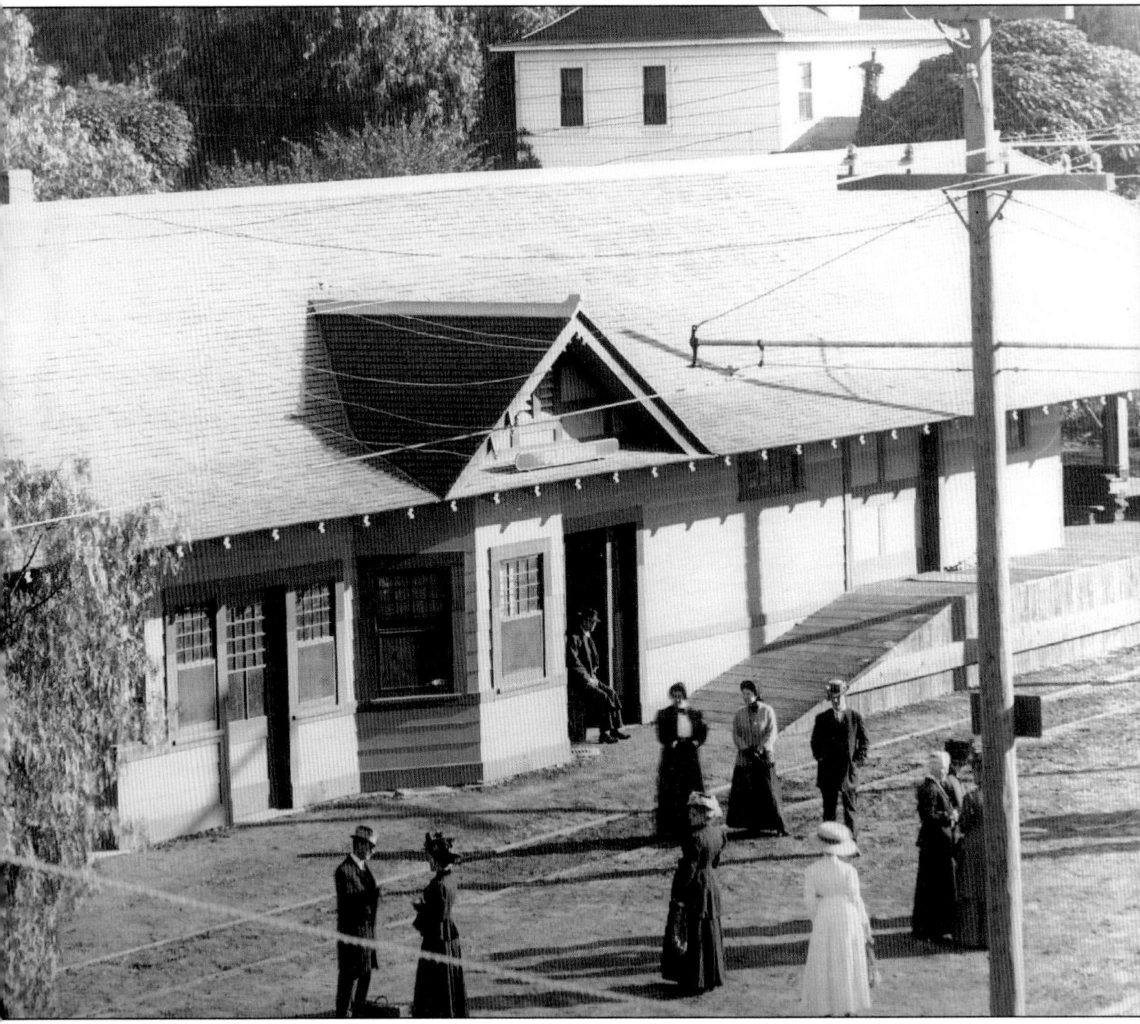

Glendorans were very proud of their new train station. Here we see people waiting for a train to take them to one of the many growing communities. (Glendora Historical Society.)

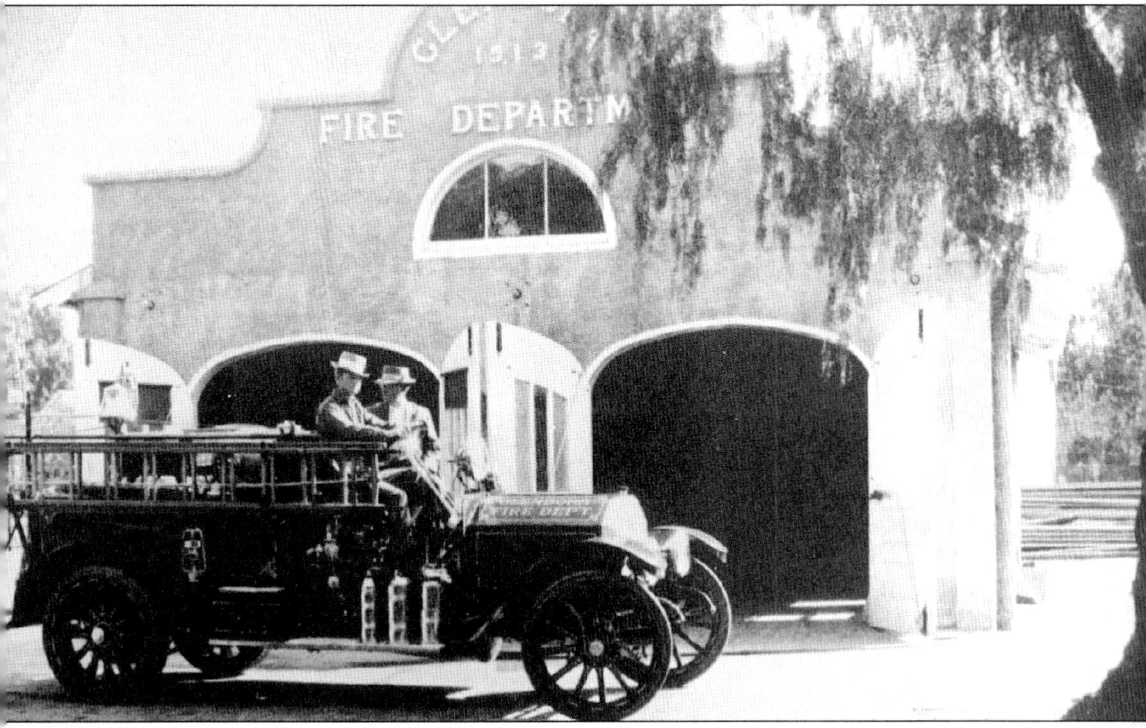

As Glendora grew, the city leaders saw the need for a fire department. The first city hall, jail, police station, and fire station complete with a modern fire engine was built on the north end of Glendora Ave. (Glendora Historical Society.)

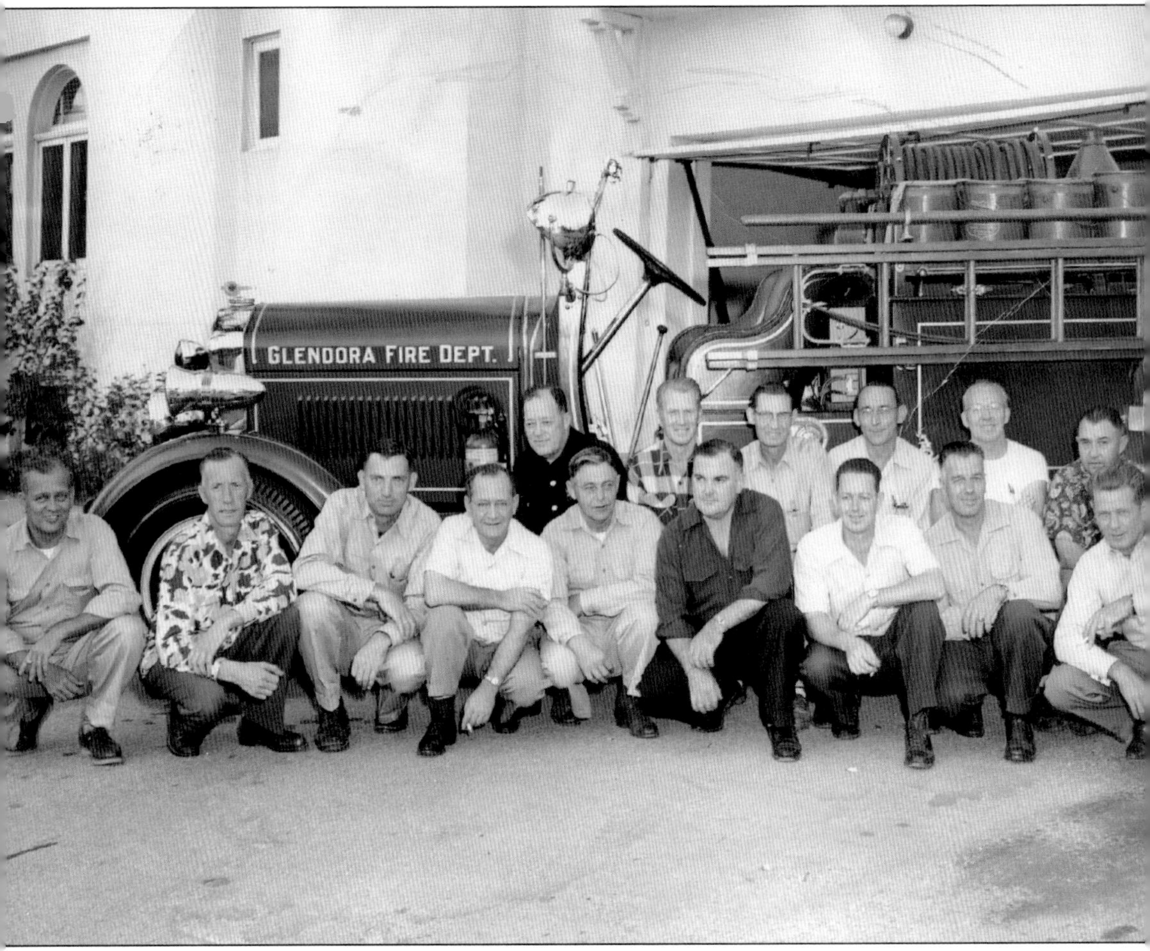

In 1953 Glendora still had its own volunteer fire department as seen here. (Glendora Historical Society.)

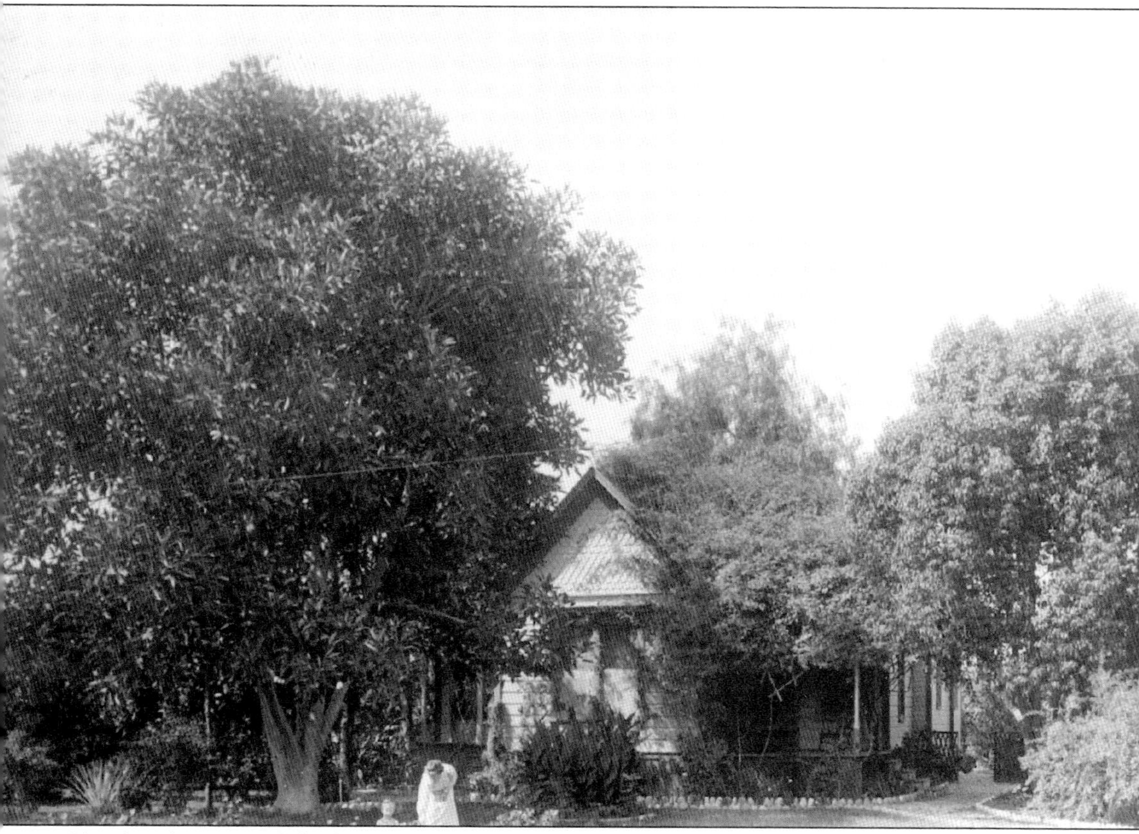

Glendora has one of the largest and oldest Morton Bay fig trees in the state of California. It is currently a state historic landmark, but in the 1930s the tree was still small and in the front yard of Emma Whistler. (Glendora Historical Society.)

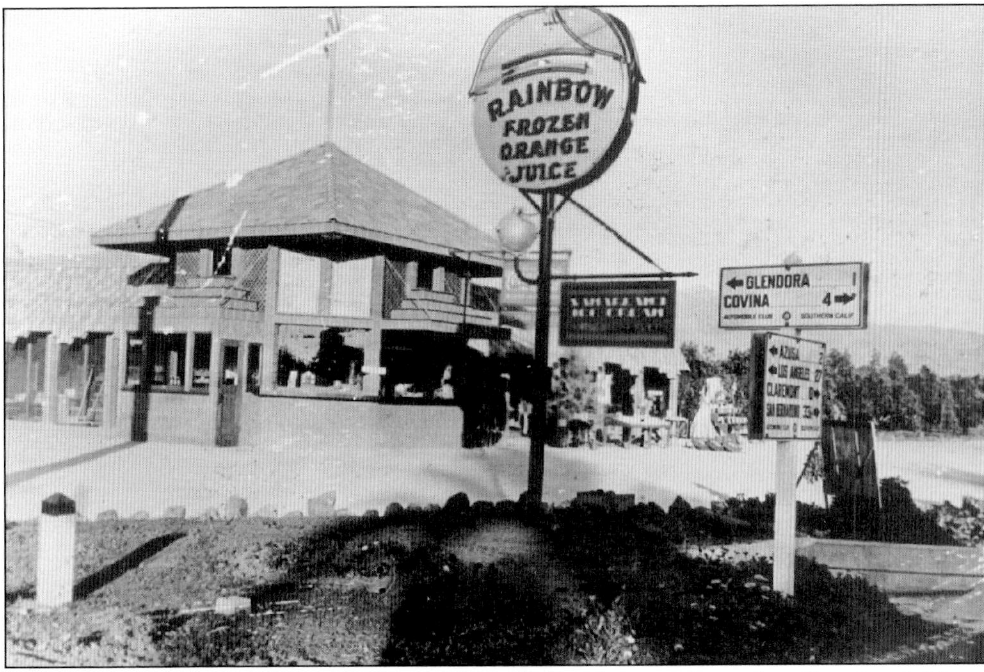

In the 1940s the youth of Glendora visited Walt Wiley's drive-in, located at Grand and Alosta, on Saturday nights for burger and fries. The building is now the Old Hickory Inn and is said to have given the McDonald brothers the idea to create a chain of hamburger restaurants. (Glendora Historical Society.)

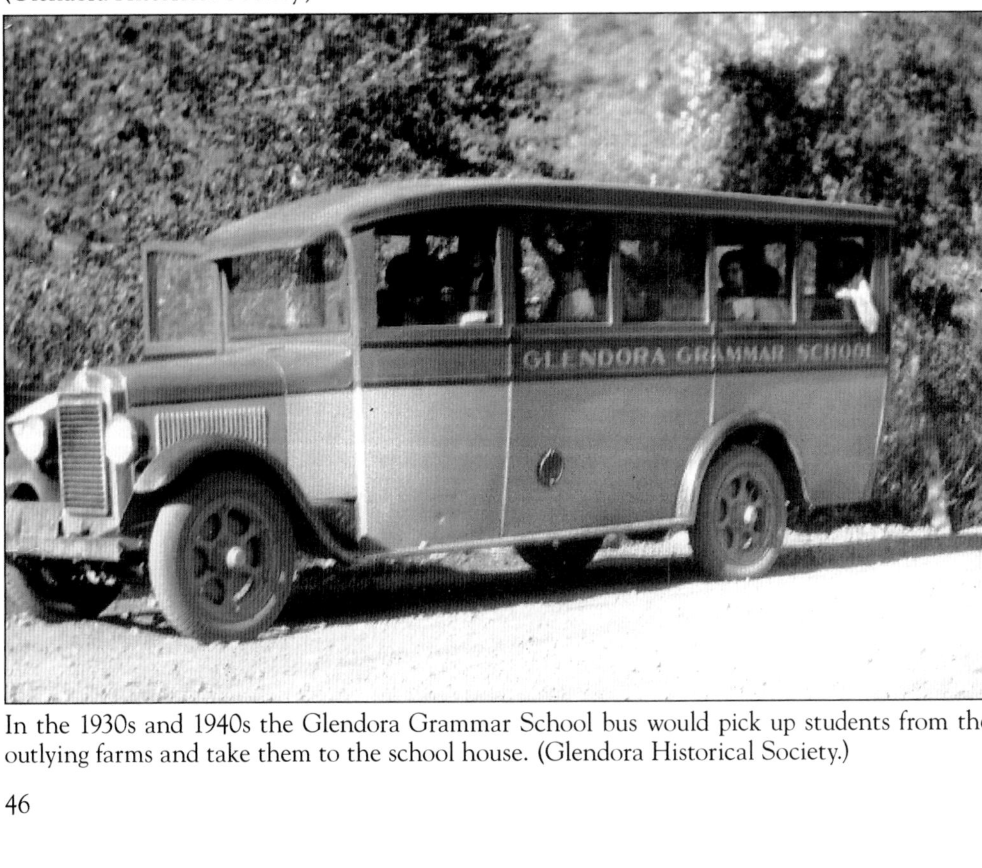

In the 1930s and 1940s the Glendora Grammar School bus would pick up students from the outlying farms and take them to the school house. (Glendora Historical Society.)

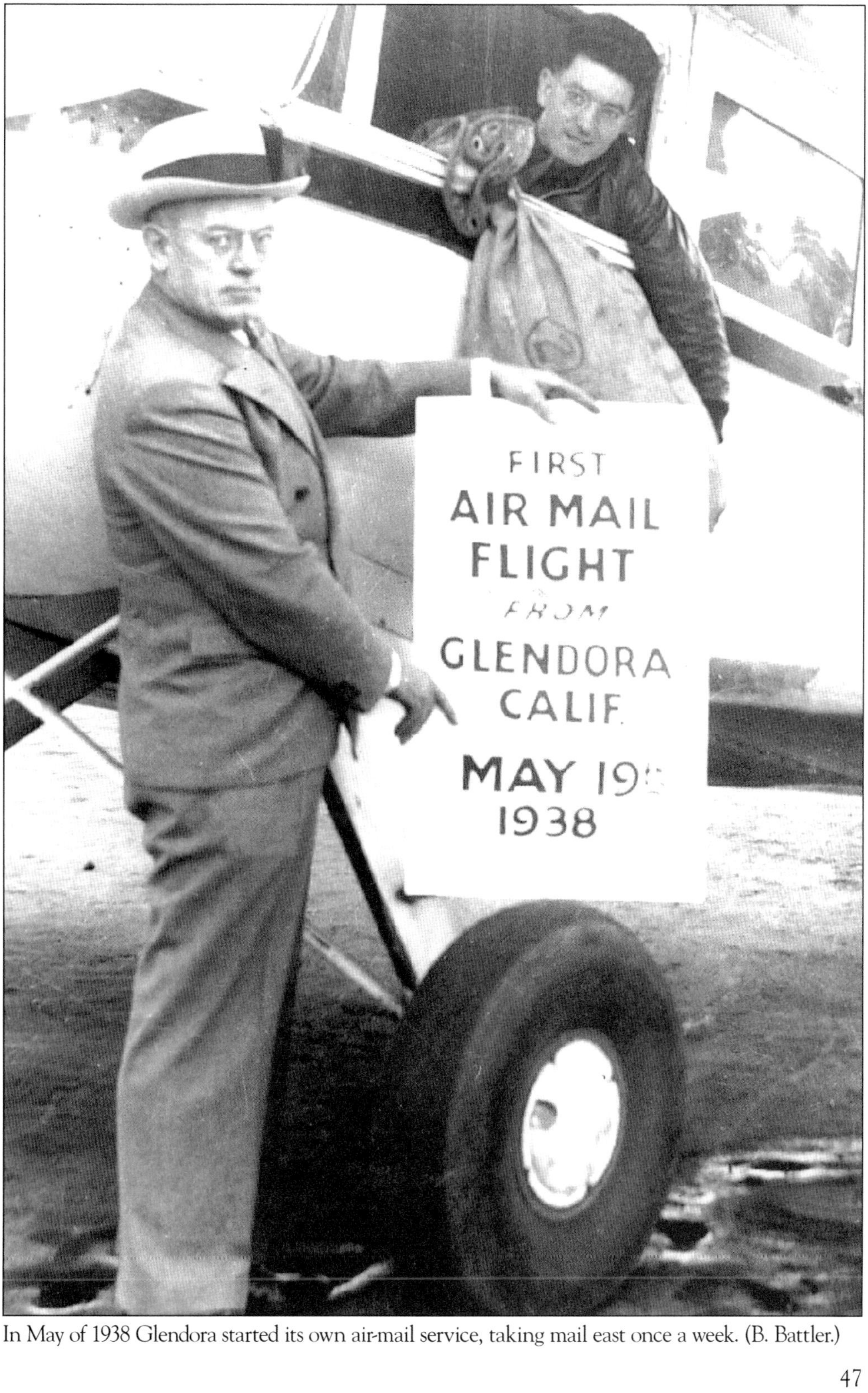

In May of 1938 Glendora started its own air-mail service, taking mail east once a week. (B. Battler.)

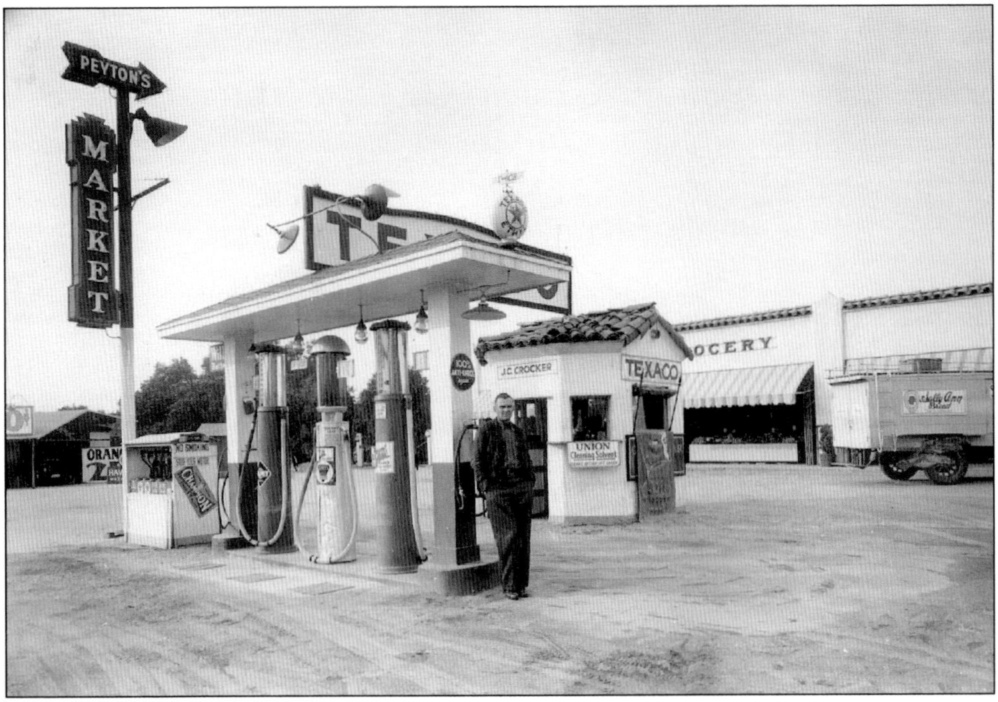

Route 66 ran along the southern part of the city of Glendora, and as automobiles drove along this historic road, the need for service stations grew. Payton's Texaco, located on the corner of Grand Ave. and Alosta Ave., met the needs of motorists. (Glendora Historical Society.)

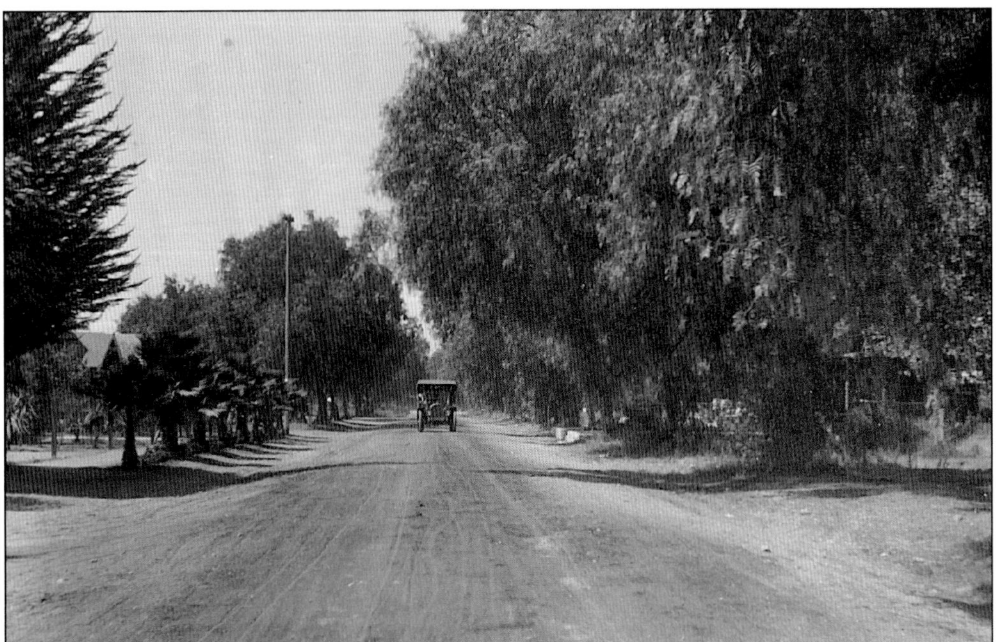

The 1930s and 1940s brought the change from horse and buggy to automobile. Roads in Glendora were paved, and it was no longer unusual to see an automobile traveling along one of the many streets of Glendora. (Glendora Historical Society.)

Three

THE CITRUS ERA

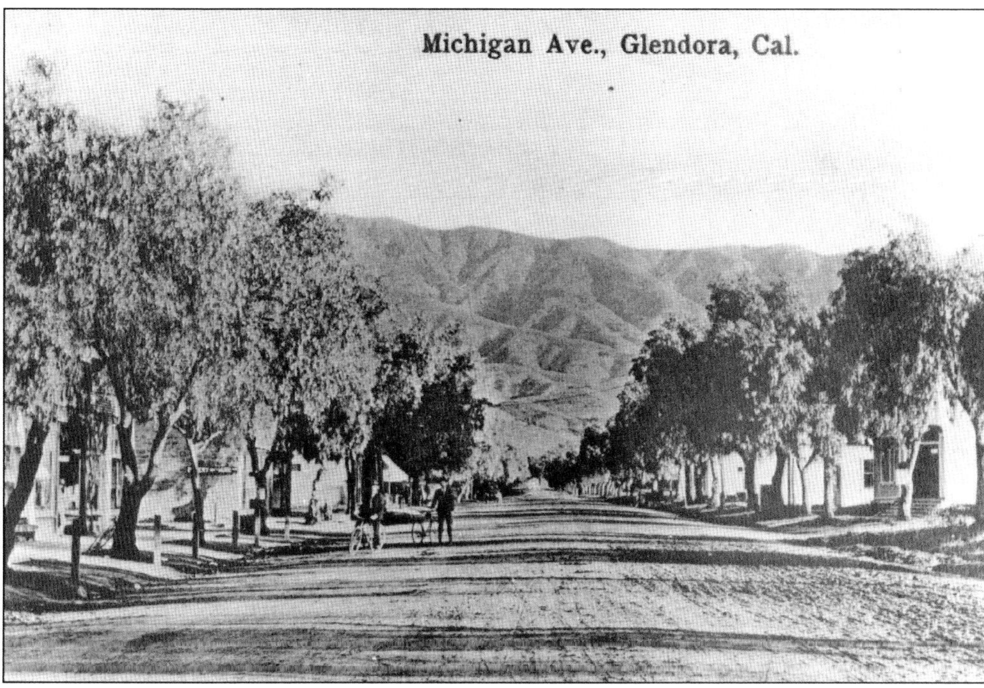

This 1930s postcard of Michigan Ave. looking north shows the tree-lined streets of Glendora. (Glendora Historical Society.)

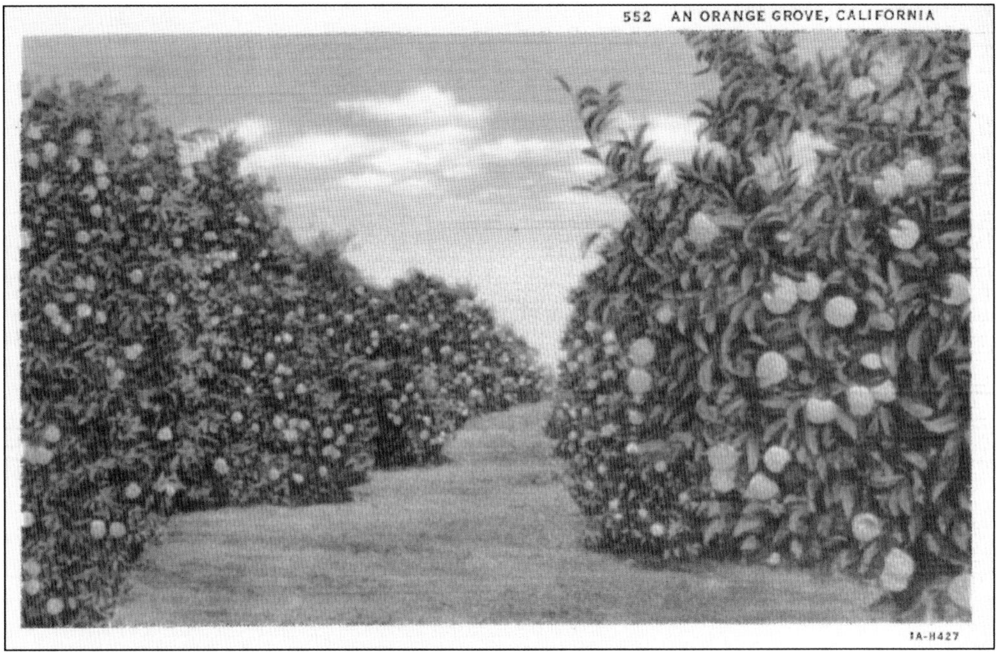

This postcard showing orange groves dates c. 1930. By this time the citrus industry had taken over the valley. (Glendora Historical Society.)

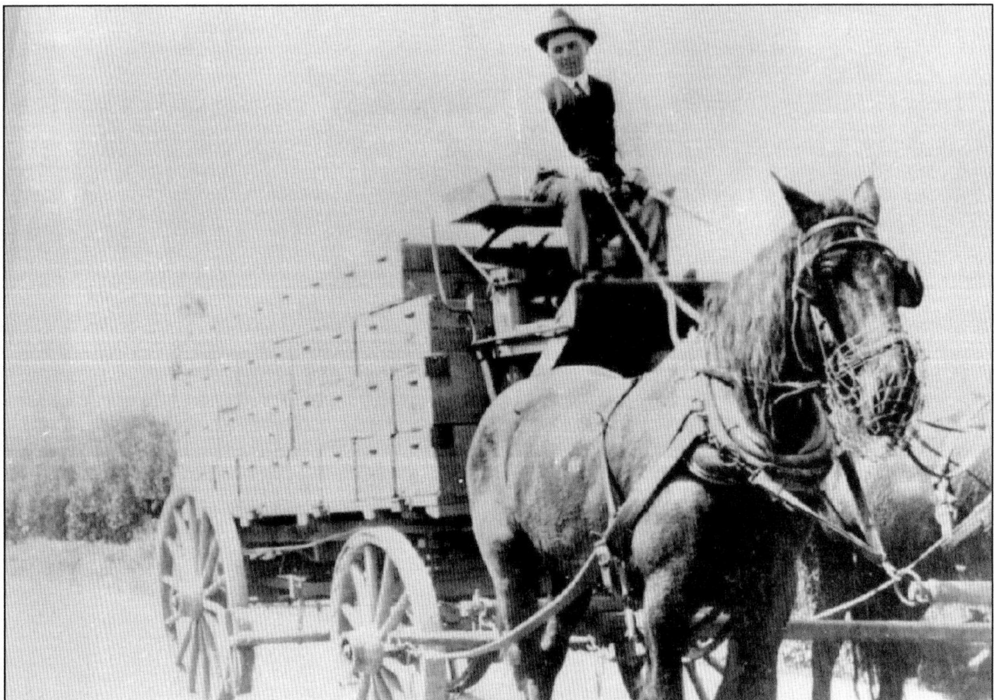
In the1890s farmers would haul their fruit by wagon to one of the many growing citrus packing houses in the area. (Glendora Historical Society.)

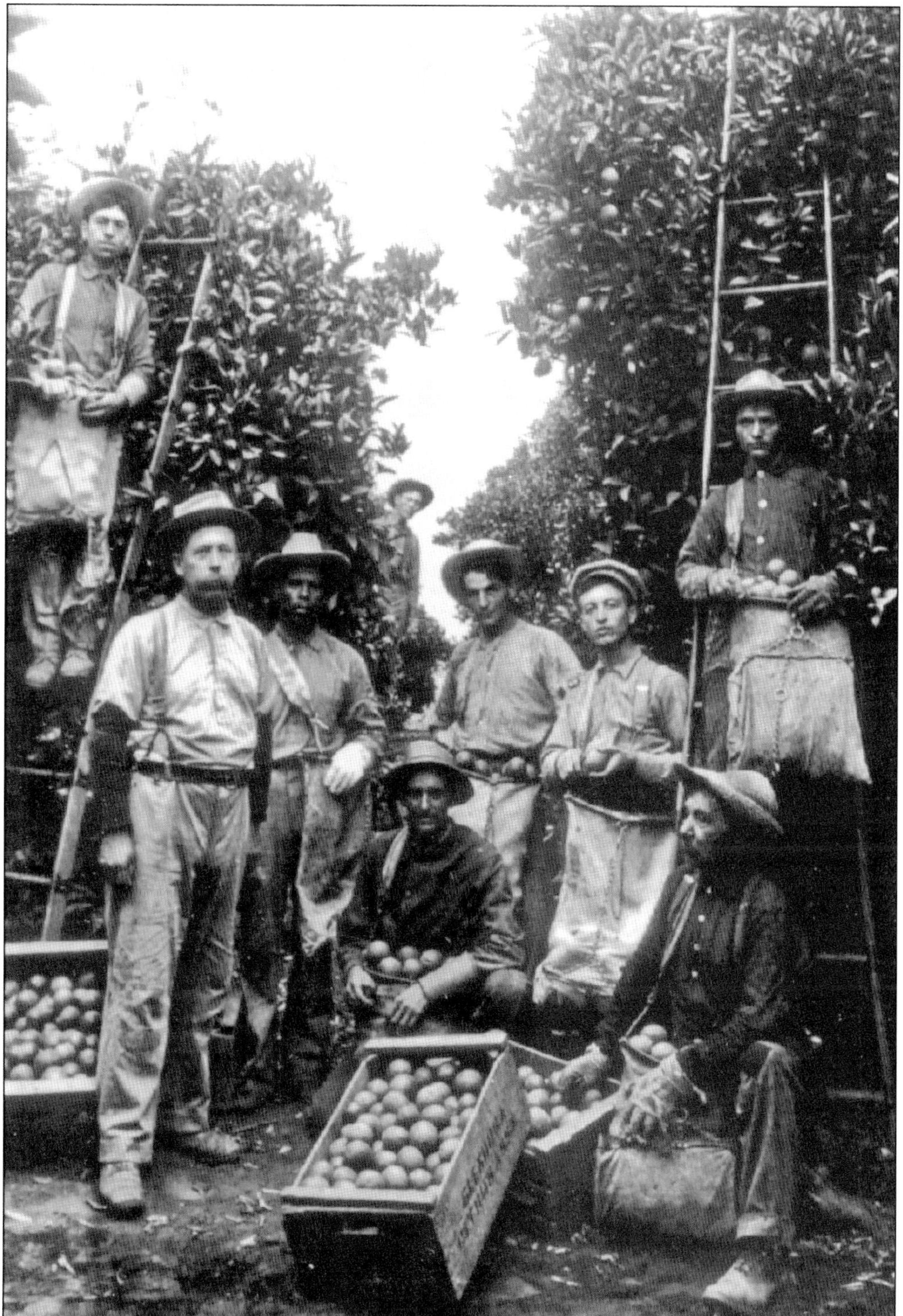

By 1900 most of the farmers in Glendora were growing lemons and oranges, and men were needed to pick all the fruit and get it to market. (Glendora Historical Society.)

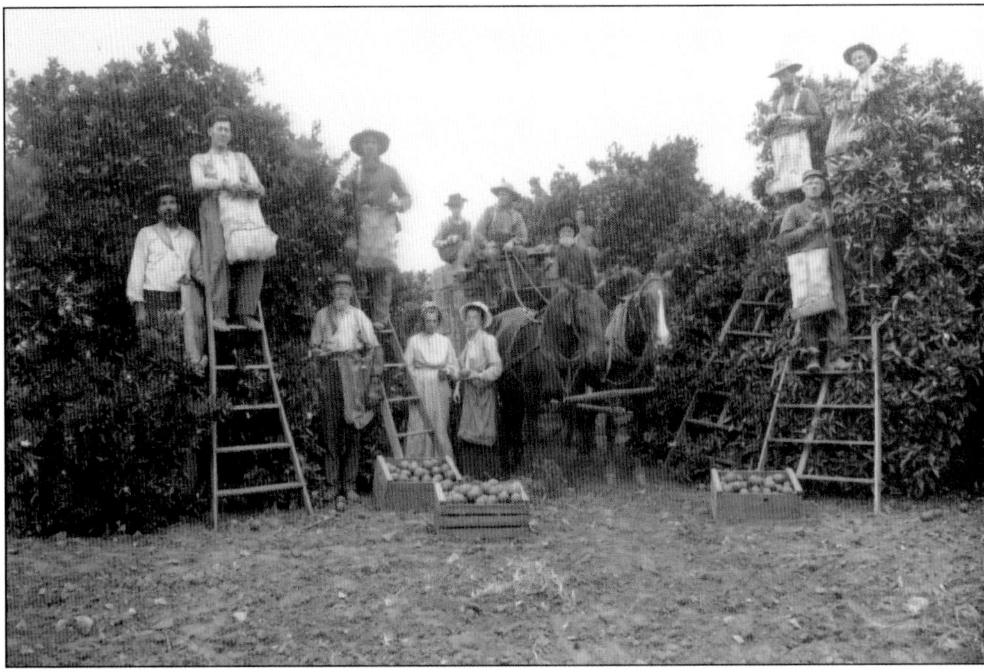

Many local families had small orchards, such as the Granda Netz Orchard, that would be tended by all of the family members during harvest season. (Glendora Historical Society.)

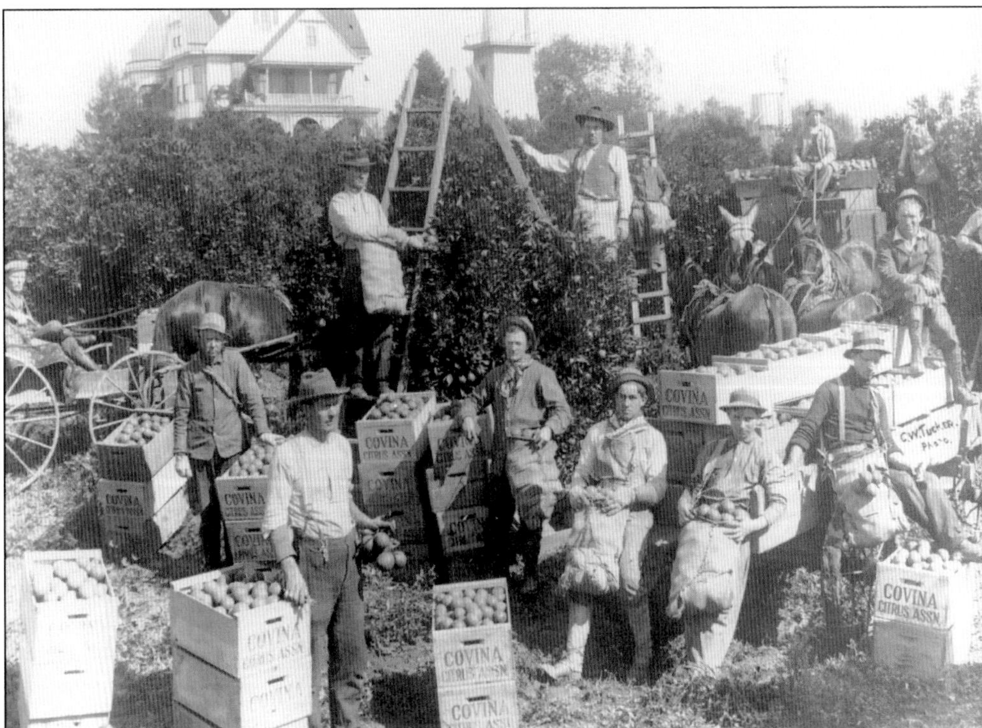

The neighboring city of Covina was also based on the citrus industry. Here a group works an orchard for the Covina Citrus Association. (Glendora Historical Society.)

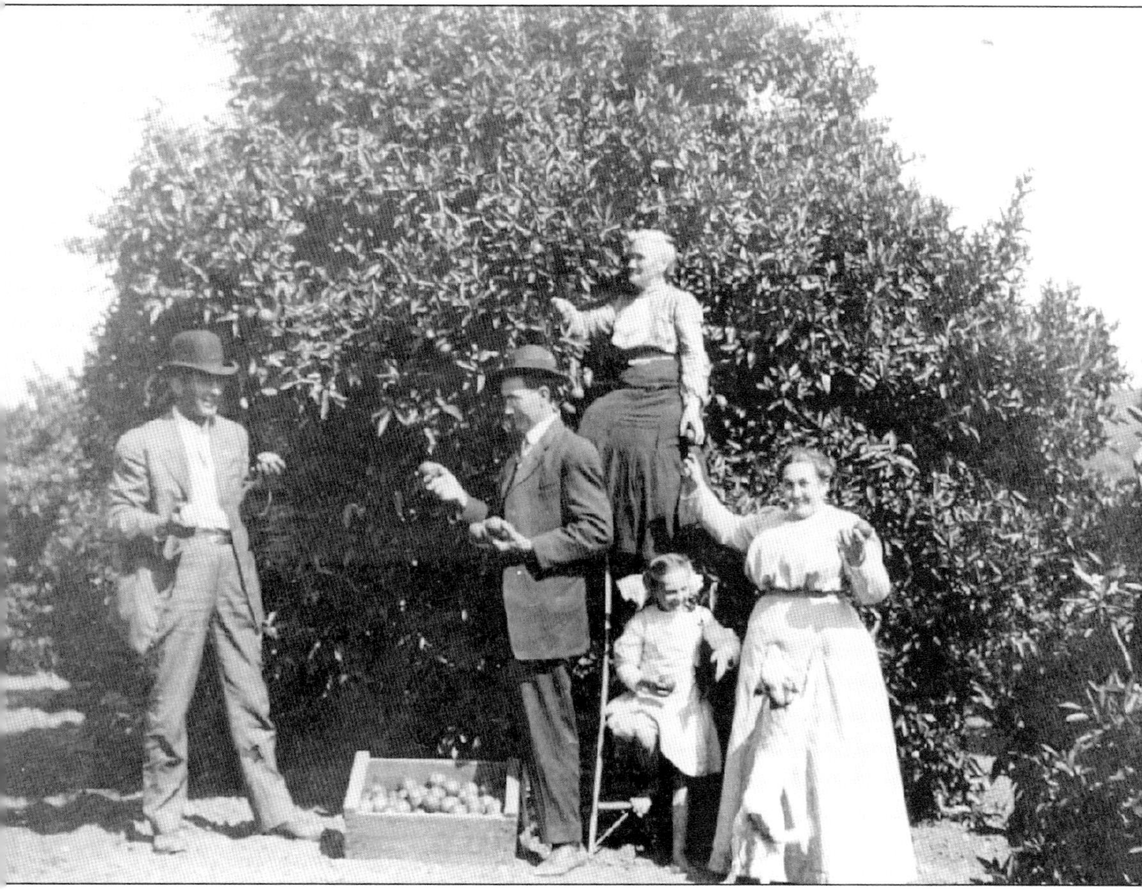

The Wilson family is seen here around 1915 in their orchard: the gentleman farmer and his family, including grandma, picking fruit. (Glendora Historical Society.)

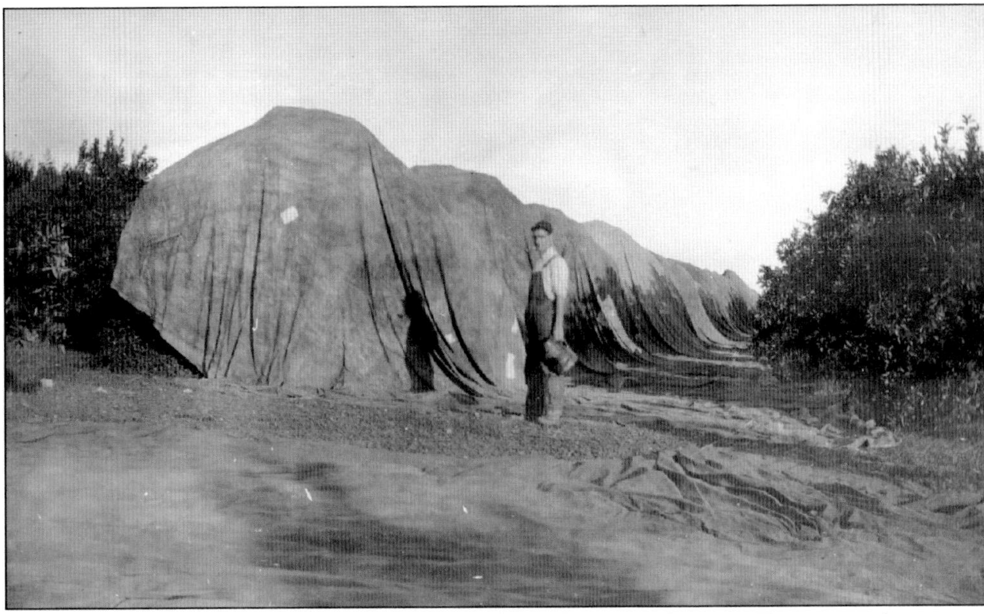

Insects are one of the many plagues that could hit the citrus farmers. To protect their crops, farmers would cover the trees with tarps . (Glendora Historical Society.)

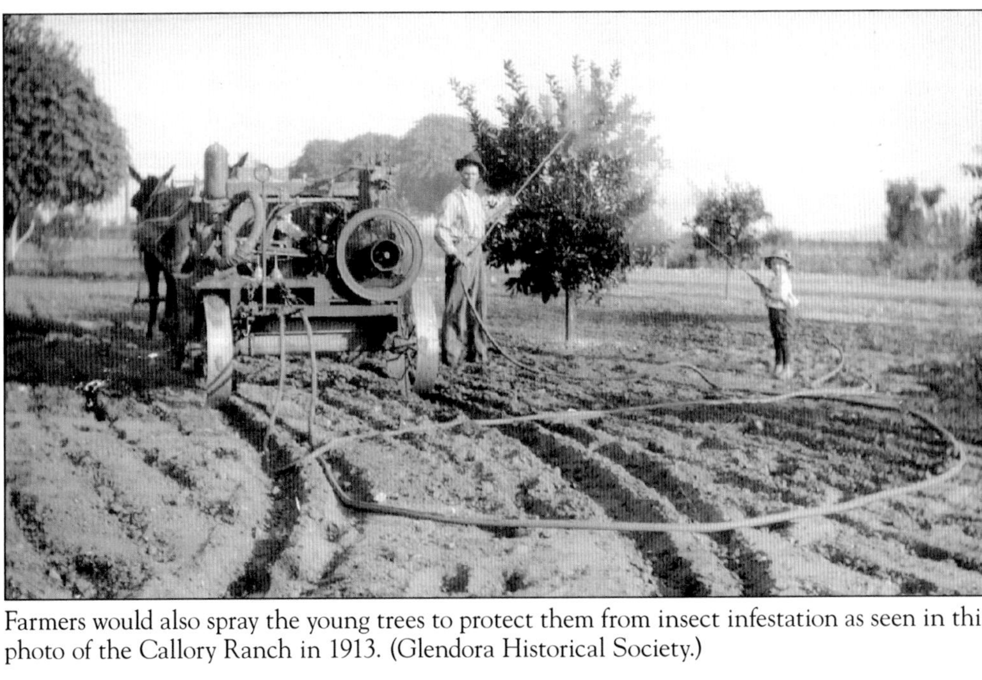

Farmers would also spray the young trees to protect them from insect infestation as seen in this photo of the Callory Ranch in 1913. (Glendora Historical Society.)

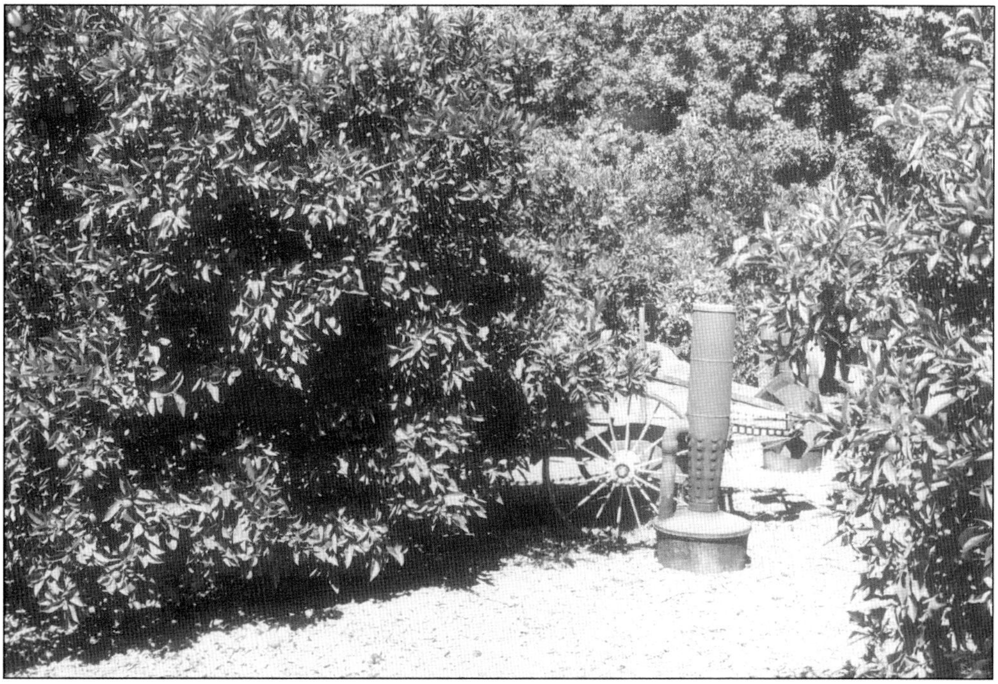

Above is a picture of orange grove with smudge pot. Smudge pots burned and were used to warm the citrus crops to keep them from freezing. Longtime residents tell stories of the smoke that would block the sun and the soot that would cover everything in the house. (J. Landers.)

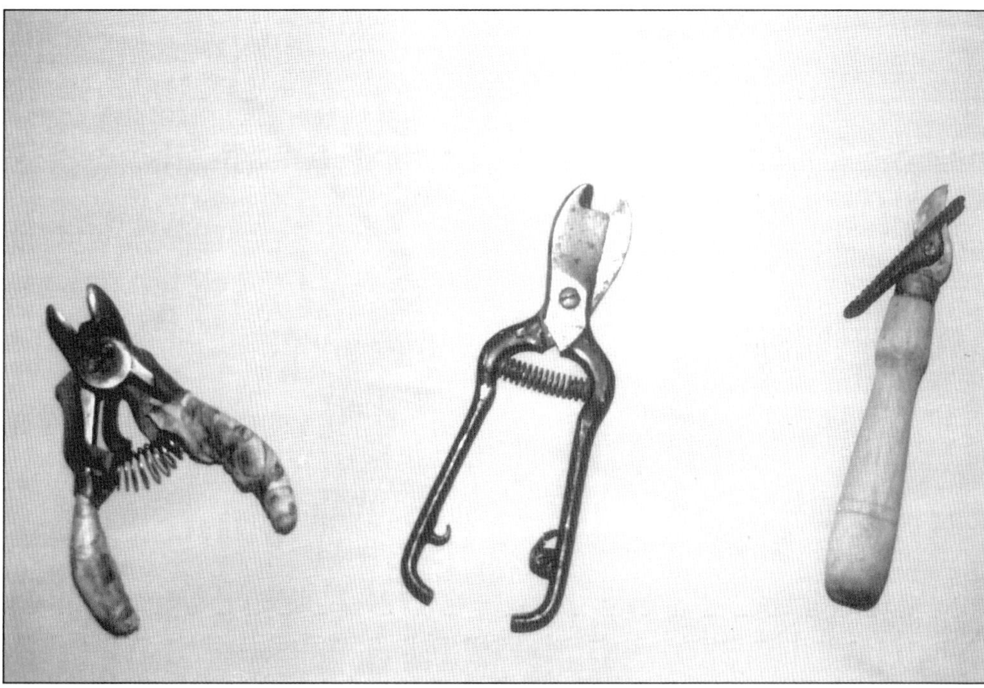

These picking tools are now housed in the Glendora Historical Society's museum. (J. Landers.)

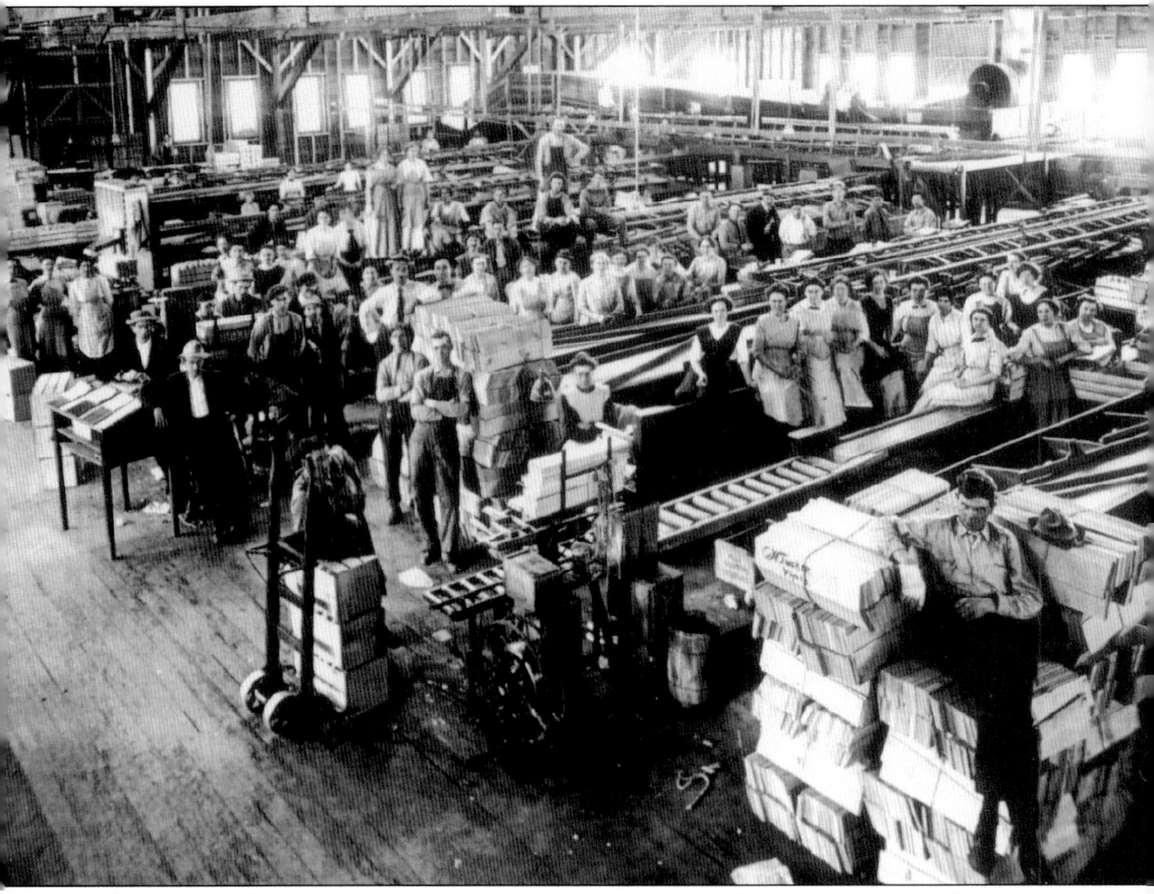

This image of a packing house dates back to the early 1900s. This is one of many such packing houses to pop up in and around Glendora, Azusa, and San Dimas. (Glendora Historical Society.)

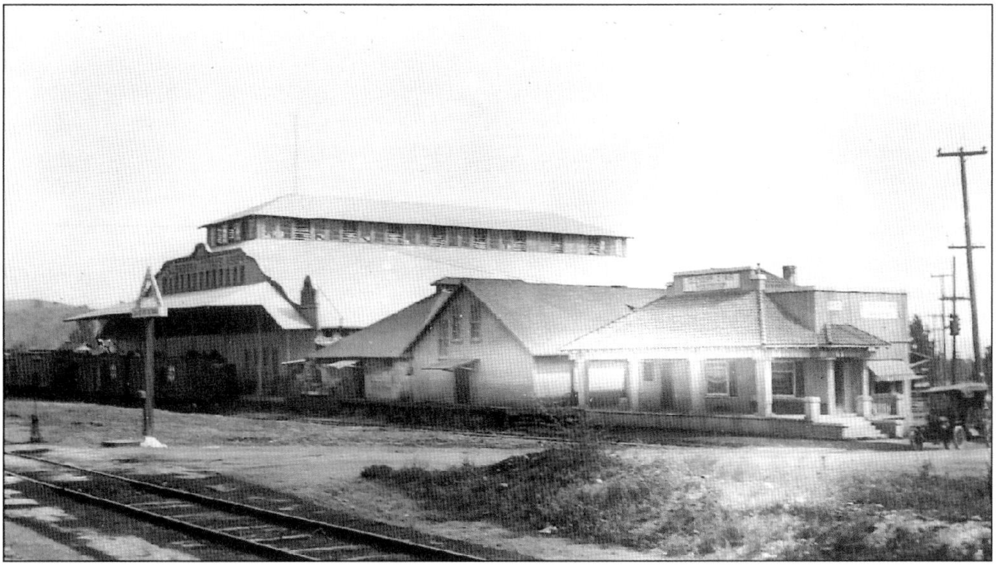

One of the first citrus packing houses in Glendora was located at Vermont Ave. and Ada. Ave. along the rail line to provide easy transport. (Glendora Historical Society.)

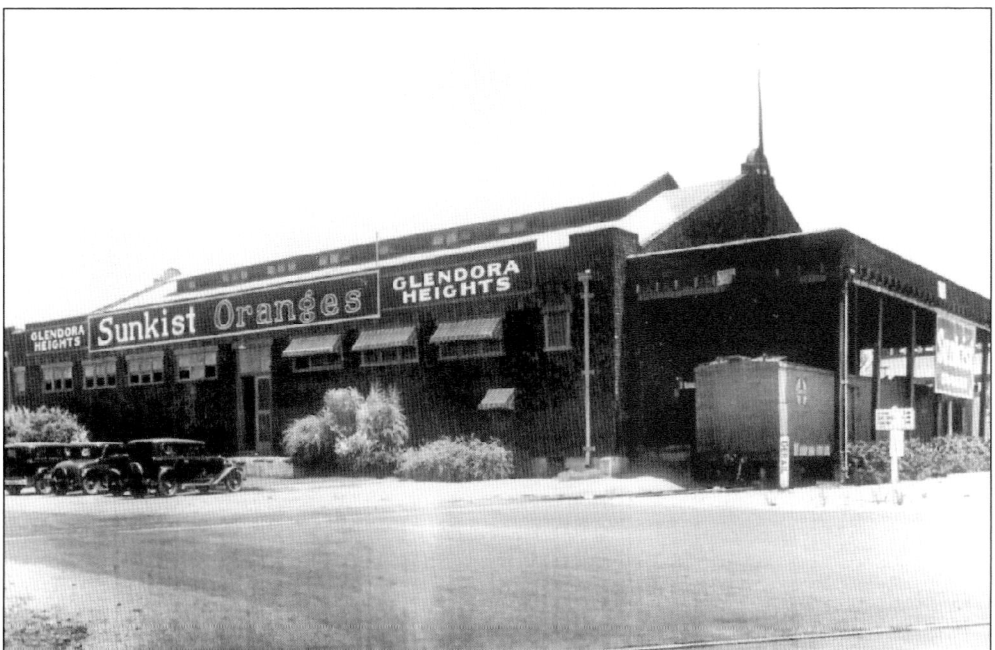

The "Sunkist Oranges" of the Glendora Heights Packing Association were loaded and transported east from this location—Grand Ave. and Foothill Blvd. (Glendora Historical Society.)

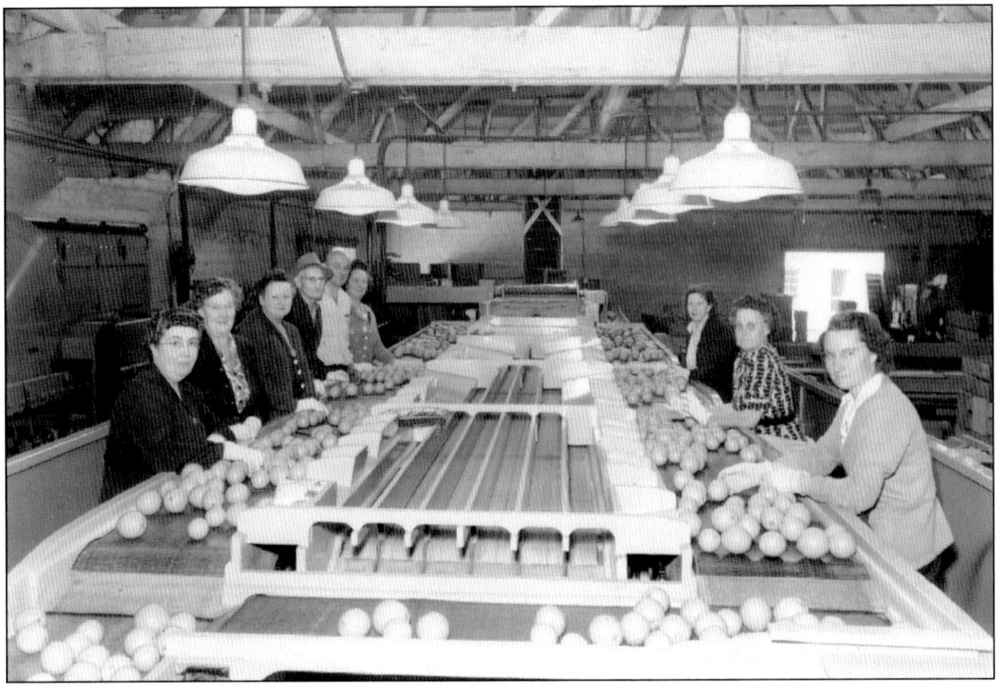

As the oranges came into the packing house, they were sized and separated as done by this Mutual Orange Packing Crew in the 1940s. (Glendora Historical Society.)

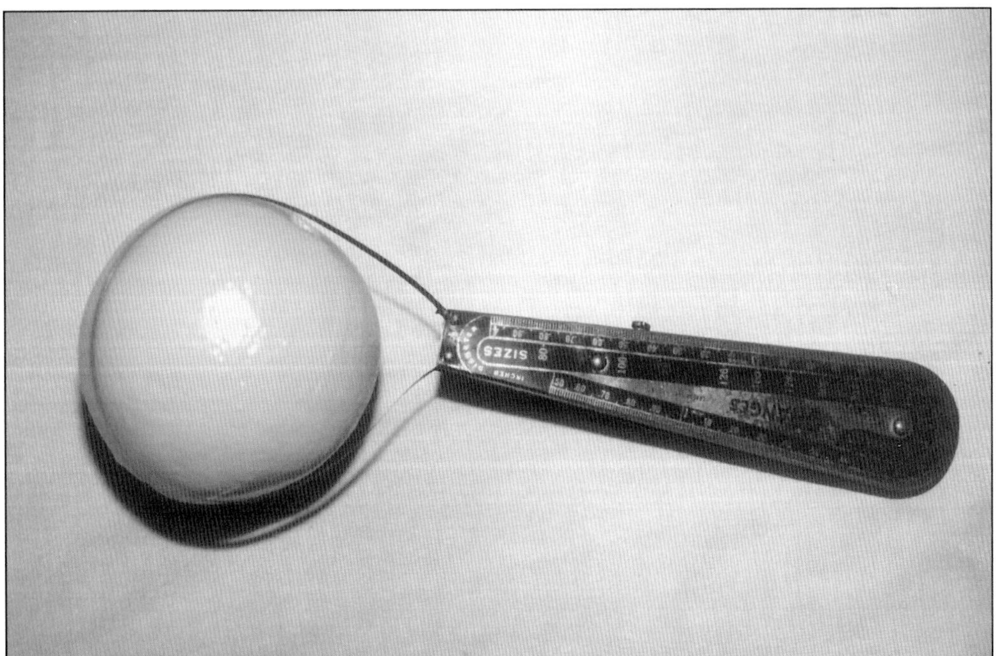

The packing houses included equipment such as this sizing ring with an orange inside. Each orange would be separated by size and placed into the proper bin for sale to consumers or for juice. (J. Landers.)

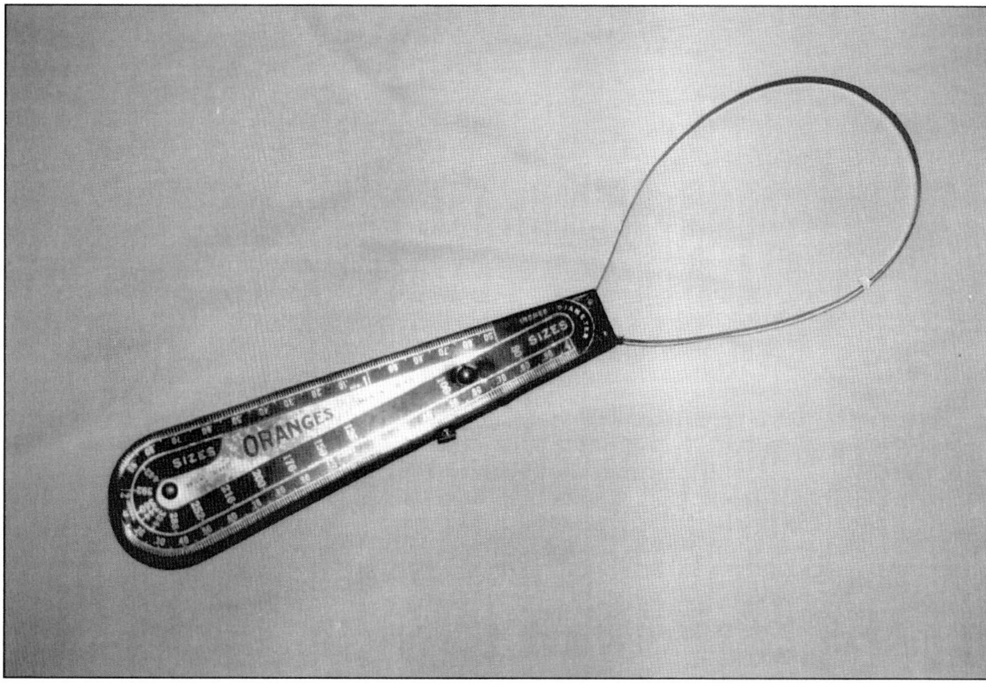

Above is an image of a sizing ring. (J. Landers.)

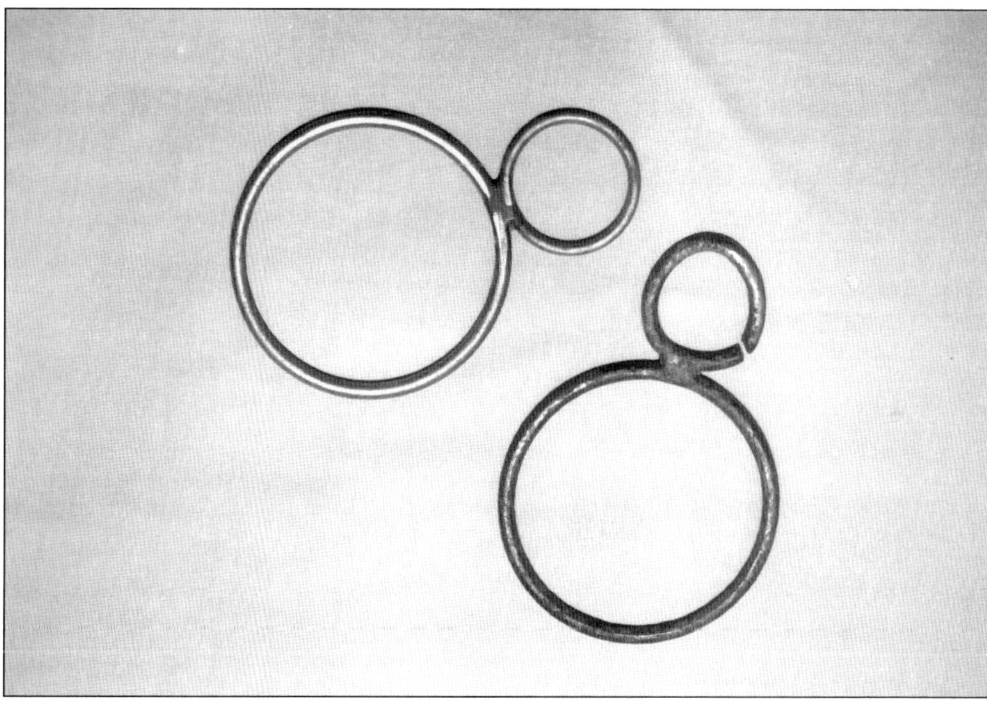

This sizing ring for lemons was used by packers to gauge quality. (J. Landers.)

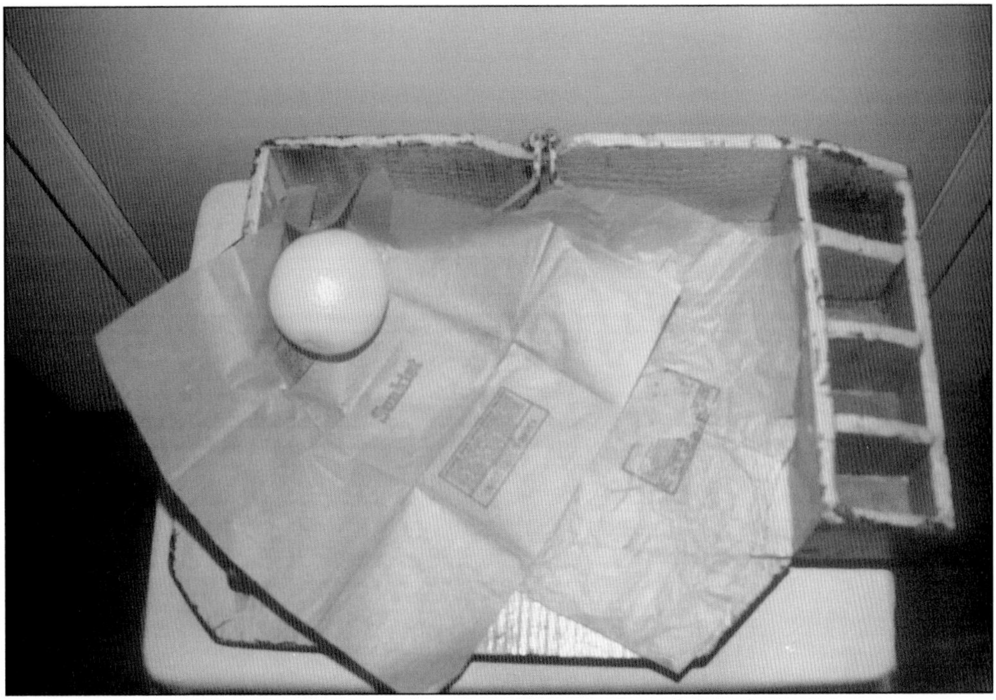

Packing house employees wrapped each orange in tissue paper and placed it in an egg carton-type container. This helped minimize bruising and mold damage during shipping. (J. Landers.)

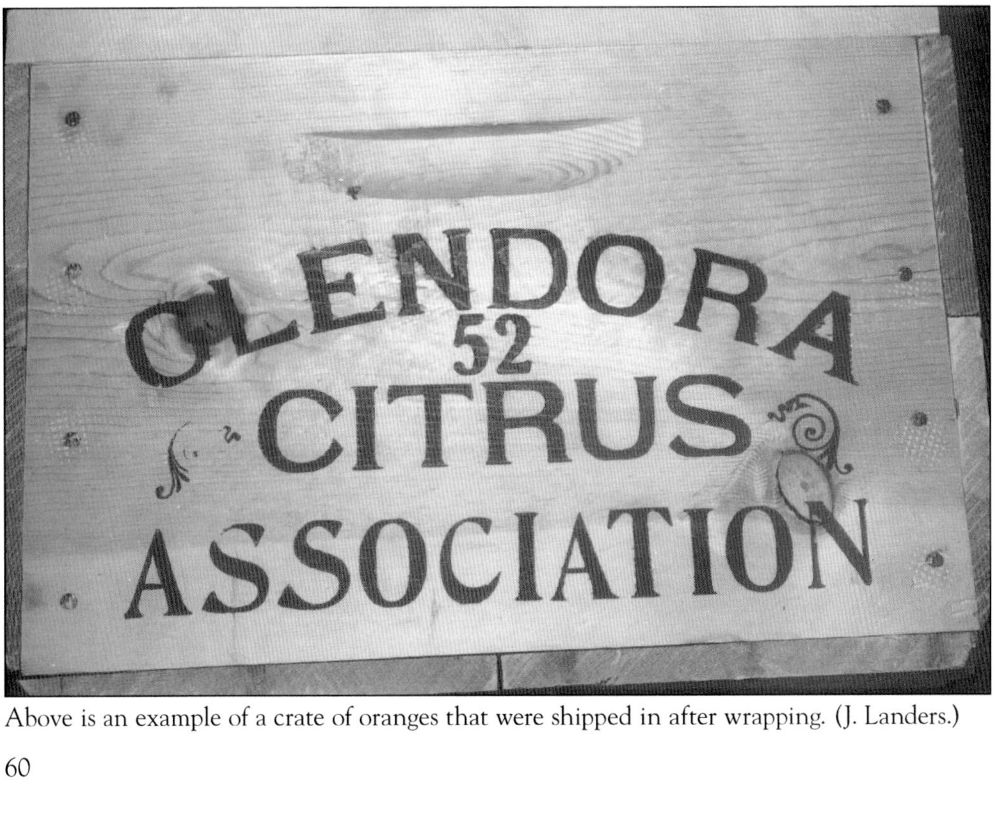

Above is an example of a crate of oranges that were shipped in after wrapping. (J. Landers.)

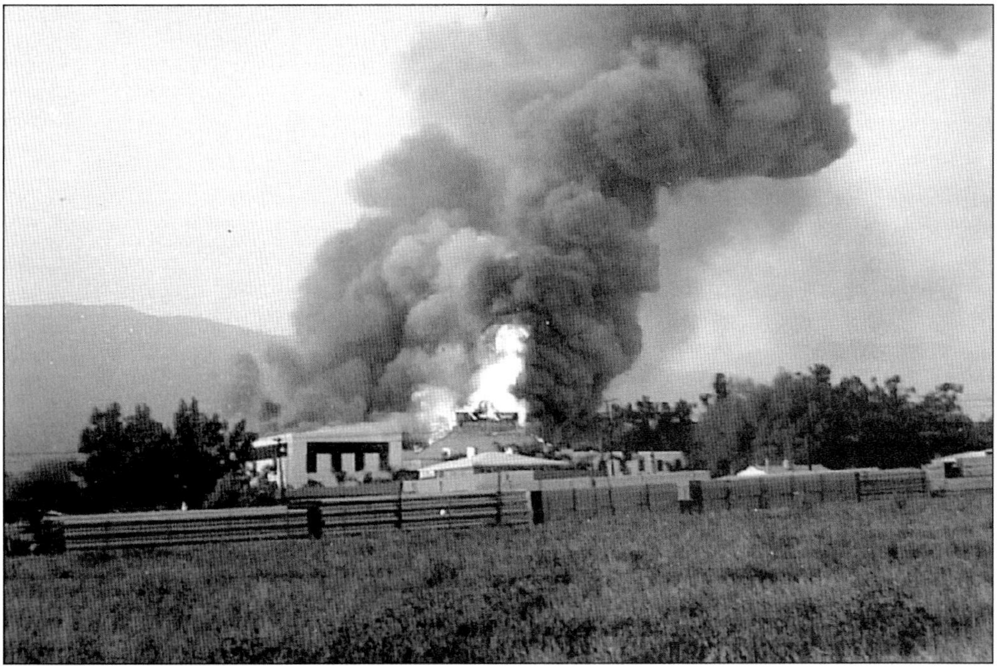

Packing houses were always threatened by fires. Machine oil and grease were regularly used to keep conveyor belts and motors working, and many wooden packing houses caught fire, like this one on Foothill Blvd. (J. Landers.)

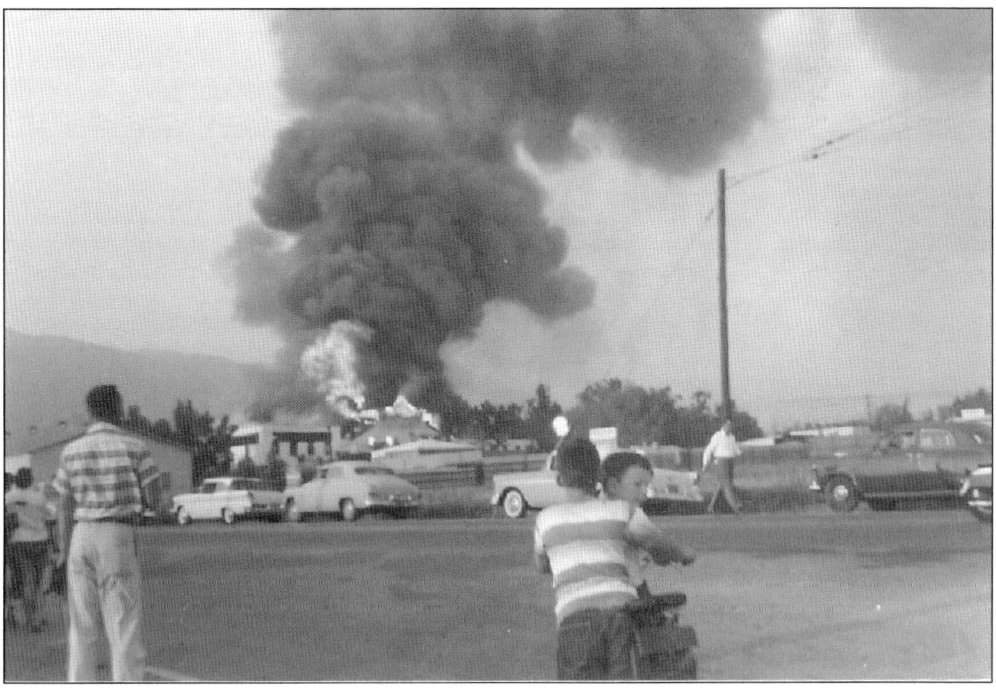

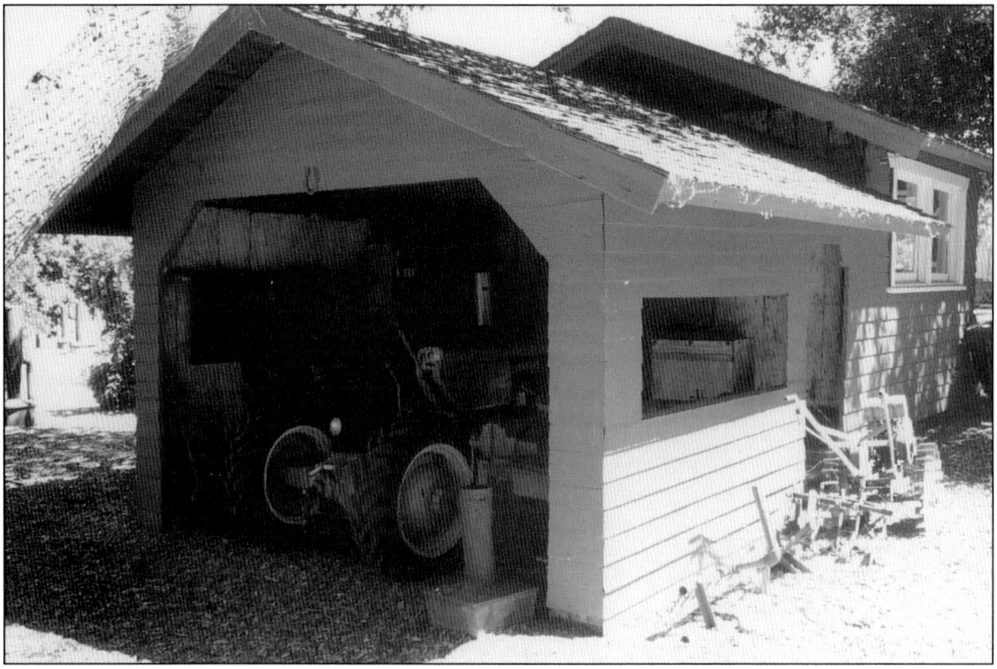

Orton Englehardt, a Glendora citrus grower, needed to find a way to irrigate his citrus trees. He developed the first impact sprinkler in this barn. (J.Landers.)

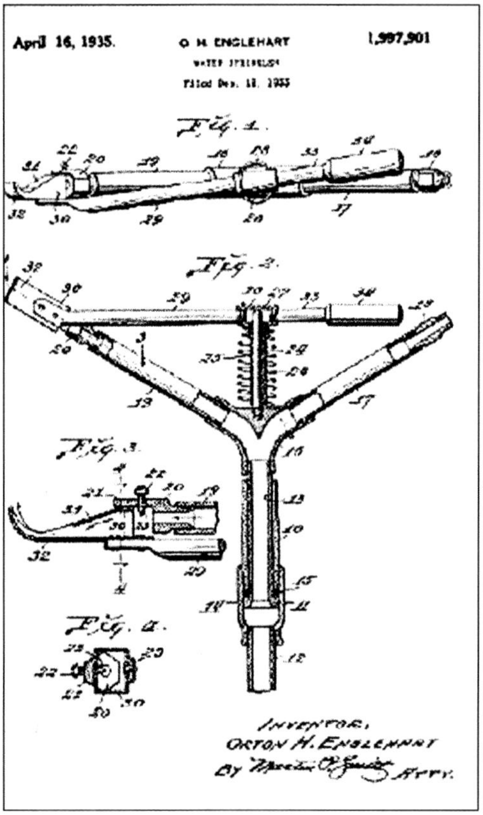

This is the patent design of the "Rain Bird Sprinkler Head." Clement La Fetra, a friend of Englehardt and a descendent of a pioneer family, saw the potential of such a device and was given the right to market the product. Thus was born a company known world wide as "Rain Bird." (Rain Bird Corp.)

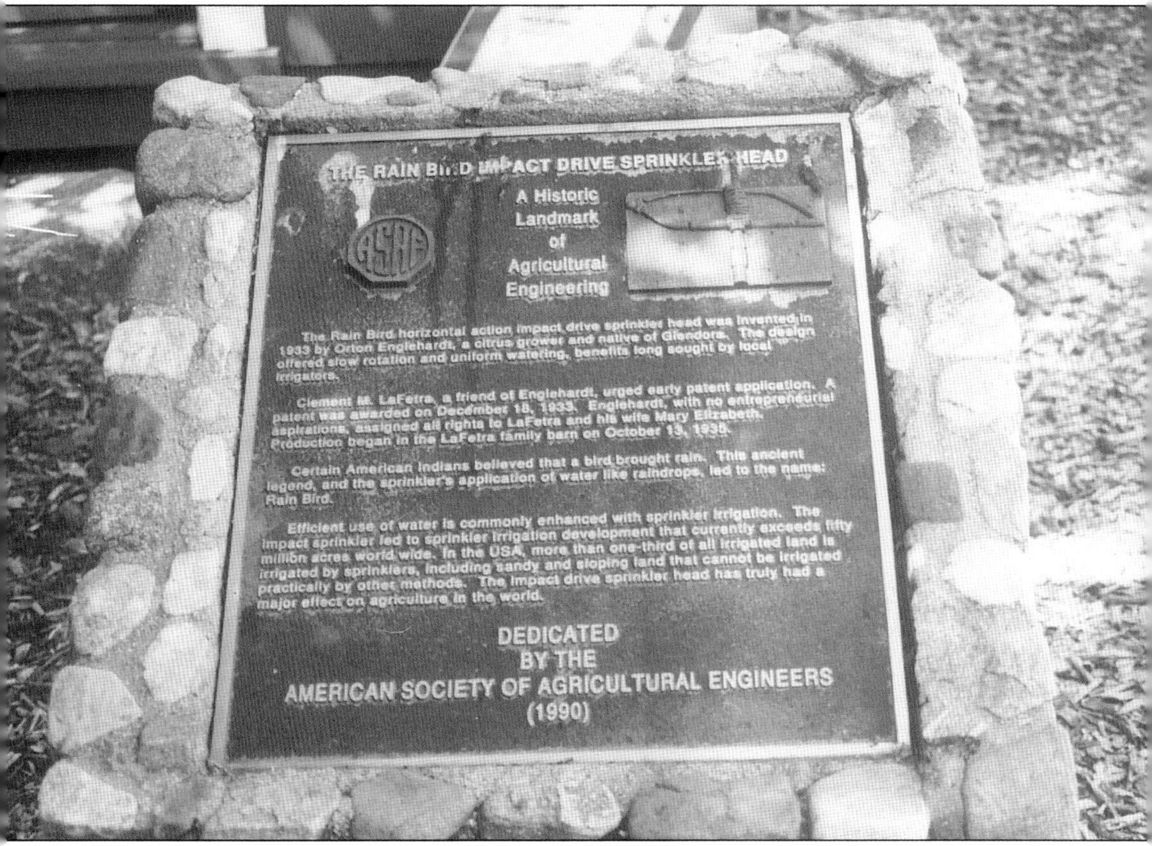

This plaque—dedicated by the American Society of Agricultural Engineering—is at the barn where Engelhardt developed the impact sprinkler. (J. Landers.)

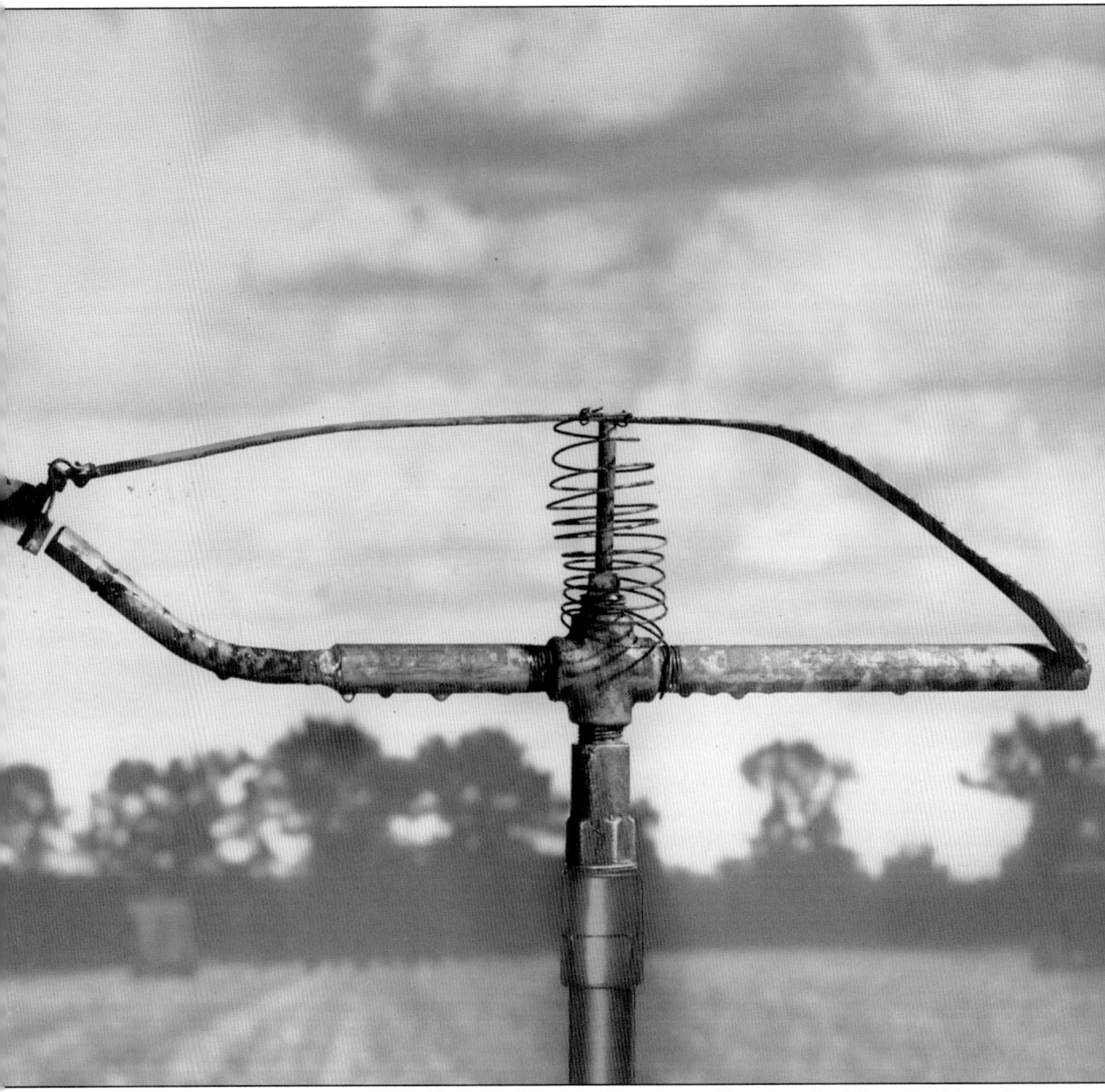

The original "impact drive" sprinkler was developed by Orton Engelhardt. (Rain Bird Int., Rain Bird Corp.)

Four

THE PEOPLE WHO CALLED GLENDORA HOME

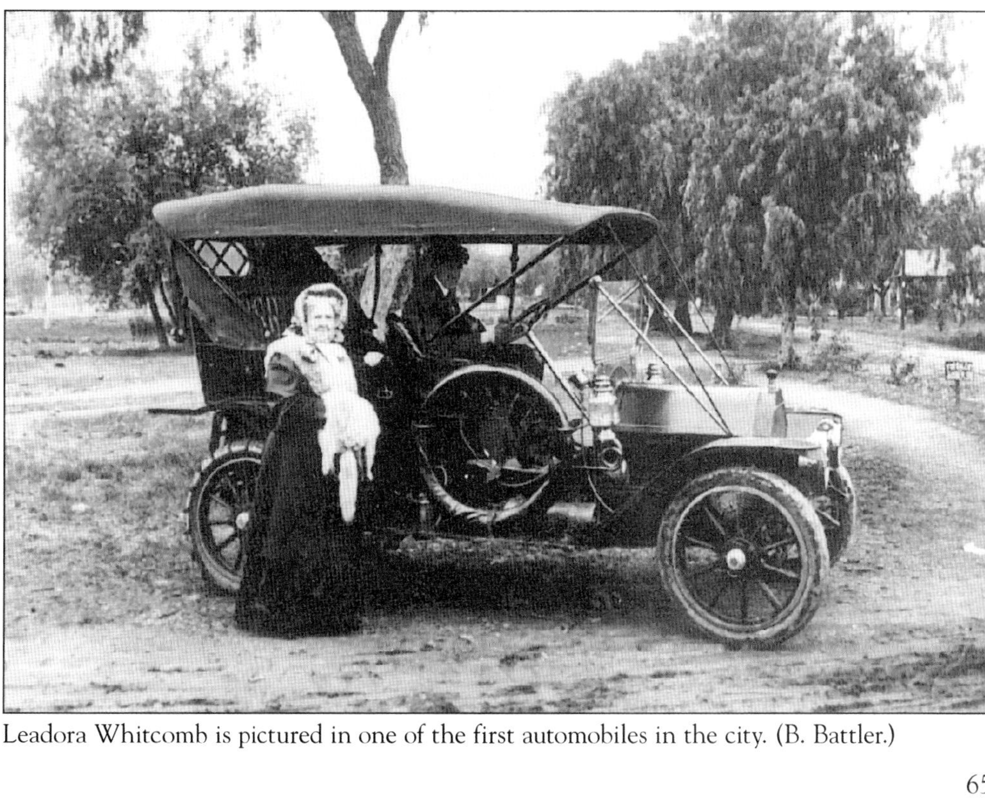

Leadora Whitcomb is pictured in one of the first automobiles in the city. (B. Battler.)

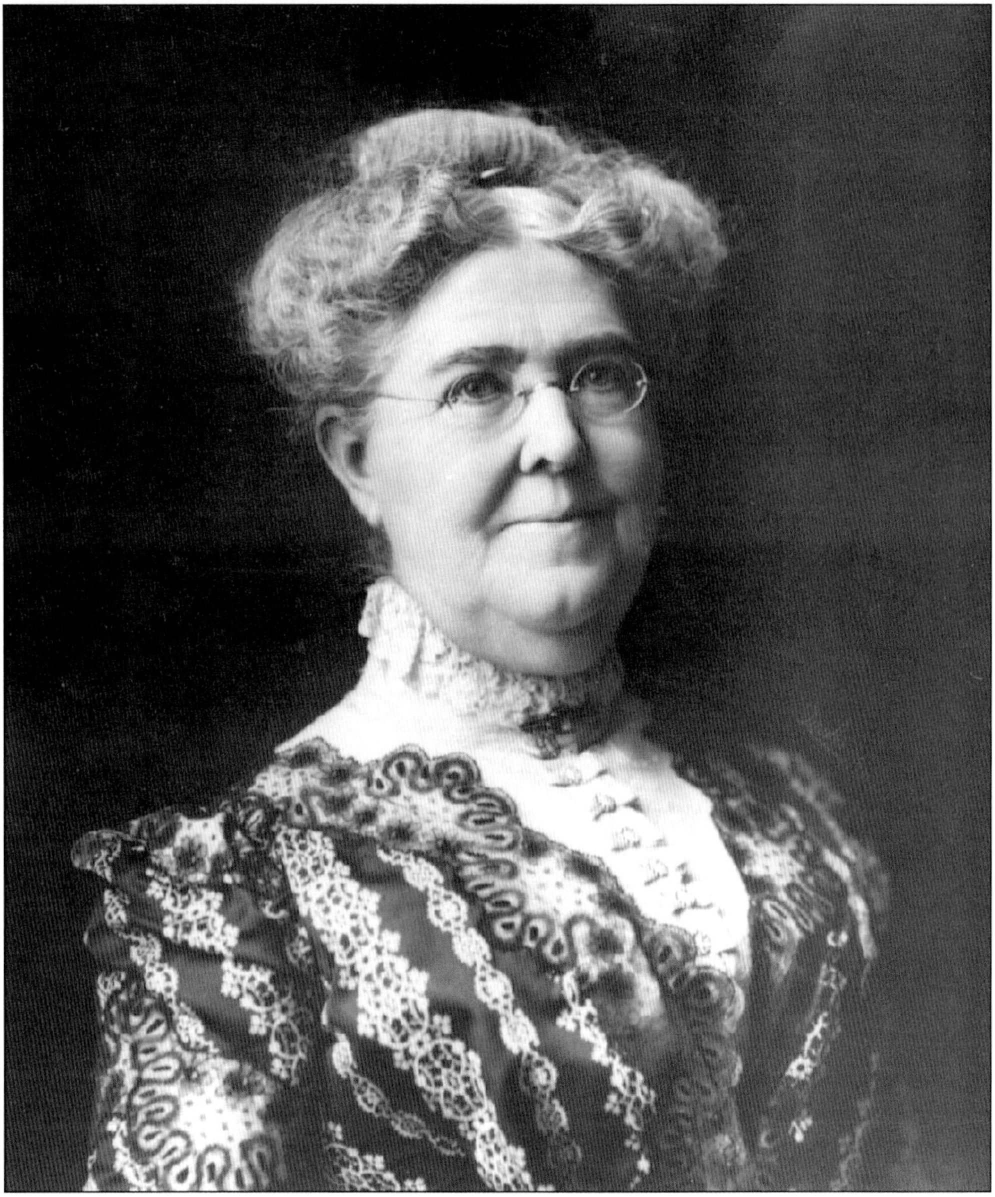

Leadora Whitcomb, wife of founder George Whitcomb, used part of her name in Glendora. (B. Battler.)

William B. Cullen is pictured here with his wife. William lost an arm in the Civil War and moved west in 1874. He built his home with lumber from an abandoned gold camp in the San Gabriel Canyon. (B. Battler.)

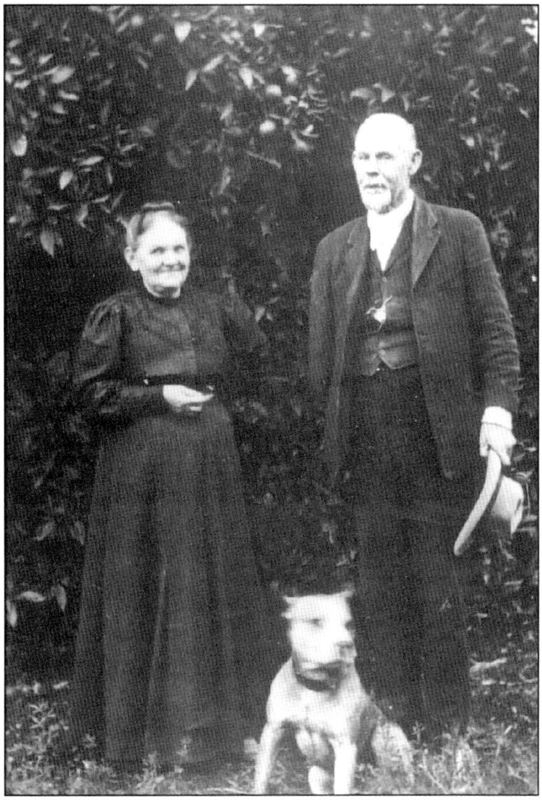

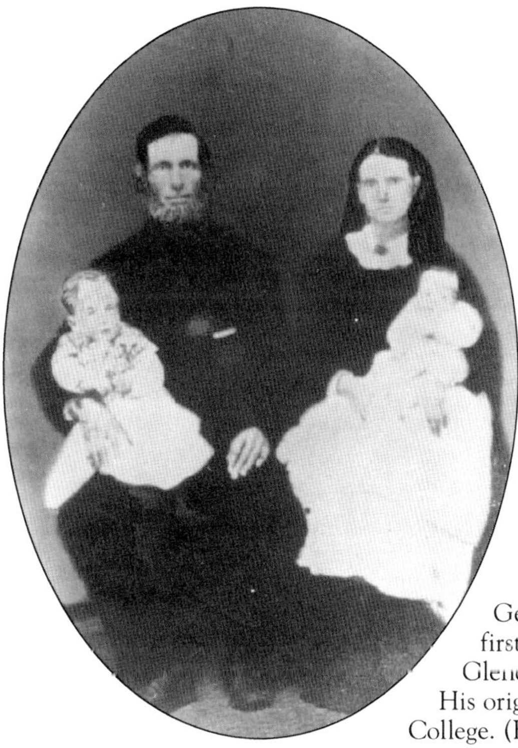

George and Livey Wright were two of the first settlers of the area that would become Glendora; George farmed, did handy work, etc. His original house stood on the site of Citrus College. (B. Battler.)

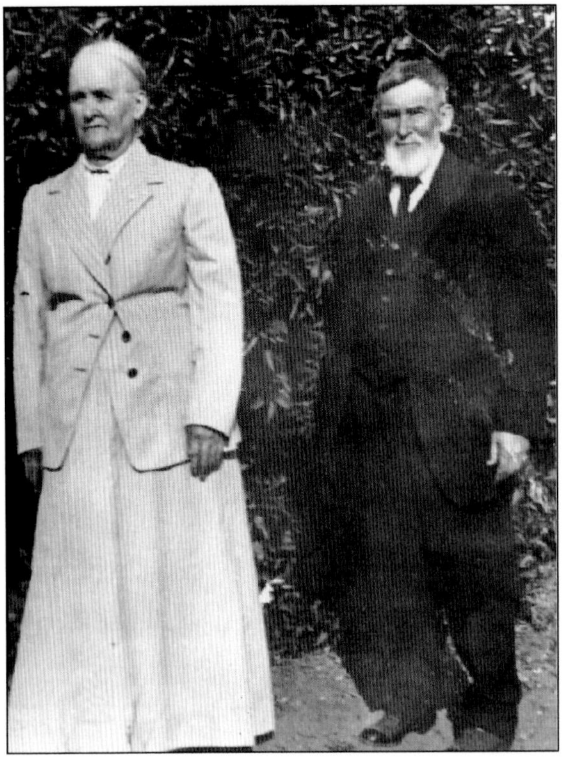

Philip and Malvina Shory were also among the original settlers and orchard growers. (B. Battler.)

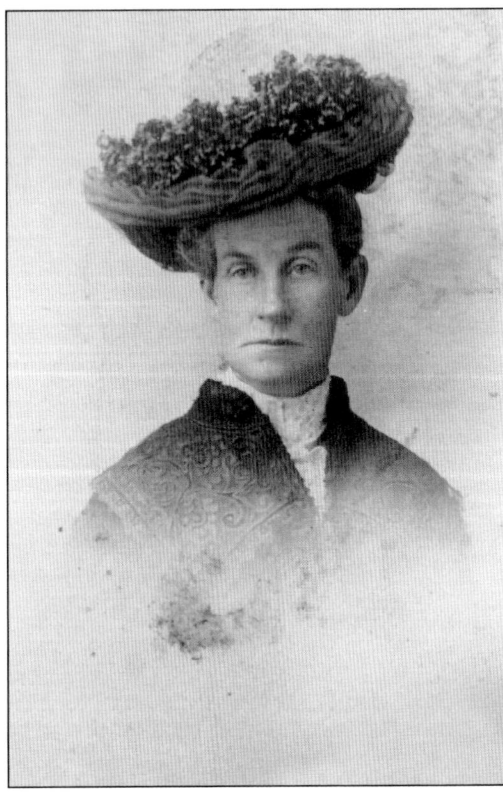

Pictured is Glendora's first librarian, Lucetta Nancy Suydam. You definitely kept quiet in her library. (B. Battler.)

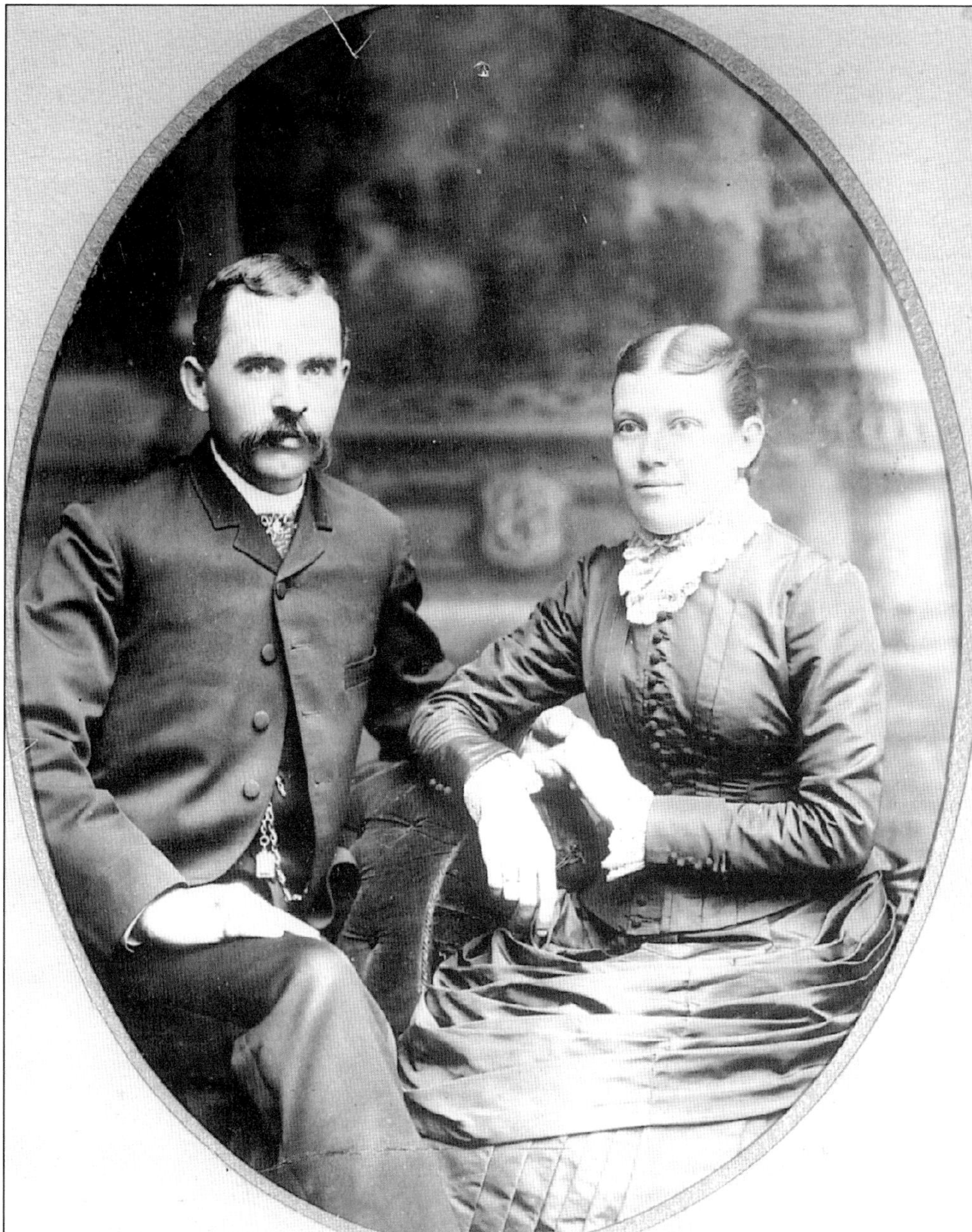

Sanford Scofield and his wife Mary are pictured above. One of the original settlers in the Glendora area, his house and orchards were near present-day Base Line road and the 210 Freeway. (B. Battler.)

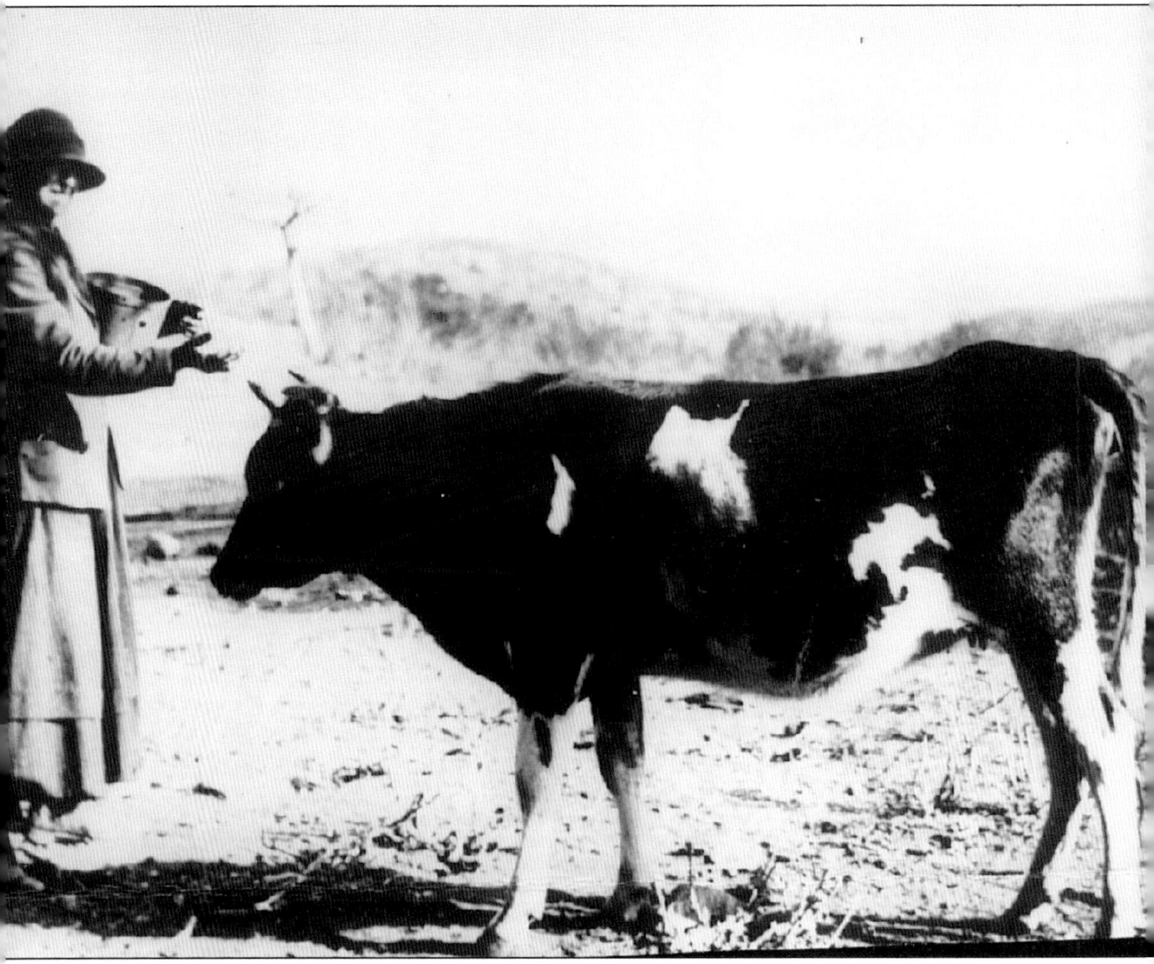

Almyra Eckles had the reputation of being able to "beat up" any man in town. (B. Battler.)

Russian immigrants moved here and began a small community after the fall of the czar. (B. Battler.)

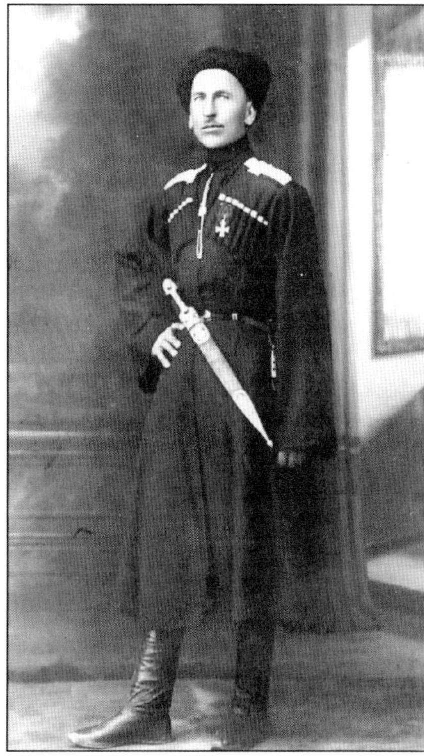

Church services are still being held on the original site. (B. Battler.)

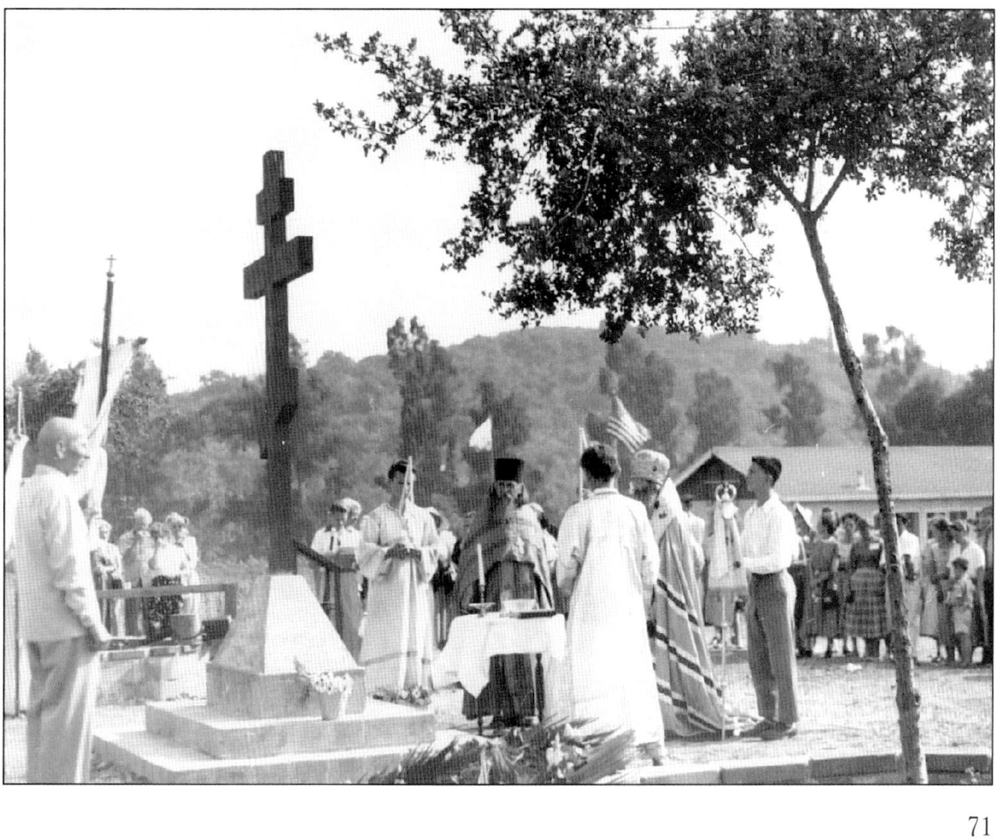

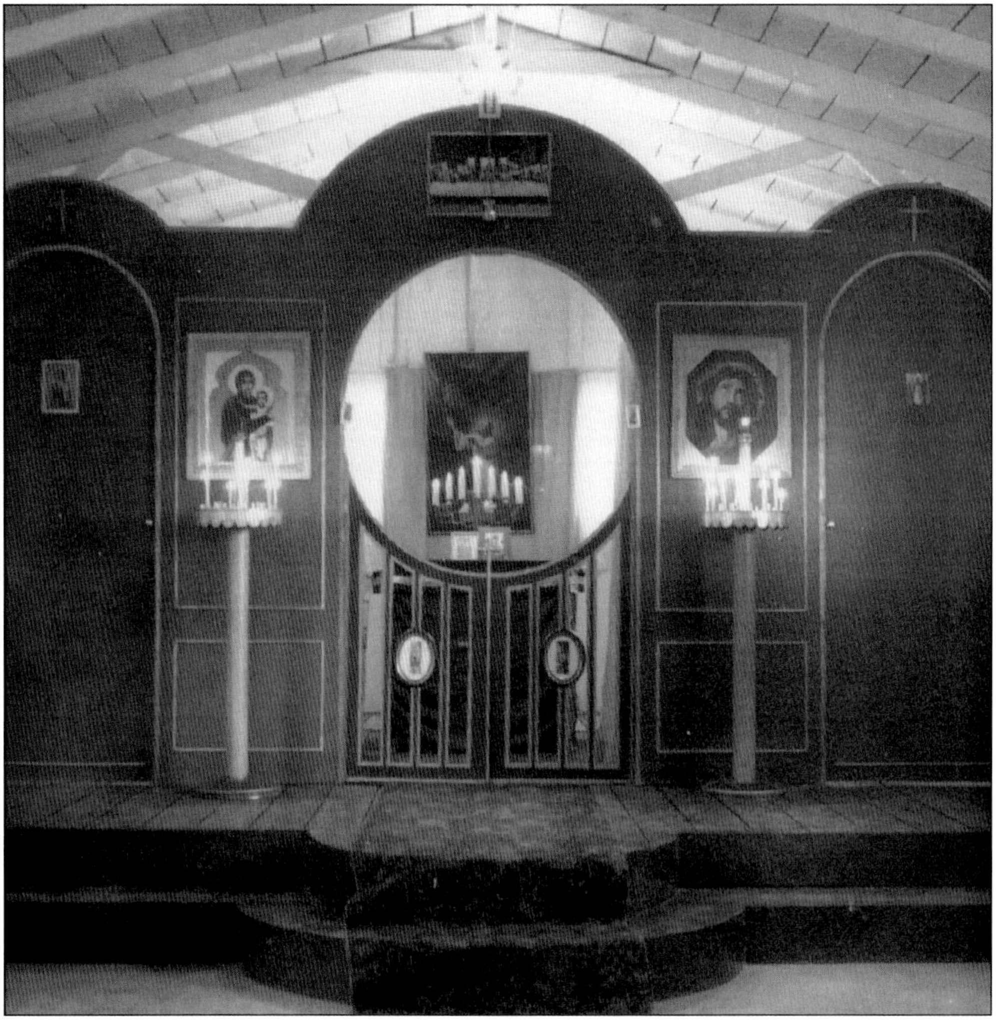

Pictured is an Russian Orthodox church altar. (B. Battler.)

James Jefferson West was one of the first people to measure and record the rainfall in the Glendora area. He was also the mayor of Glendora from 1916–1918. (B. Battler.)

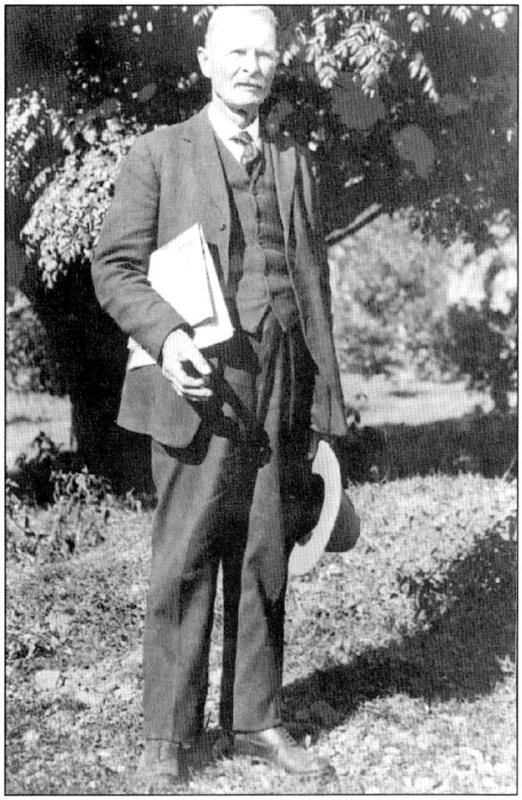

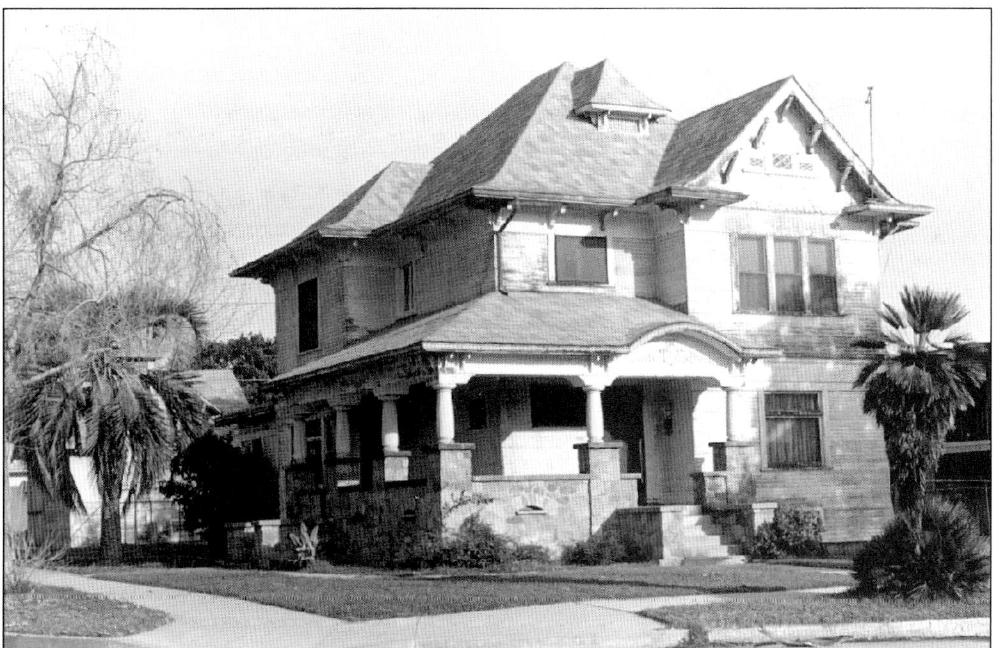

The house that West built still stands behind City Hall. (B. Battler.)

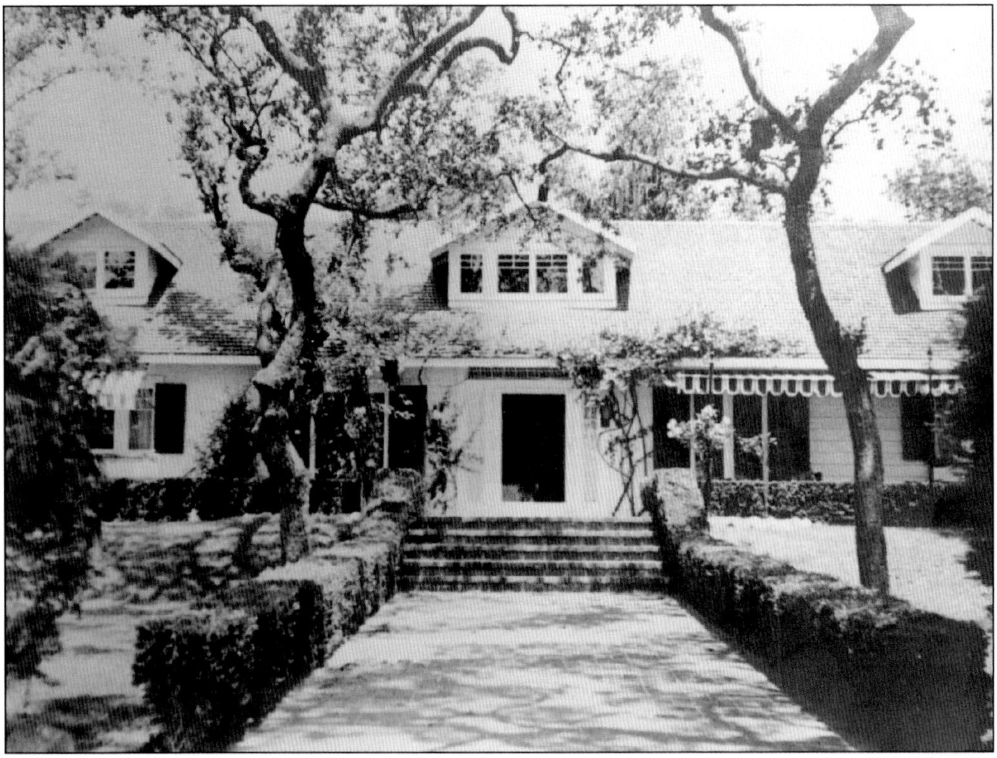

Actress Mary Miles's pictures for Metro were *The Fairy and The Waif*, *Dimples*, and *Lovely Mary*. She lived in Glendora and bought her house along with the guest house next door. (B. Battler.)

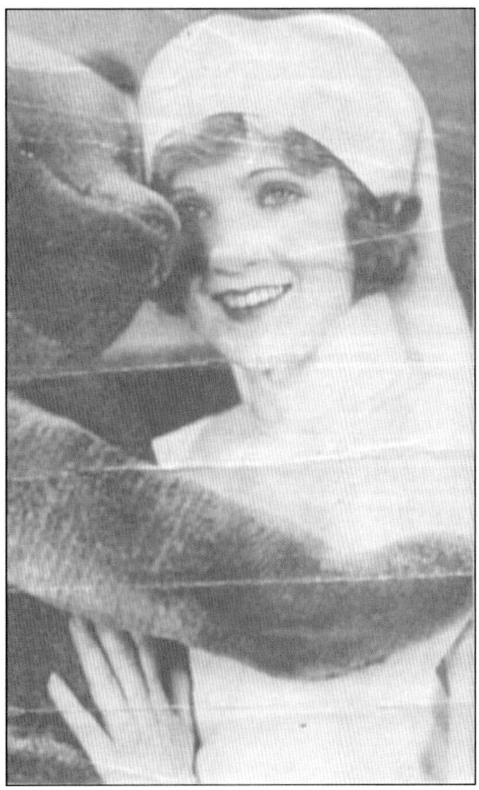

Mary Miles is seen here in a publicity shot from the 1920s. (B. Battler.)

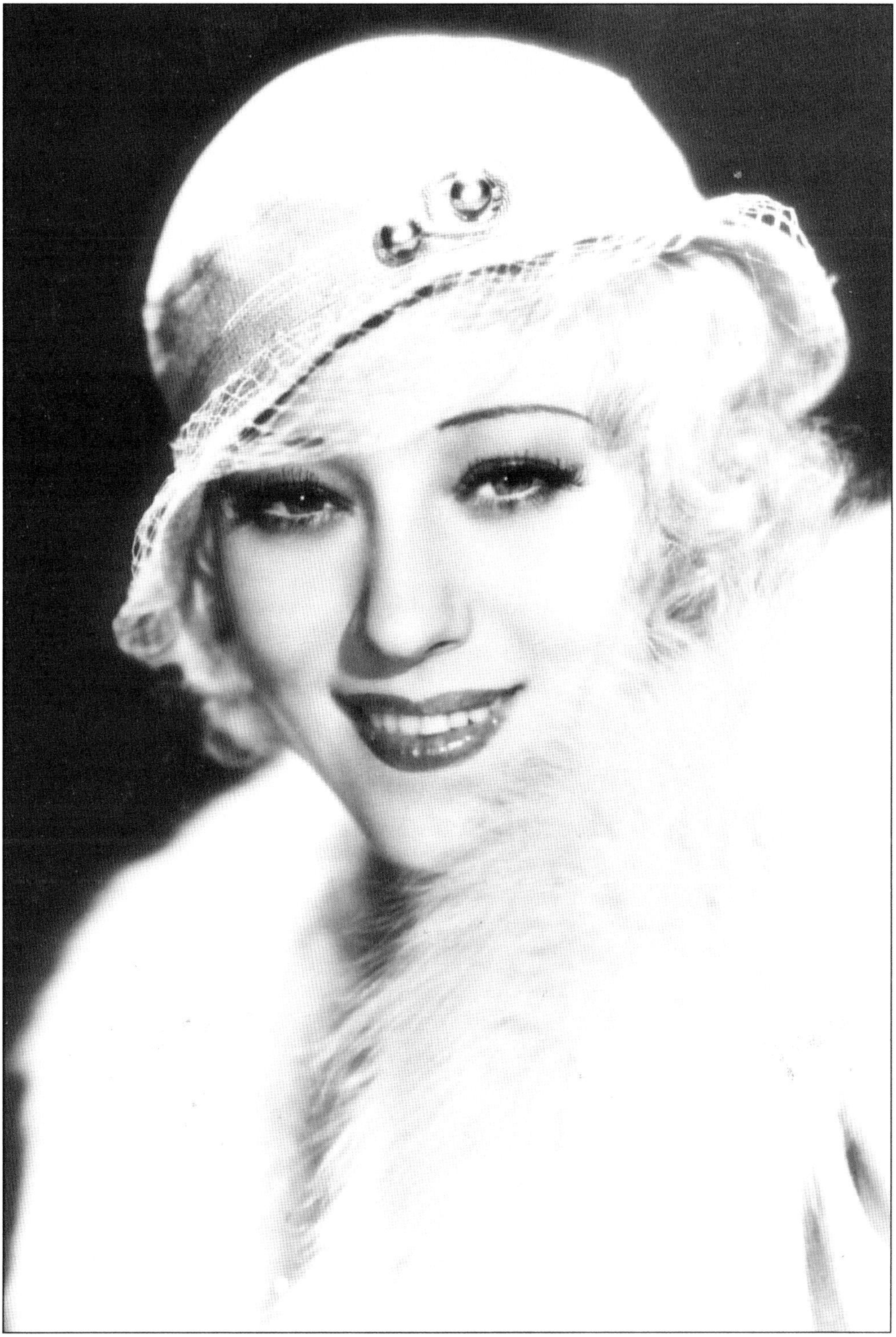

During the 1930s World's Fair, Sally Rand became a household name as a result of her famous "fan dance." She moved to Glendora and became part of the community. (B. Battler.)

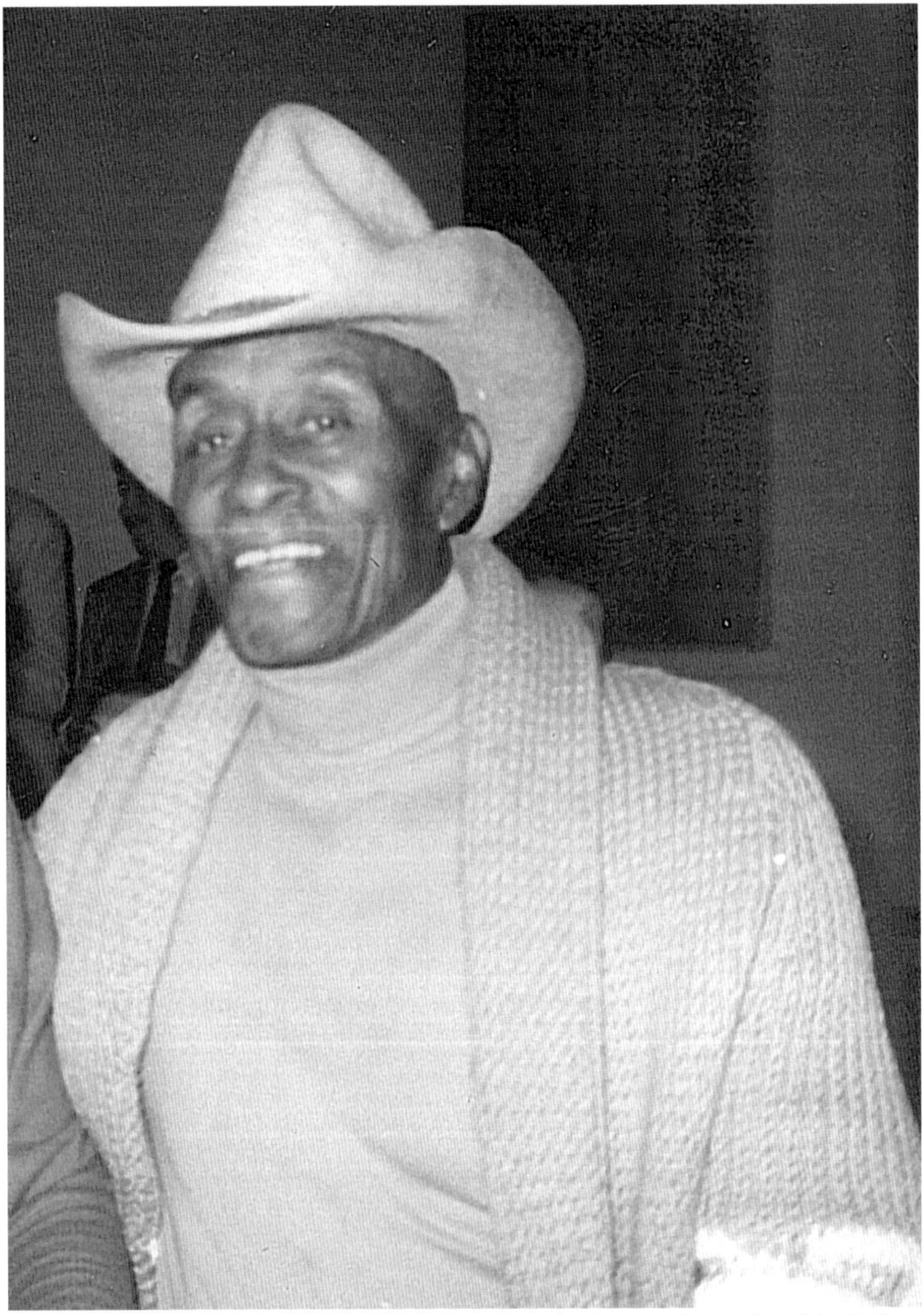

From engaging in gladiator fights in the Colosseum to leading a column of Buffalo Soldiers across the Western Frontier, Woody Strode was pioneer in American films. He was also an active member of the Glendora Historical Society. (B. Battler.)

Five

The Art of Citrus Labels

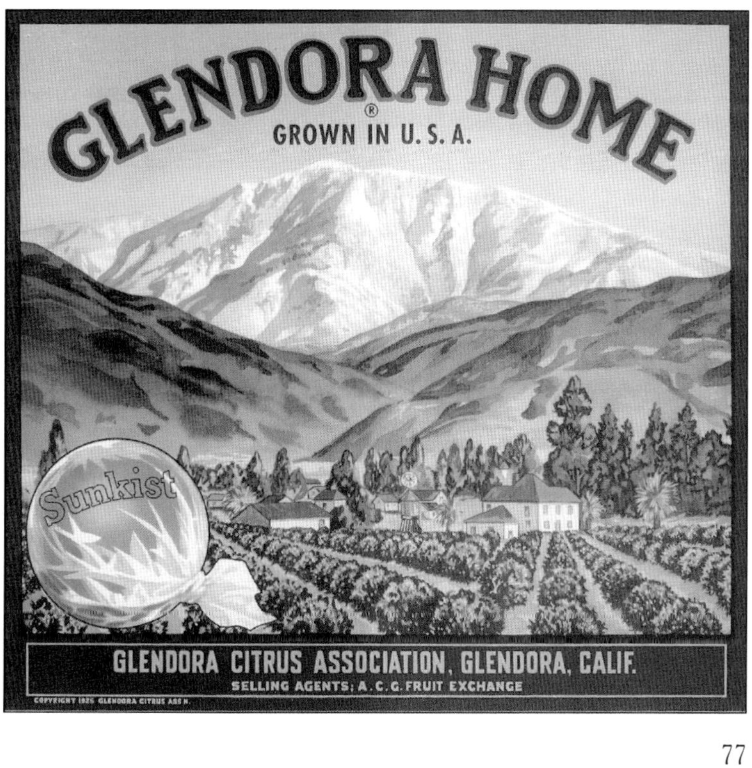

The Glendora Home brand of navel oranges artwork shows Glendora snug against the foothills with a snow-capped Mt. Baldy in the center. (Huntington Library.)

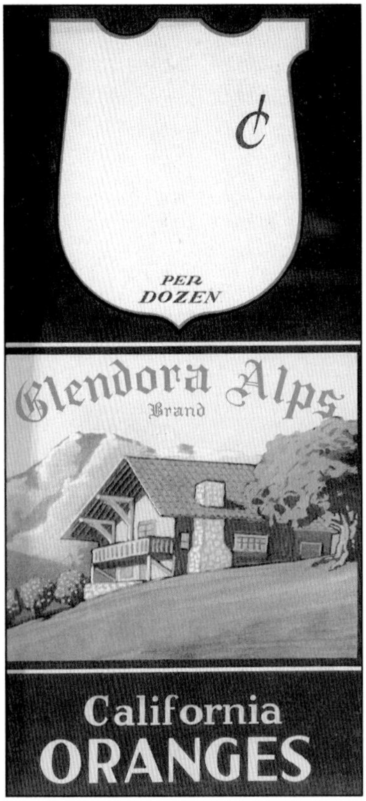

A Glendora Alps box-end has a place for the price of the fruit as well as a picture of the company's logo—a traditional Swiss Alps chateau. (Huntington Library.)

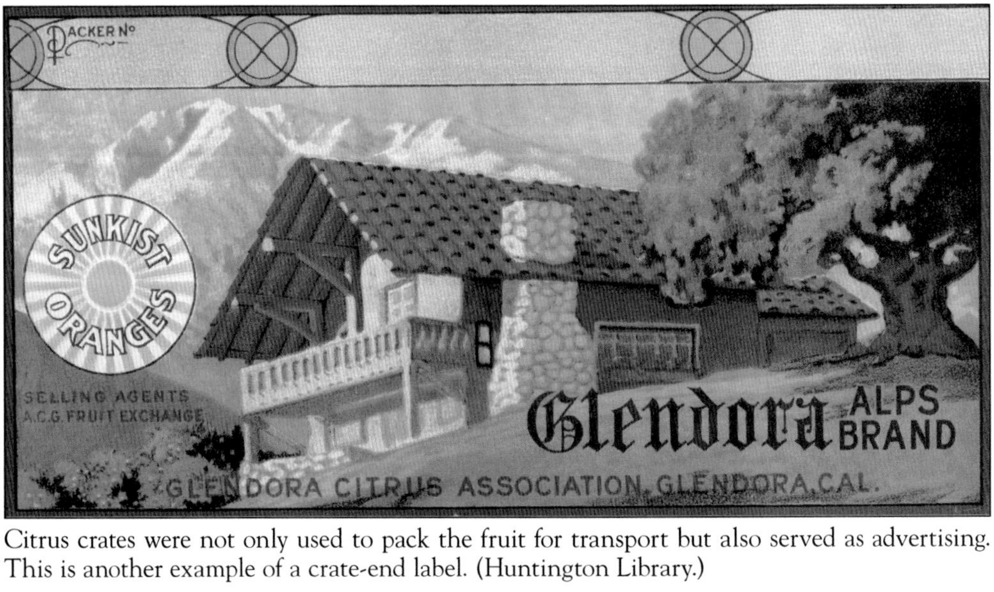

Citrus crates were not only used to pack the fruit for transport but also served as advertising. This is another example of a crate-end label. (Huntington Library.)

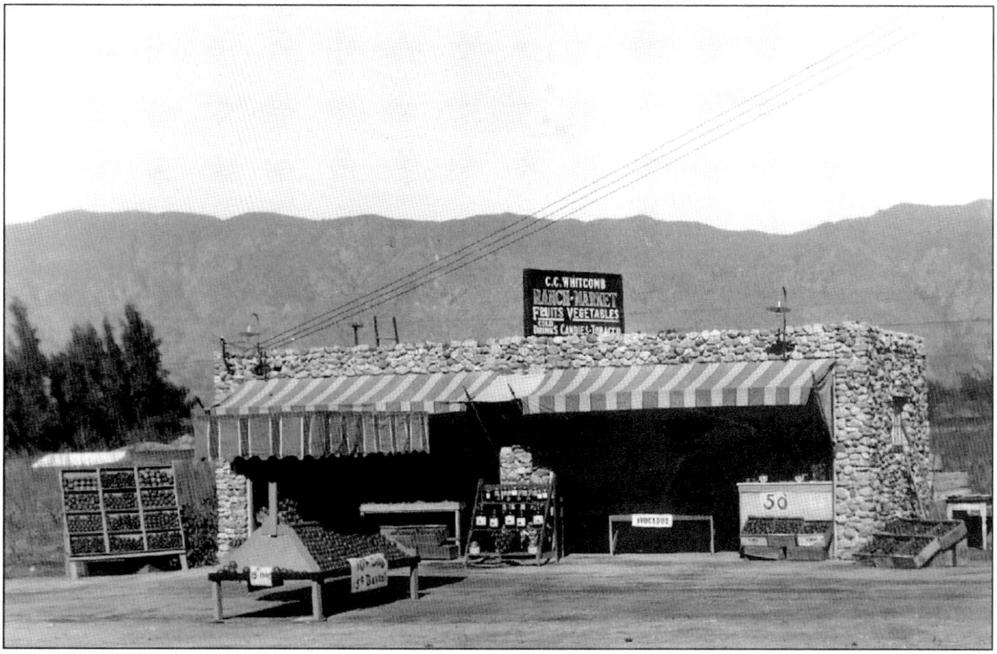

As Route 66 became the main highway to travel into Los Angeles, many of Glendora's citrus growers set up roadside stands to sell their fruit. This particular stand was run by Leadora Whitcomb along Foothill Blvd. (Huntington Library.)

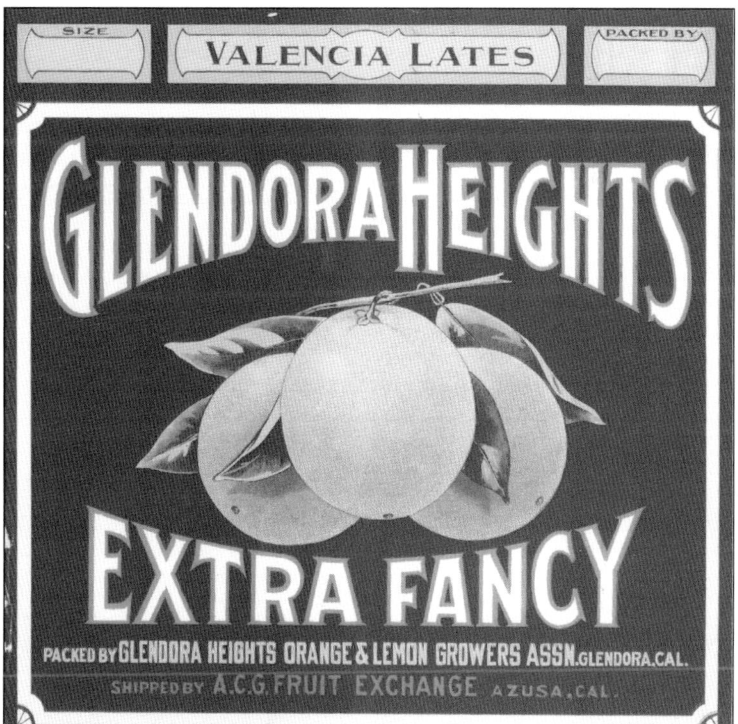

Pictured at right are Glendora Heights Valencia Oranges. Art and advertising were important in selling the fruit. Advertisers would display only perfect oranges on the citrus crate labels to show the buyer that they were the best. (Huntington Library.)

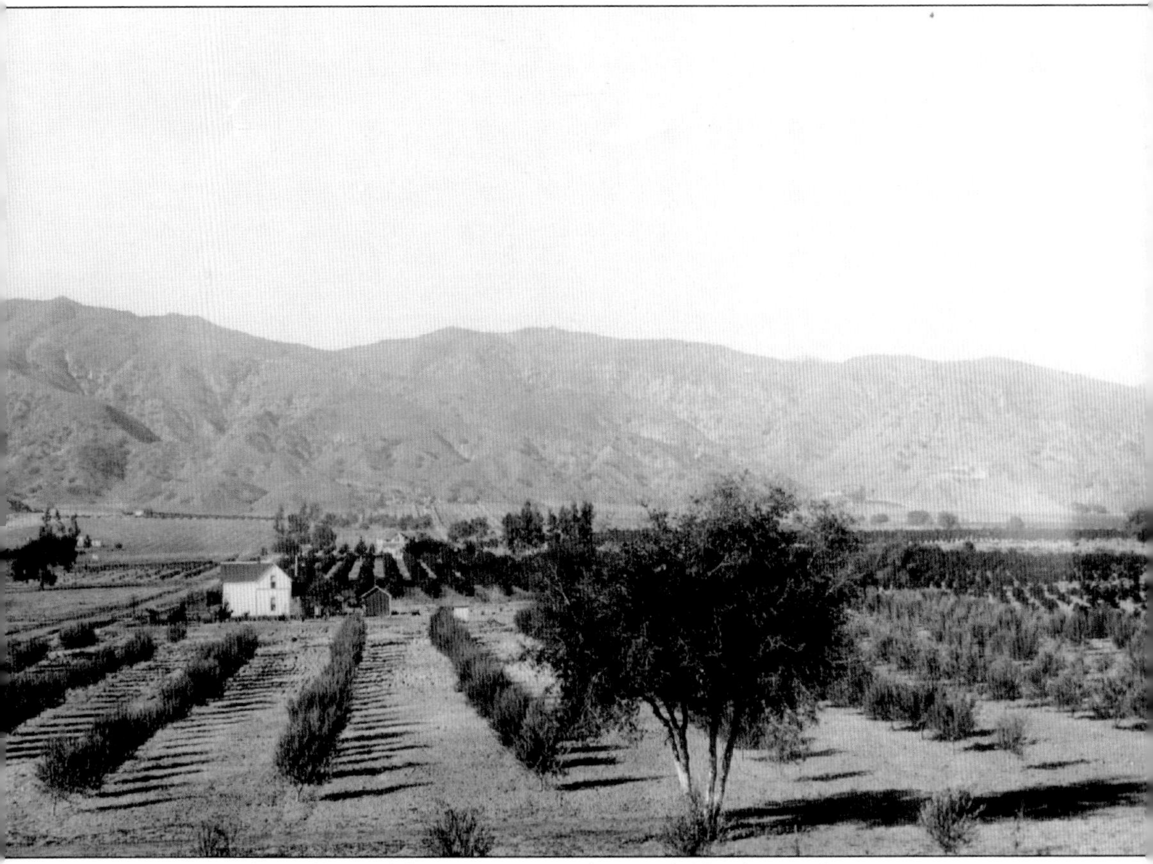

Lemons were also well suited for growing in and around Glendora and were given great care in packing and shipping. (Glendora Historical Society.)

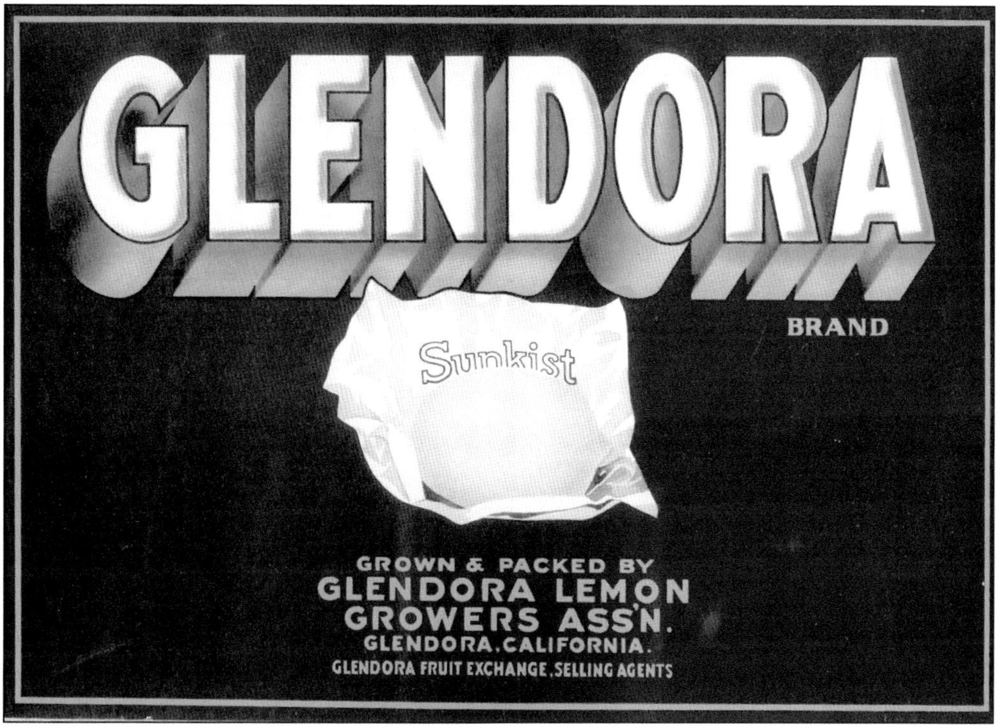

The Glendora Lemon Growers Association label shows a bold name and the tender care with which they handle their product. (Huntington Library.)

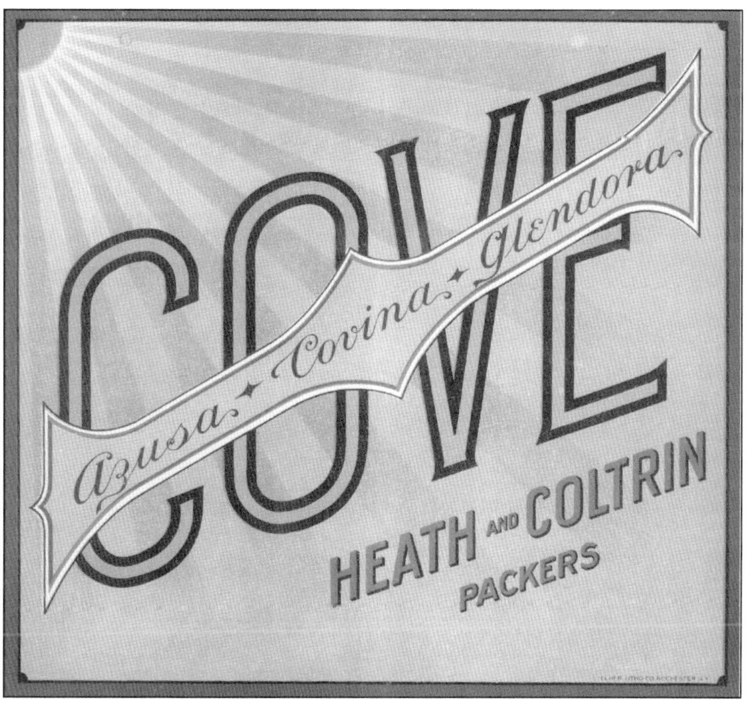

Many of the towns in the San Gabriel Valley were close together, so many farmers banded together and created their own citrus association to handle the buying and selling of the fruit. (Huntington Library.)

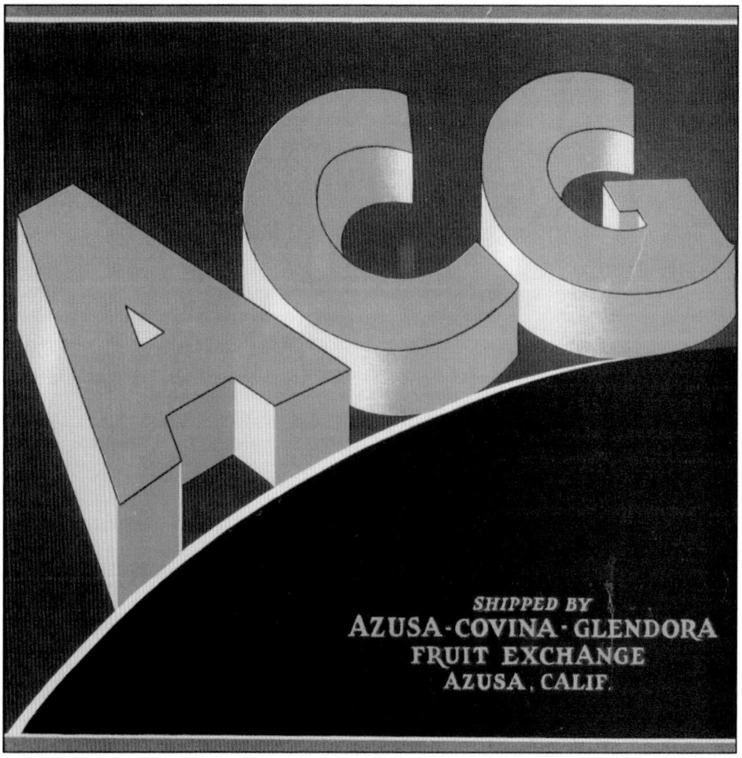

Sometimes the citrus label art was nothing more than the simple use of the first letters of the towns names as here with ACG: Azusa-Covina-Glendora Citrus Association. (Huntington Library.)

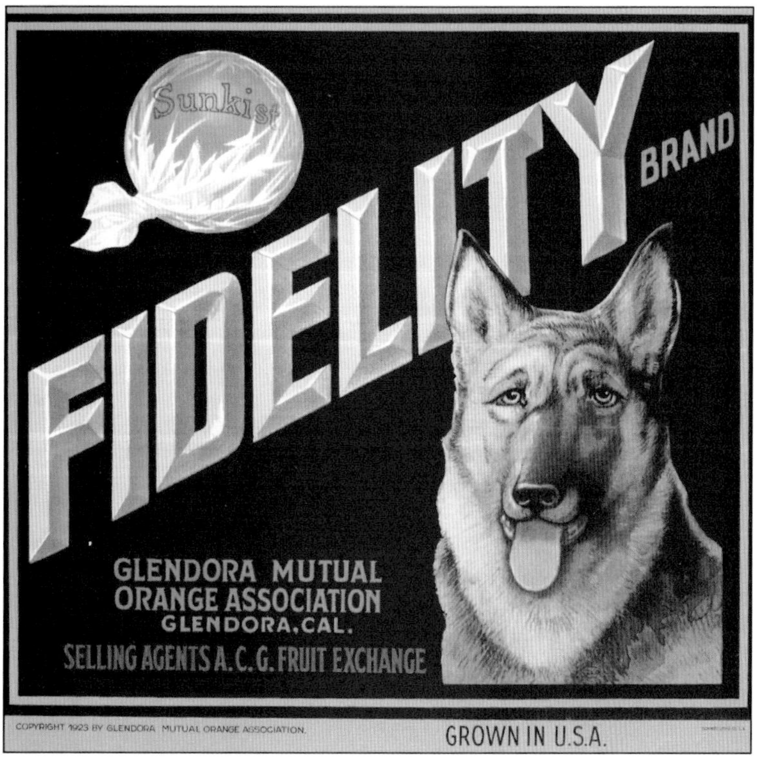

Buyers could depend on the quality of the Fidelity Brand of the Glendora Mutual Orange Association. (Huntington Library.)

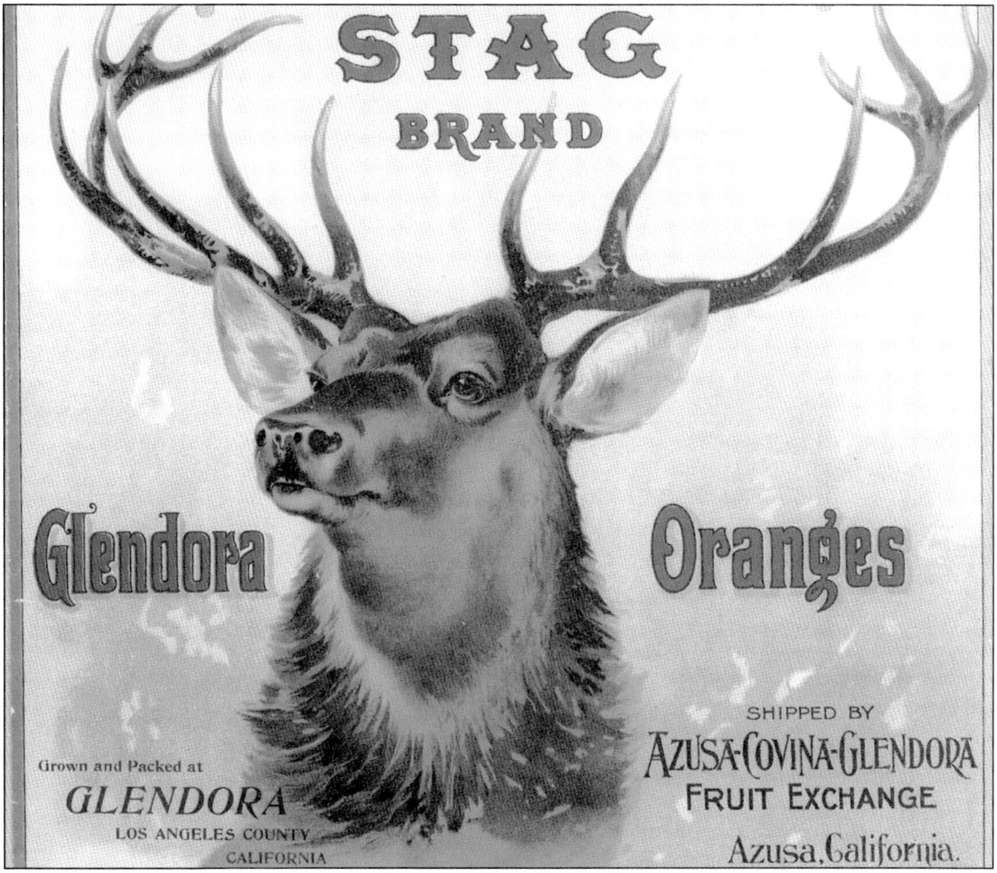

Often the art that was used on the citrus labels reflected the times and the accepted symbols of strength and dependability, as in this Stag Brand of the Azusa-Covina-Glendora Citrus Association. (Huntington Library.)

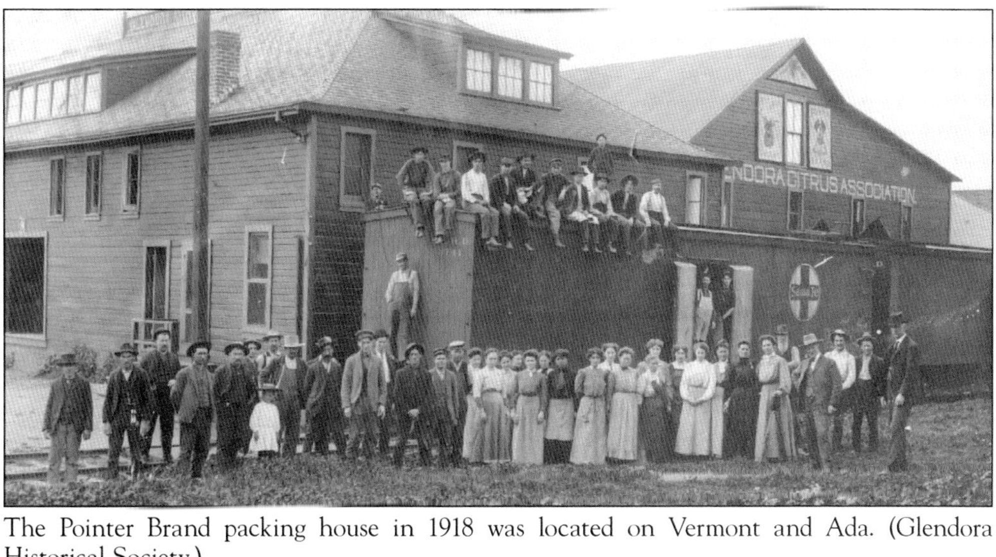

The Pointer Brand packing house in 1918 was located on Vermont and Ada. (Glendora Historical Society.)

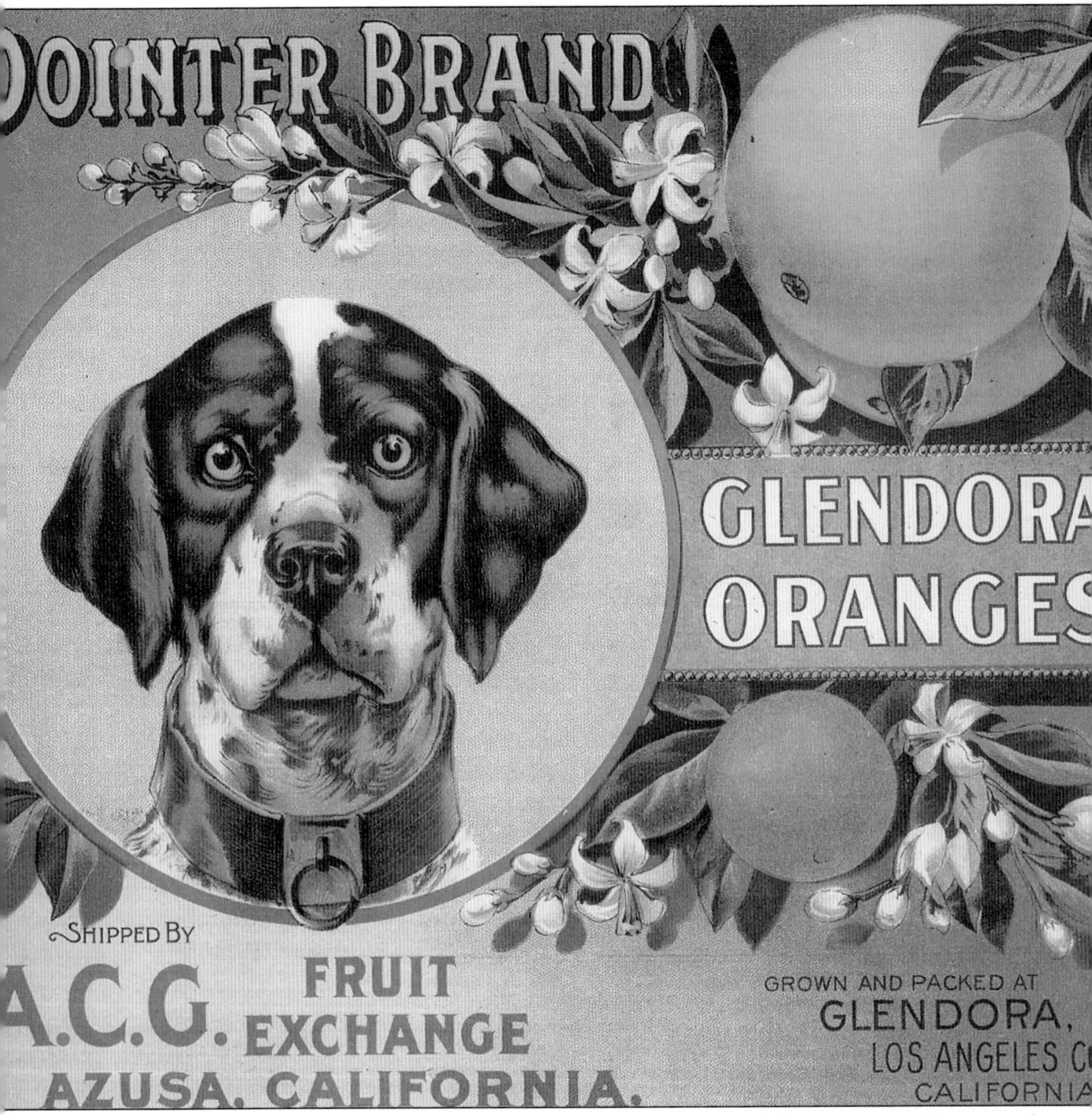

The art work of the Pointer Brand of oranges shows the beauty of the orange in all stages of growth, from flower to green fruit to ripe and ready-to-eat orange. Many of the logos were picked from family pets or favorite symbol. (Huntington Library.)

In the Hunter Brand crate label from the 1920s a young man who is ready to go on the hunt takes a Hunter orange to eat. (Huntington Library.)

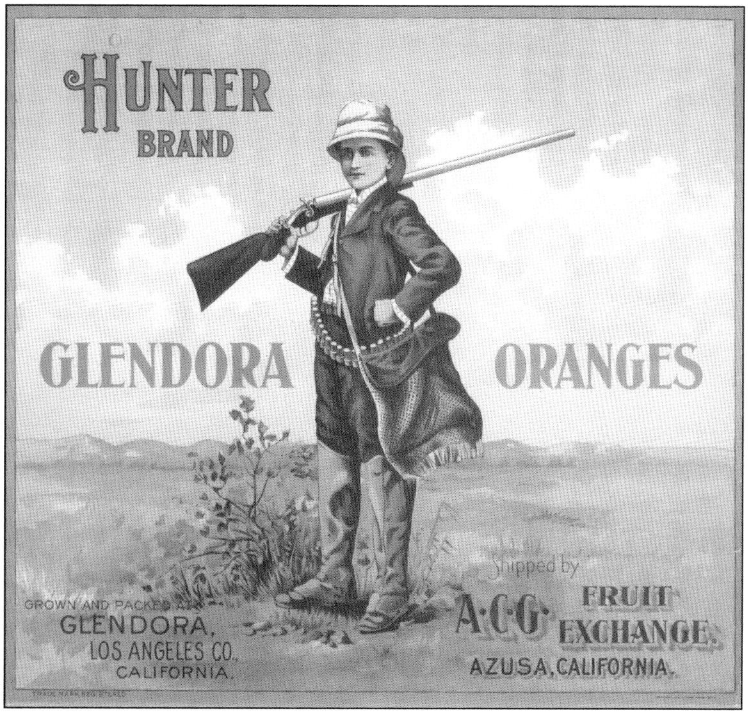

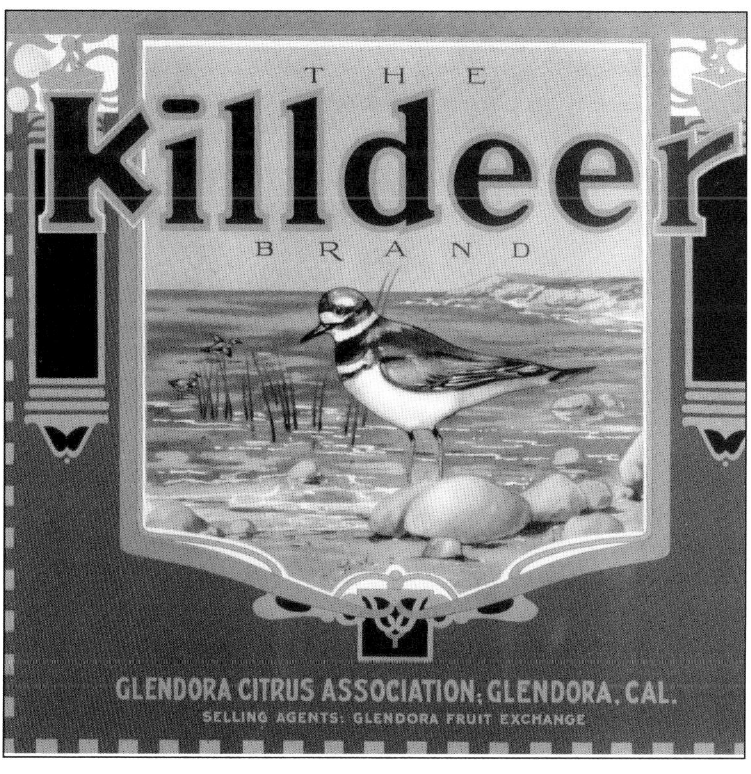

The Killdeer Brand uses the Pacific Ocean as a backdrop and a bird as its logo. Glendora is 50 miles inland from the Pacific coast. (Huntington Library.)

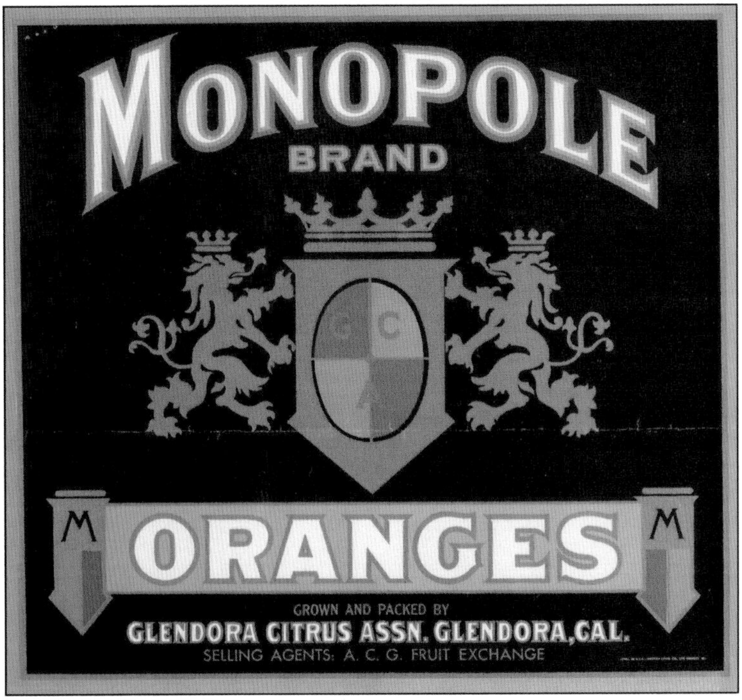

The Monopole Brand of oranges is seen to the left. (Huntington Library.)

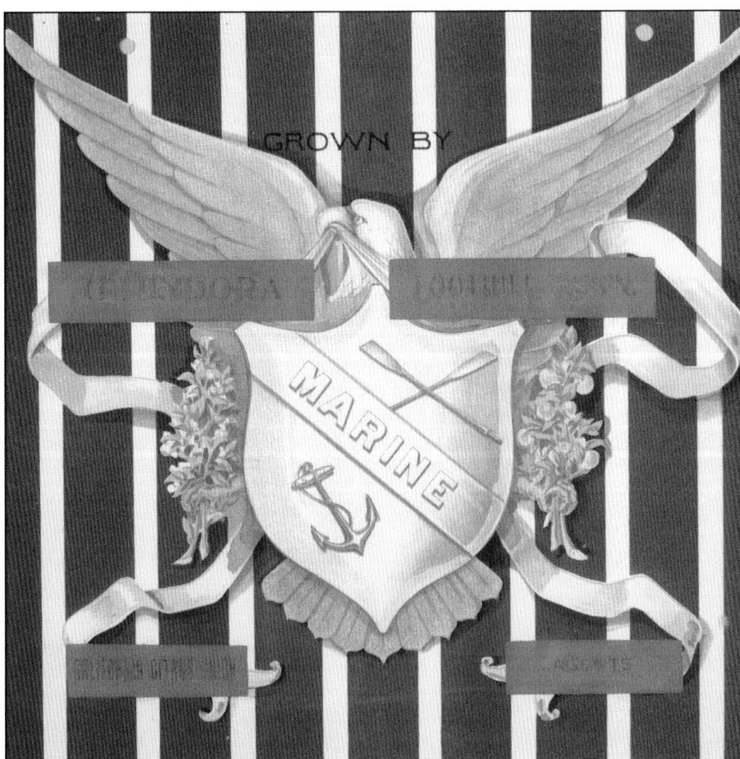

During World War II Glendora still produced citrus and would ship it overseas, as evidenced by this c. 1940 Marine Brand Citrus cratelabel. (Huntington Library.)

Five

From Citrus to Suburb

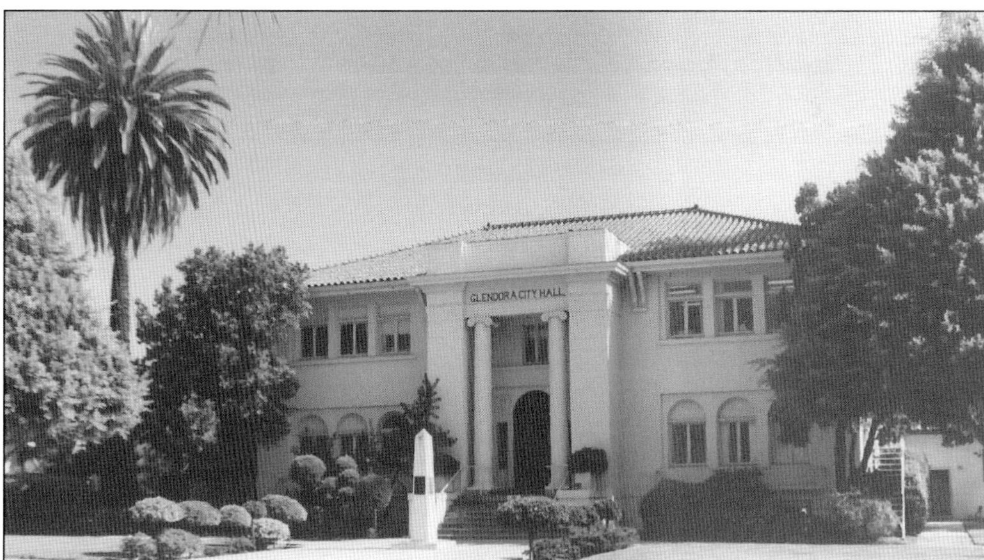

As Glendora grew in size and population, a proper city hall was needed. In 1921 the city fathers built the current city hall to house the government and city offices. This was the second city hall; the first being the old fire station built in 1913. (J. Landers.)

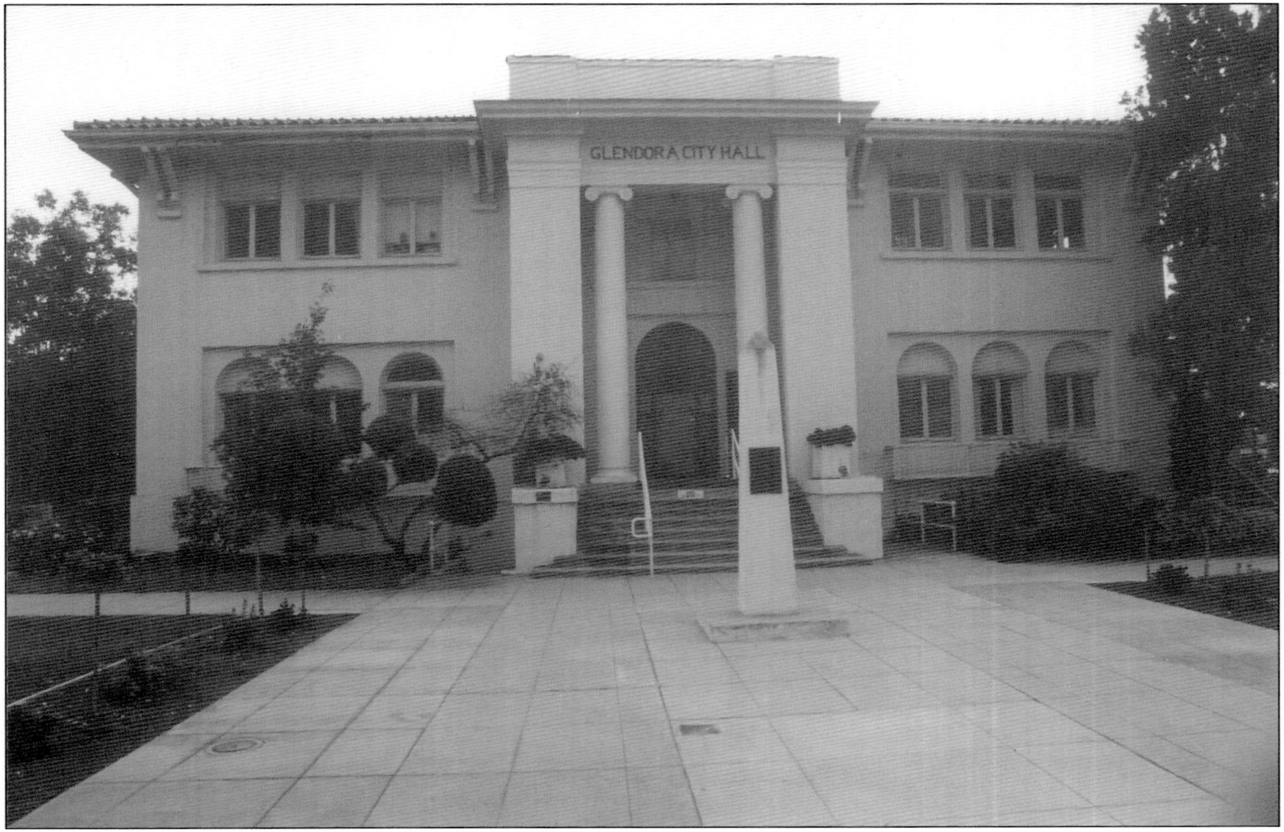

Here is a view of city hall with the time capsule obelisk in front. (J. Landers.)

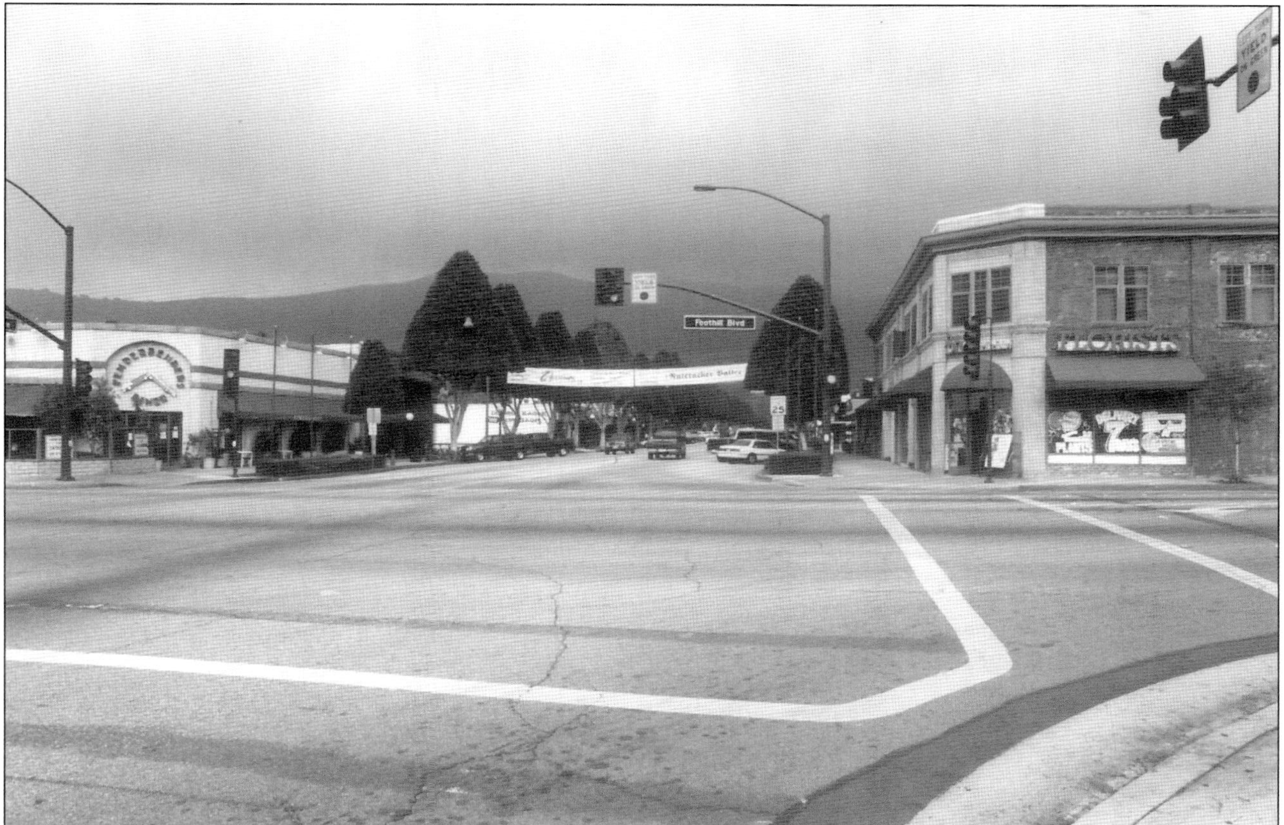

This section of Glendora Ave. north shows some of the original buildings that still exist. (J. Landers.)

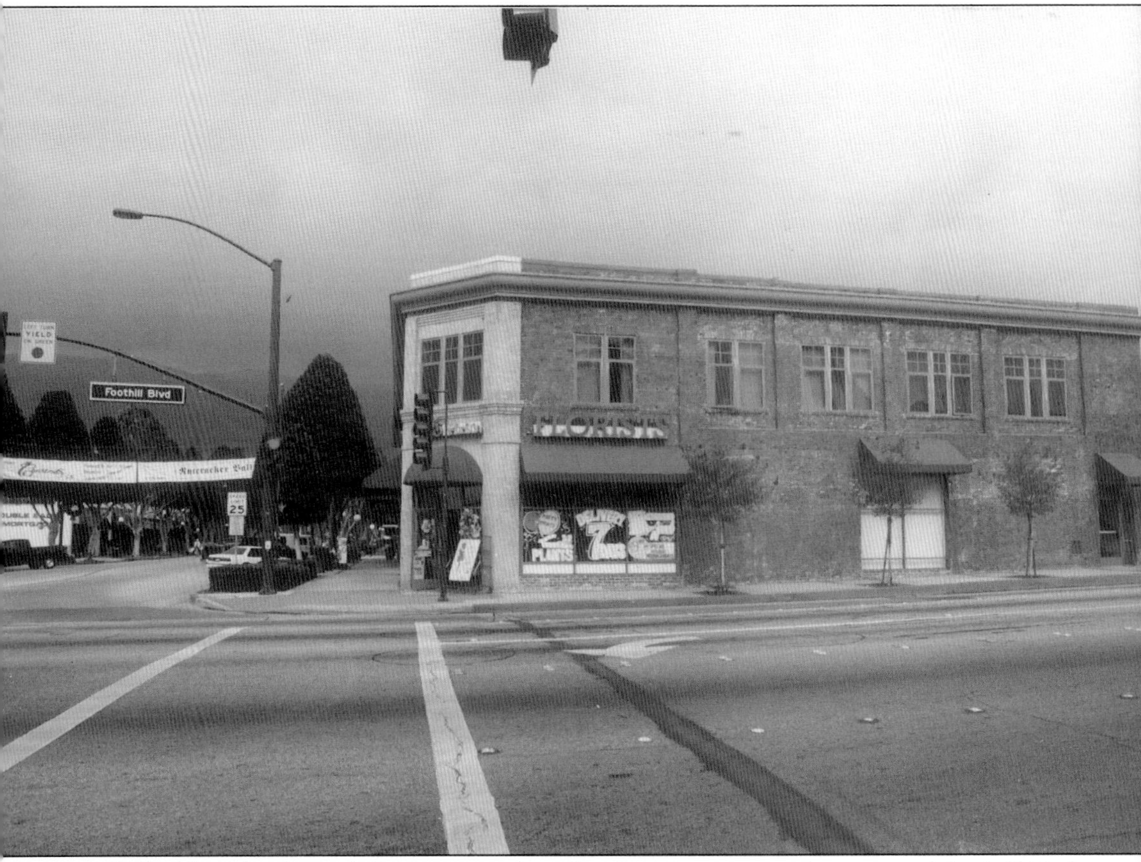

The building that housed the grocery and market that was once on the corner of Foothill Blvd. and Glendora Ave. is still in use today. It is still a prominent building that people see as they enter the "Village" of Glendora. (J. Landers.)

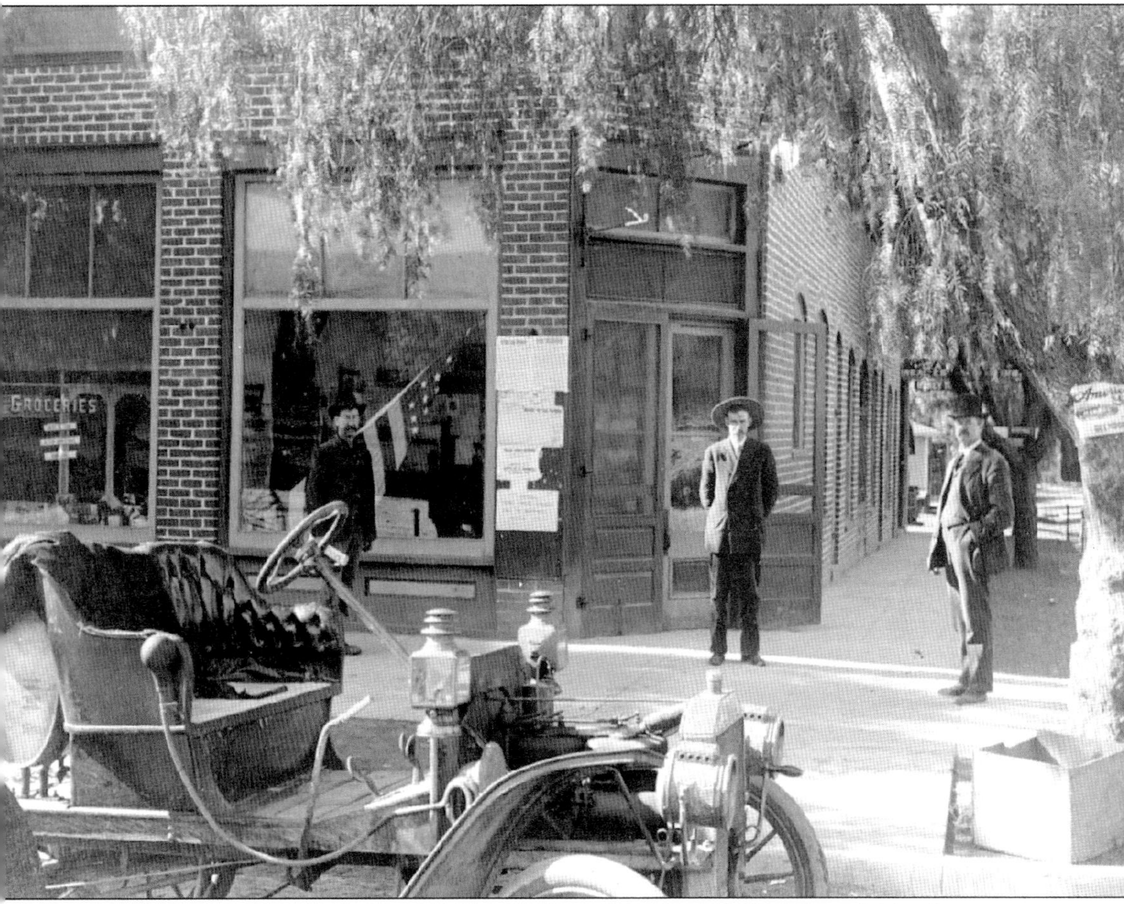

The Village Grocery and Market in 1913 on the corner of Foothill Blvd. and Glendora Ave is seen in this image. (Glendora Historical Society.)

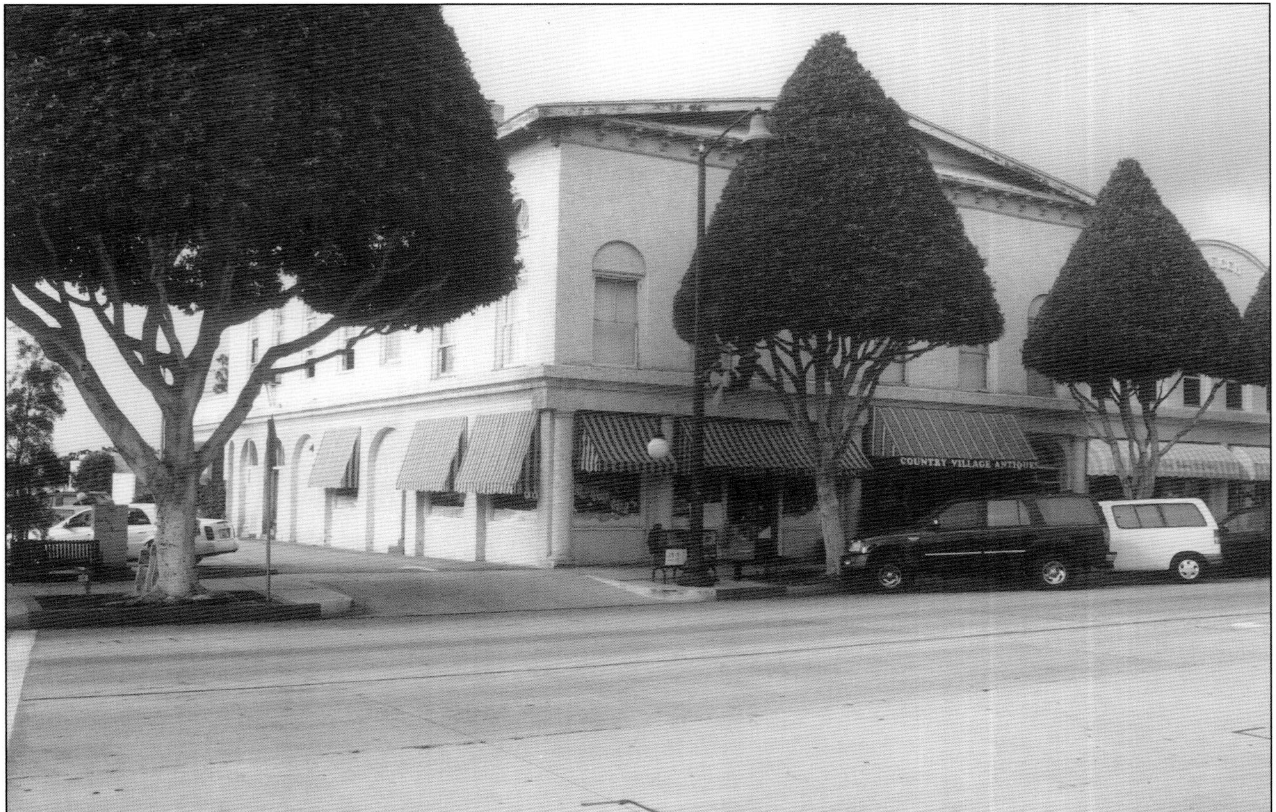

Glendora's opera house has undergone many changes and is no longer the center for culture and entertainment, but it is used for community programs, a restaurant, and antique stores. (J. Landers.)

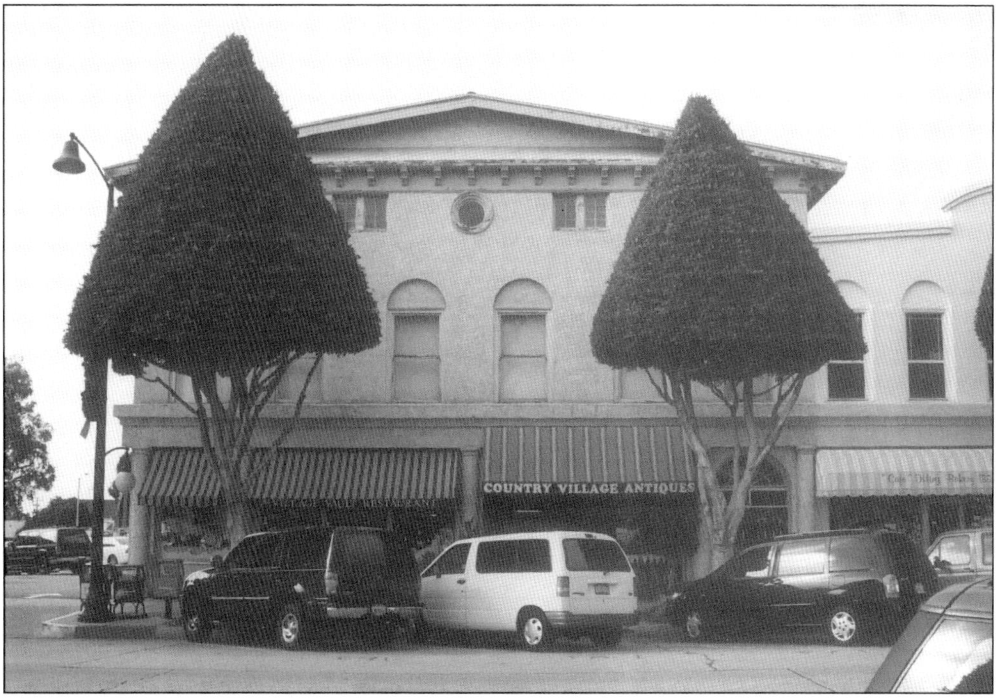

Pictured is a frontal view of the opera house today. (J.Landers.)

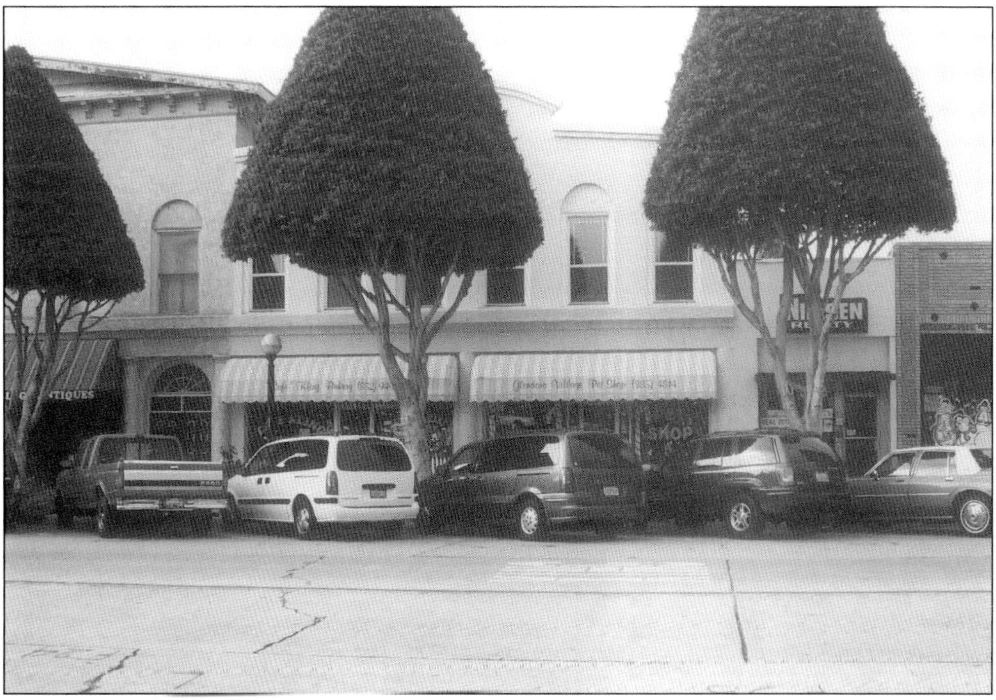

The Glendora Village Pet Shop and the Cafe Kling Bakery still use the building that once held the Glendora Market and the upstairs office of Dr. Odell. (J. Landers.)

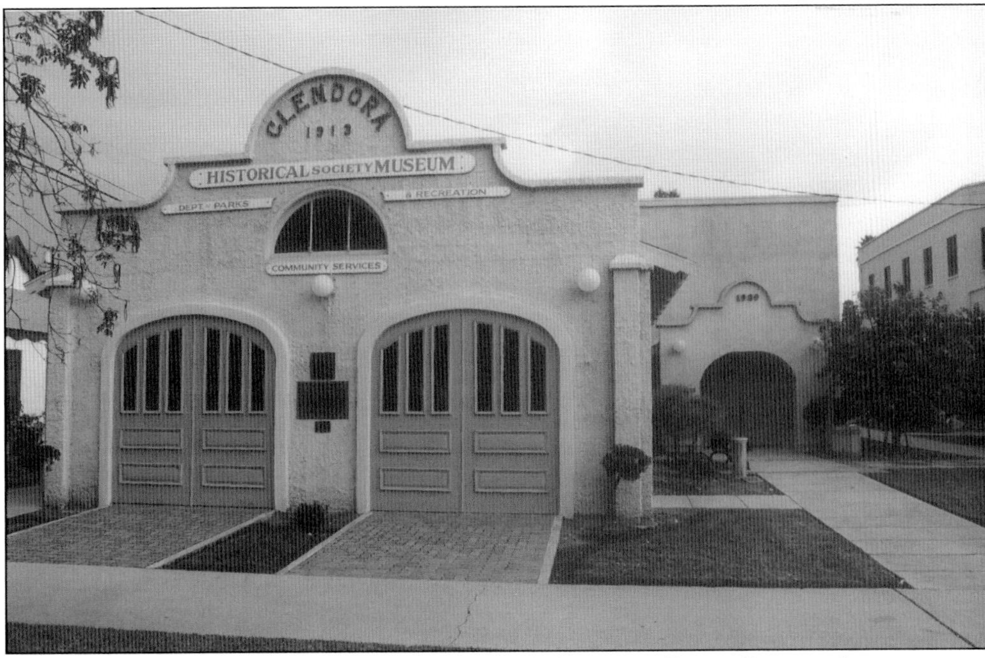

Glendora's original city hall and fire station served the city well. It still serves the community by housing the memories and history of a diverse city as the site of the Glendora Historical Museum. (J. Landers.)

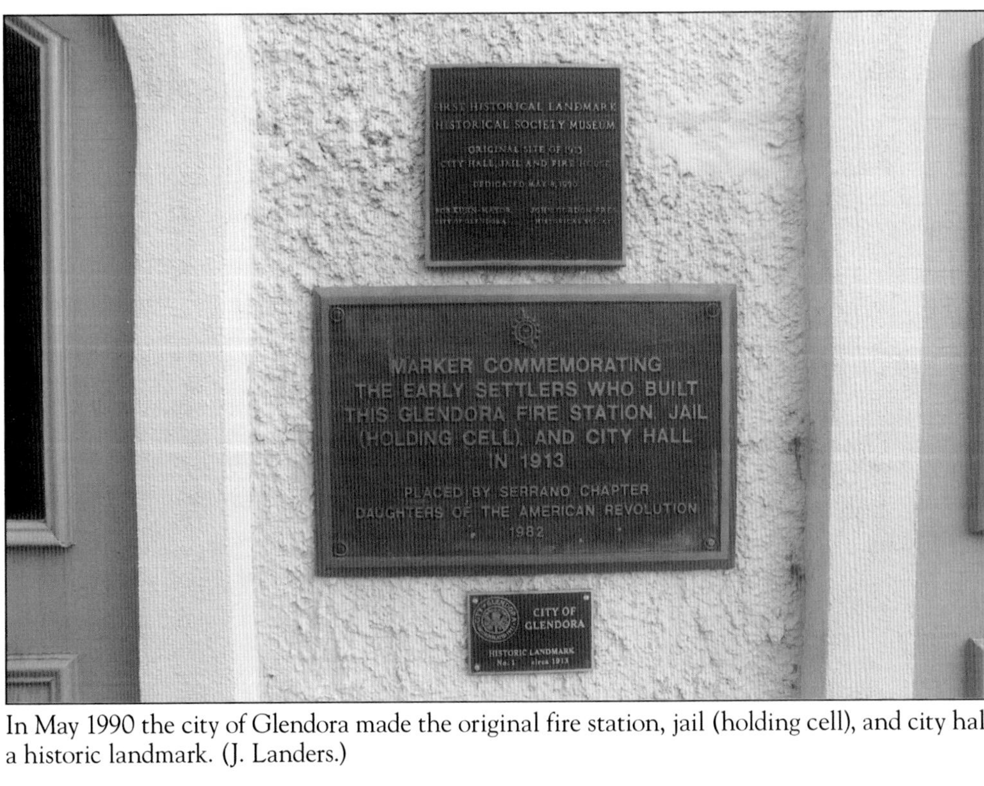

In May 1990 the city of Glendora made the original fire station, jail (holding cell), and city hall a historic landmark. (J. Landers.)

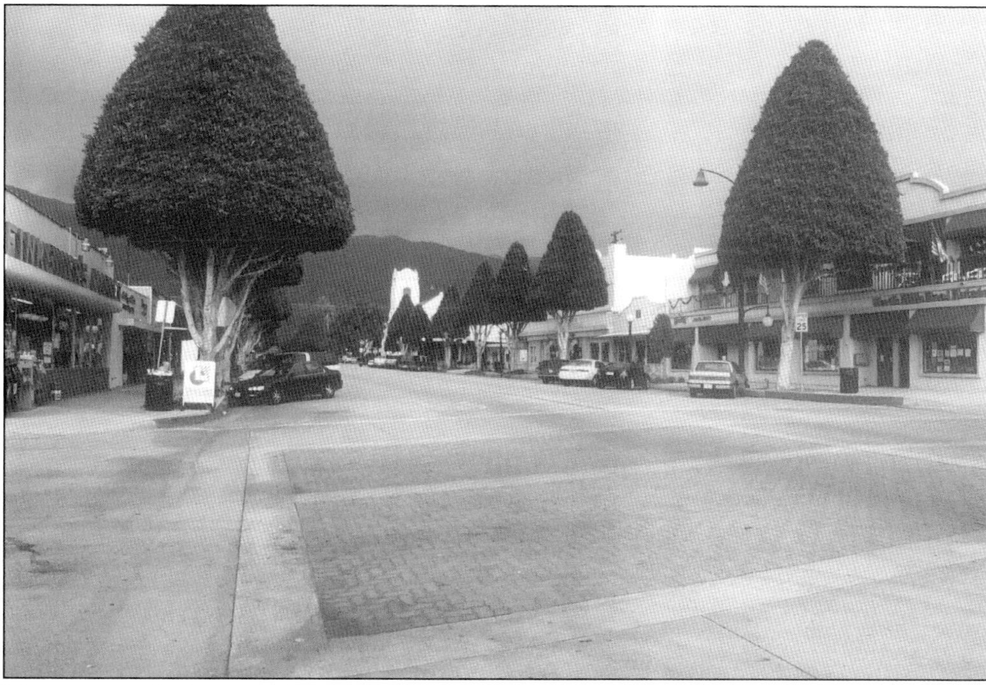

This is a view looking north on Glendora Ave as it appears today. (J. Landers.)

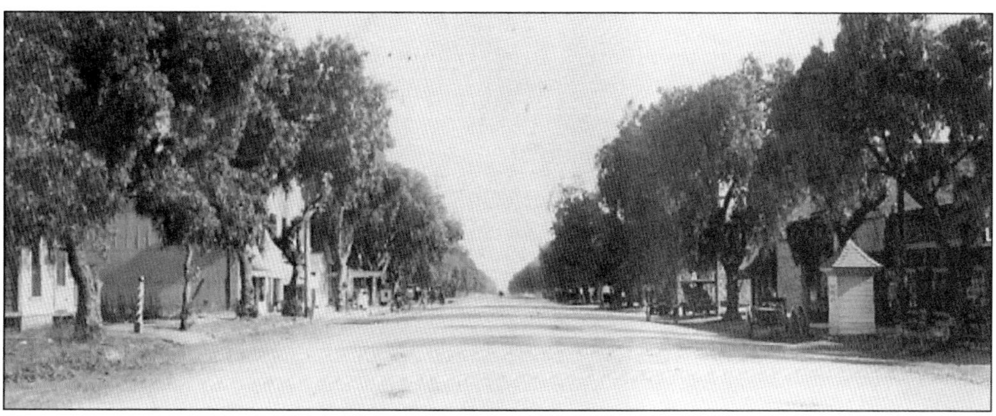

This is a panoramic view of Glendora Ave. was taken in 1880.

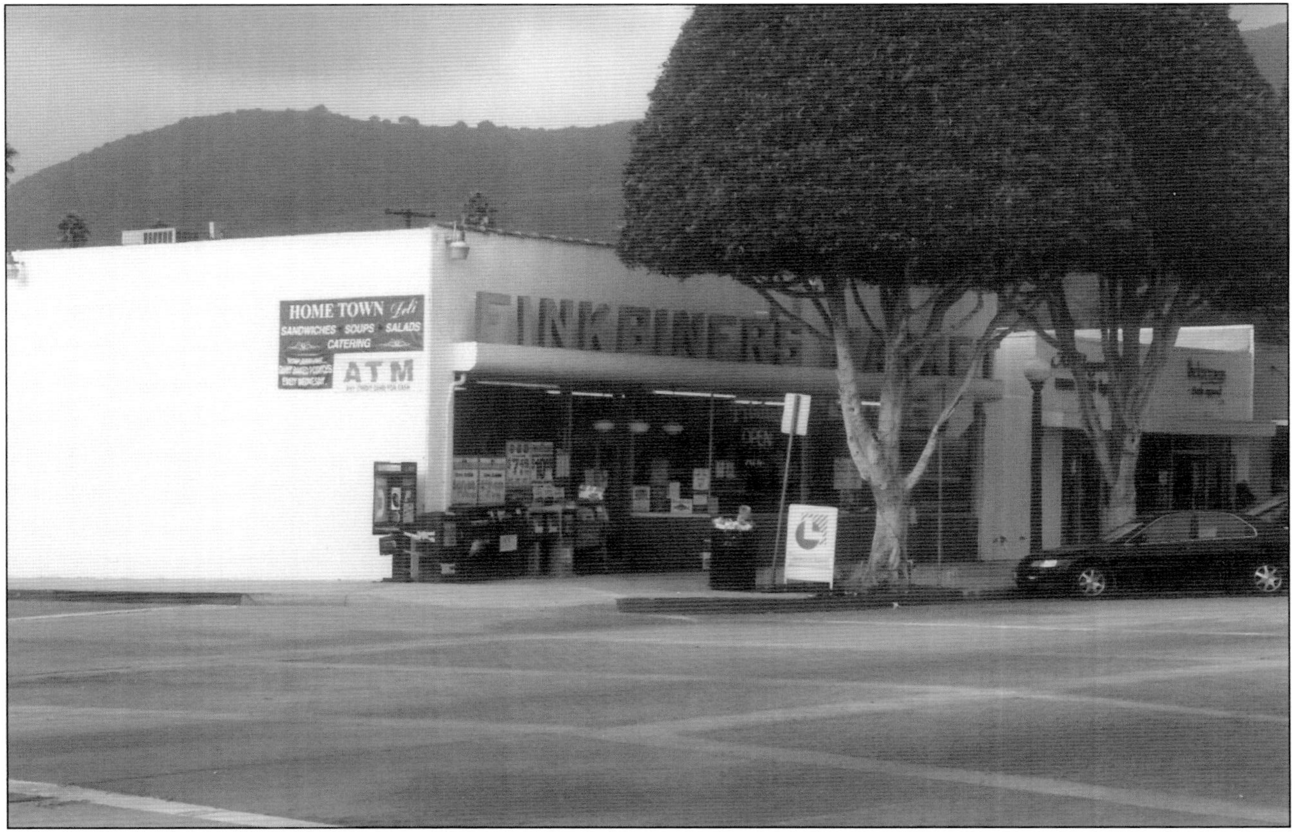

Joe Finkbiner was one of Glendora's mayors and also one of the city's prominent businessman. (J. Landers..)

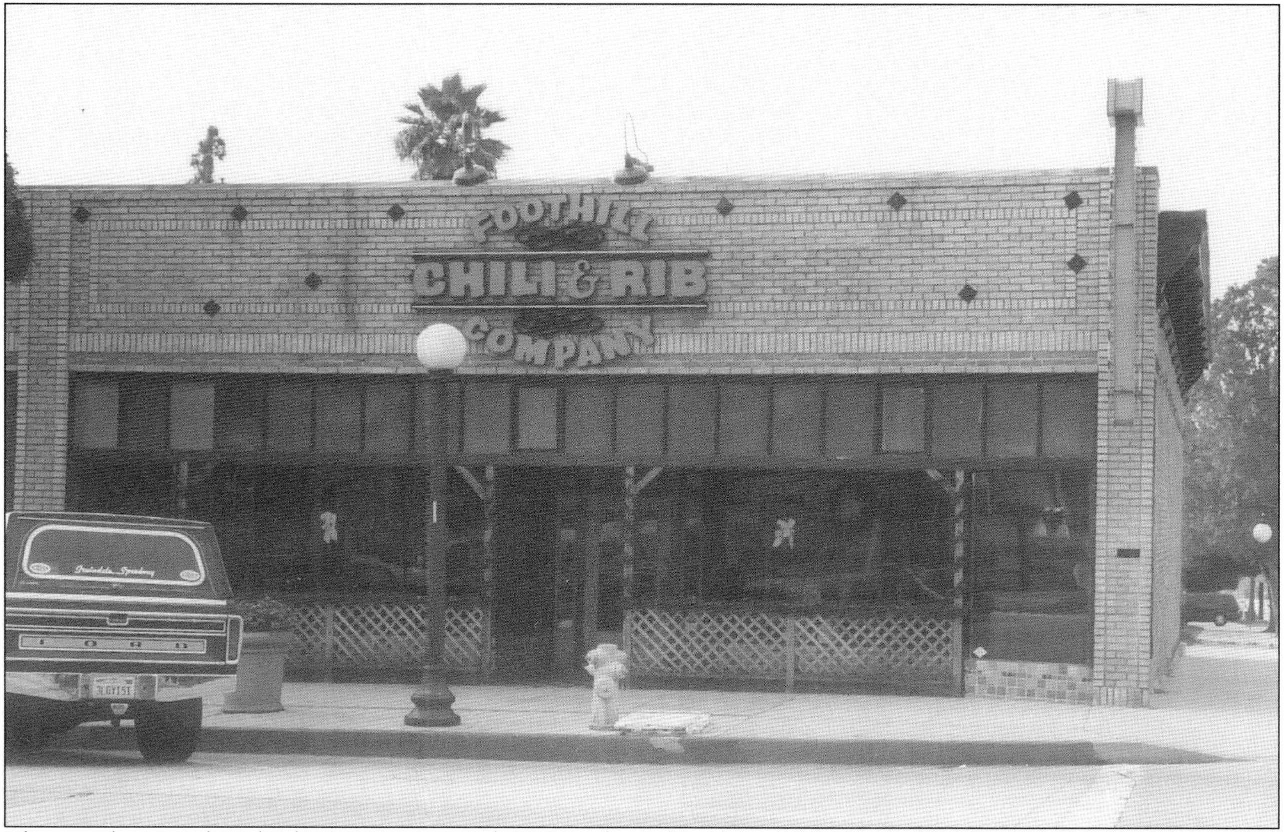

The Matthews and Walmsley Grocery Store has gone through a number of changes through the years, first becoming a hardware store and now home to the Foothill Chili and Rib Company. (J. Landers.)

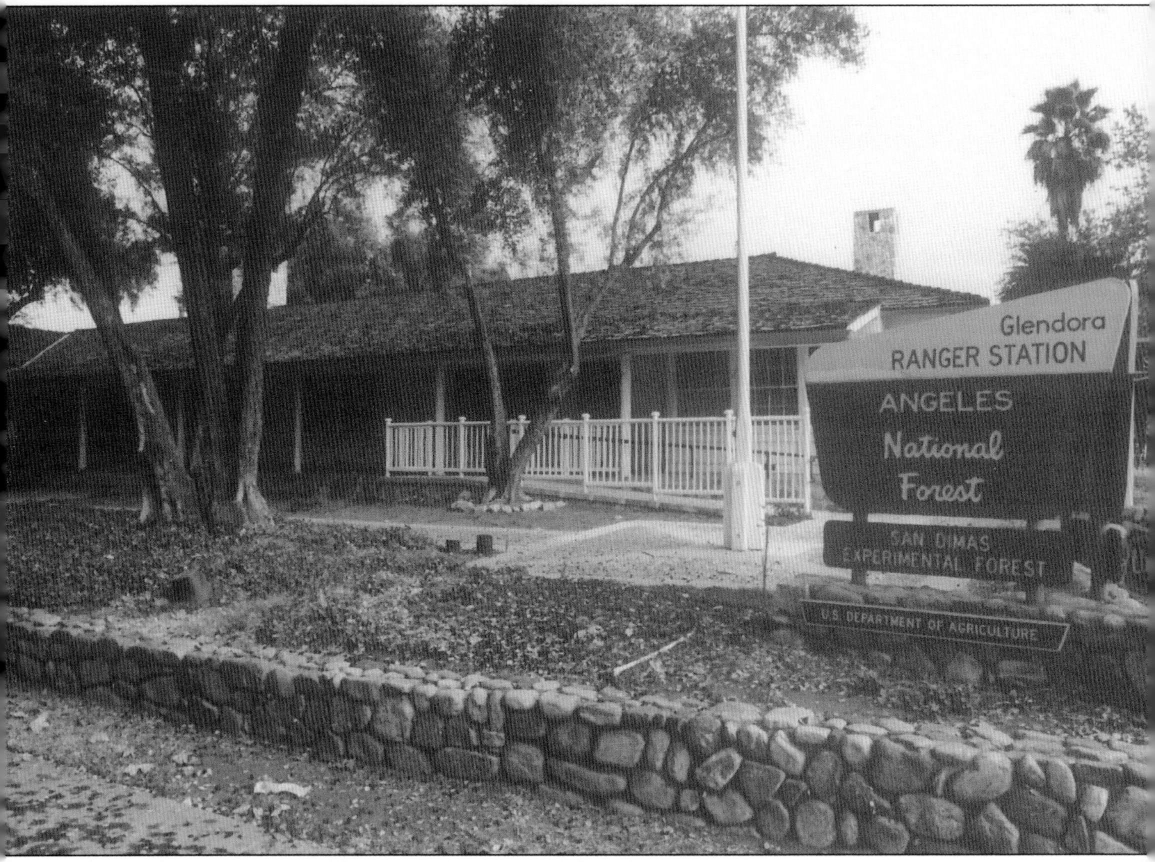

Glendora is nestled at the base of the San Gabriel Mountains. It is one of the gateways to the many recreation spots and sightseeing stops of the area. The U.S. Forest Service has a ranger station in Glendora that oversees all of forest parks and experimental conservation forest lands in the Los Angeles National Forest. It was built in the 1920s, and its architecture anchors Glendora in its past. (J. Landers.)

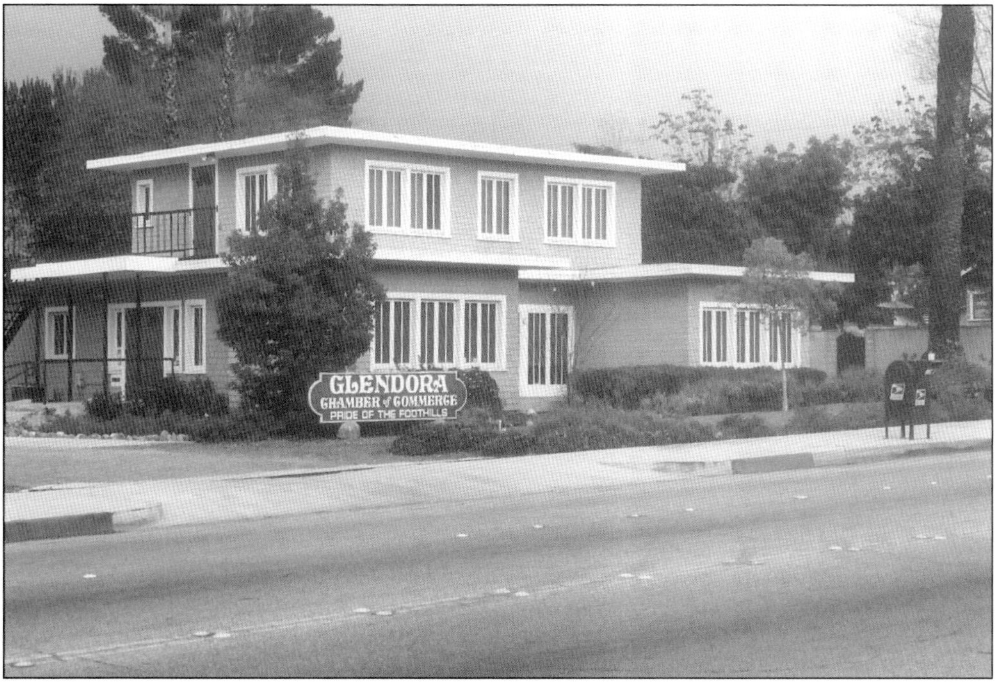

Many of the Crafts-style homes that are found around the city have also been given a new lease on life for the Chamber of Commerce and other law and business offices. (J. Landers.)

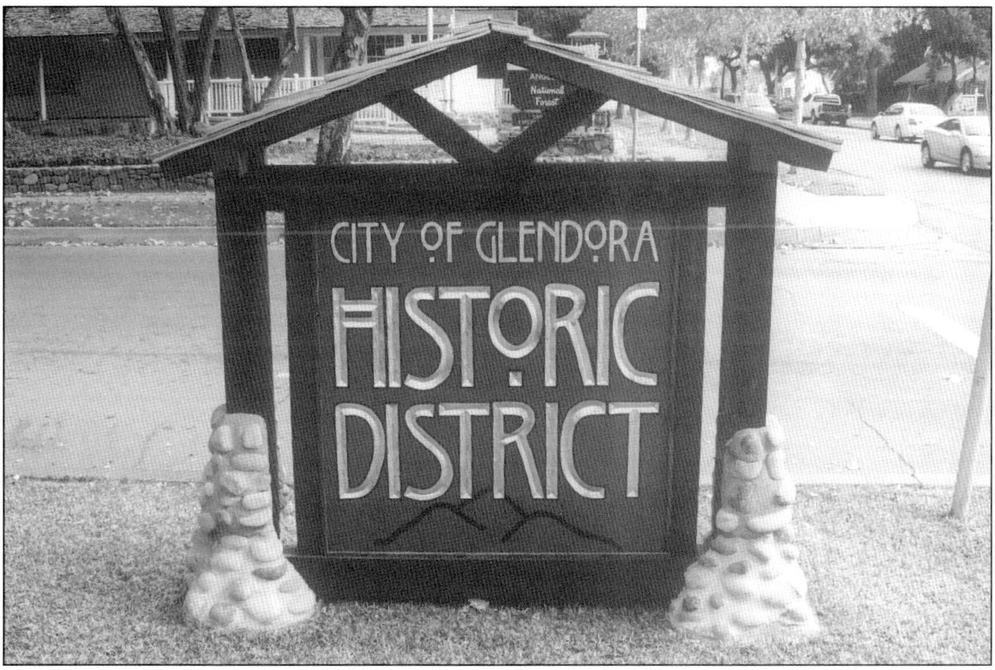

In the rush to embrace the 21st century, many local communities have allowed many of their historic homes and buildings to fall under the wrecking ball. Glendora's saw the need to preserve a bit of their rich and wonderful past and created an Historic District. This district will save and help to restore and maintain many of the original buildings around the Village. (J. Landers.)

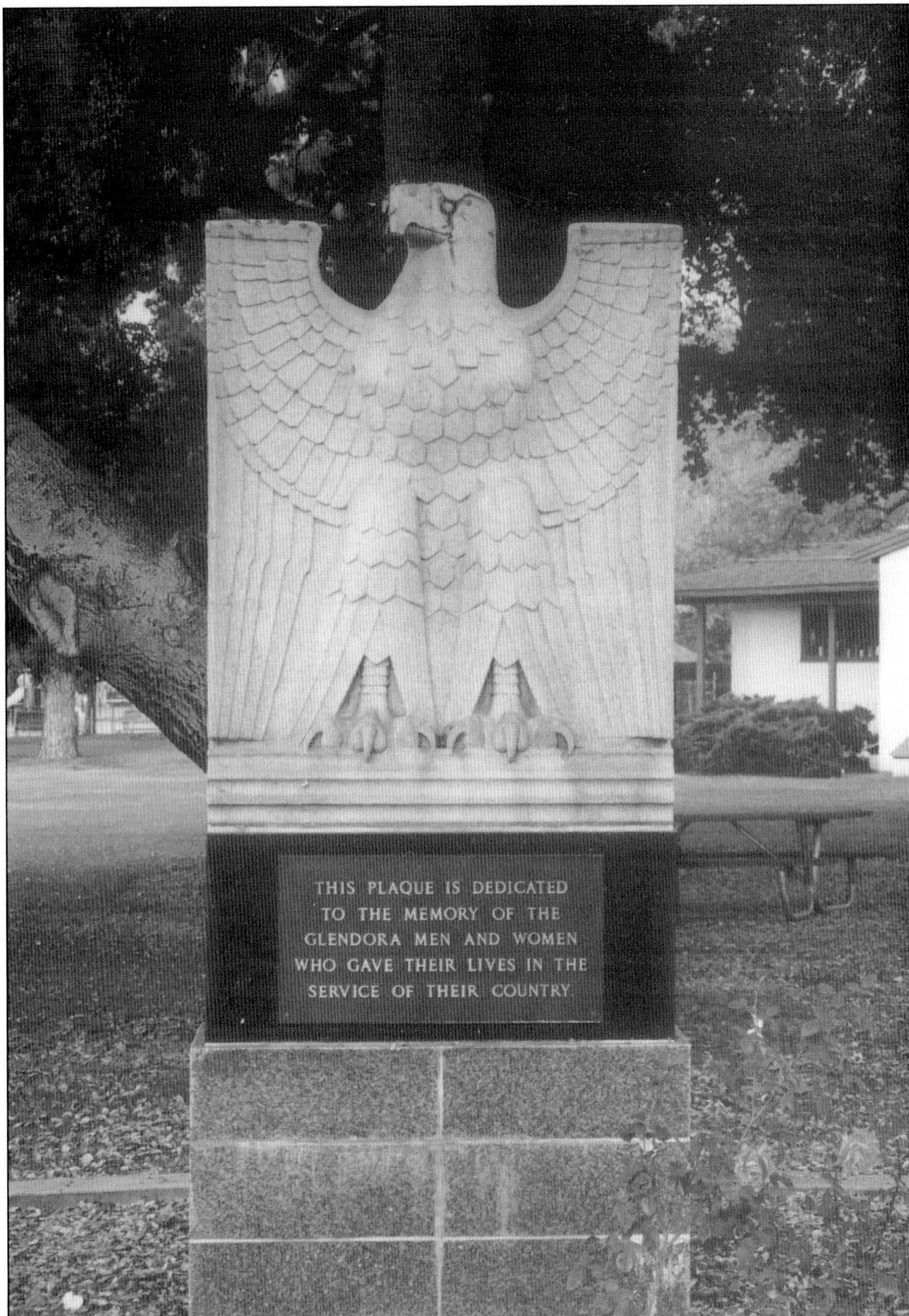

The men and women of Glendora have always answered the call to help defend the country in timse of war. The city dedicated this memorial to all who sacrificed their lives in the 1950s. (J. Landers.)

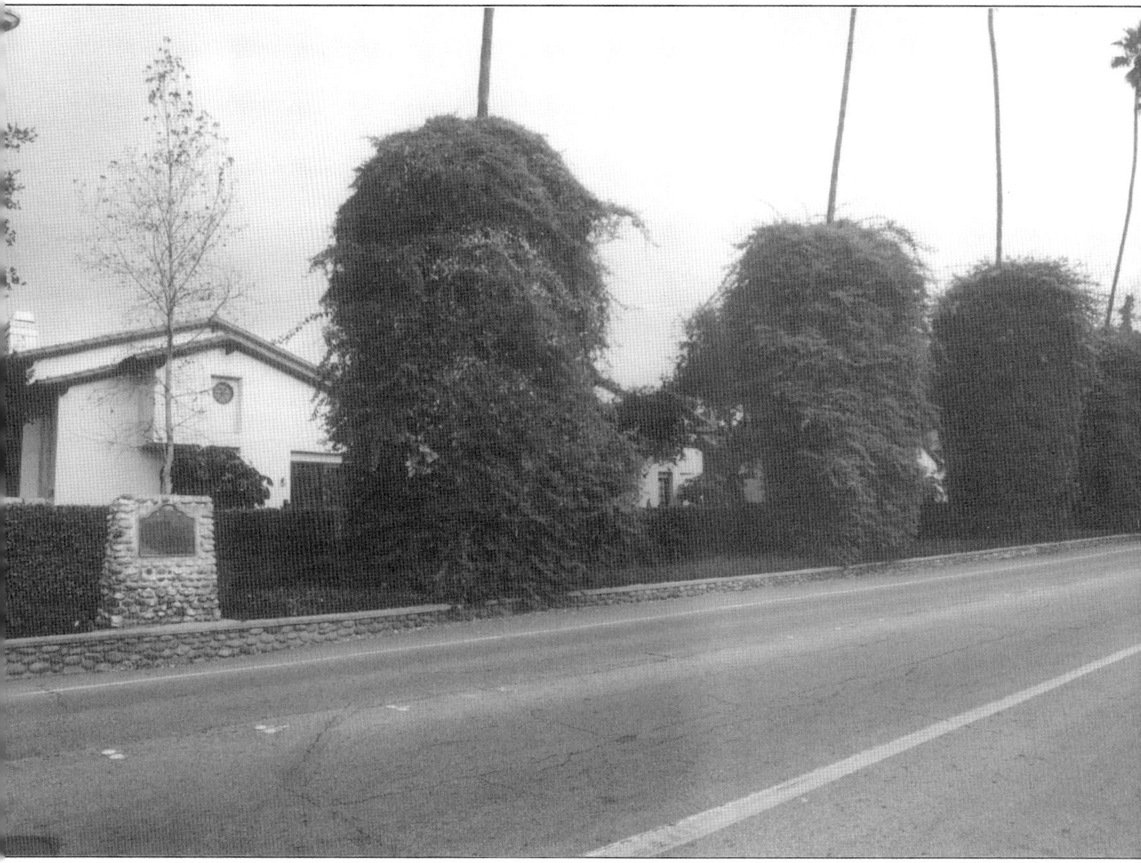

As one travels down Bennett Ave. just east of the Village shopping district, one finds a row of bougainvillaea lining the north side of the street. These bougainvillaea were planted in 1901 by the R.W. Hamlins family who were early citrus growers and are a California Historical Landmark. (J. Landers.)

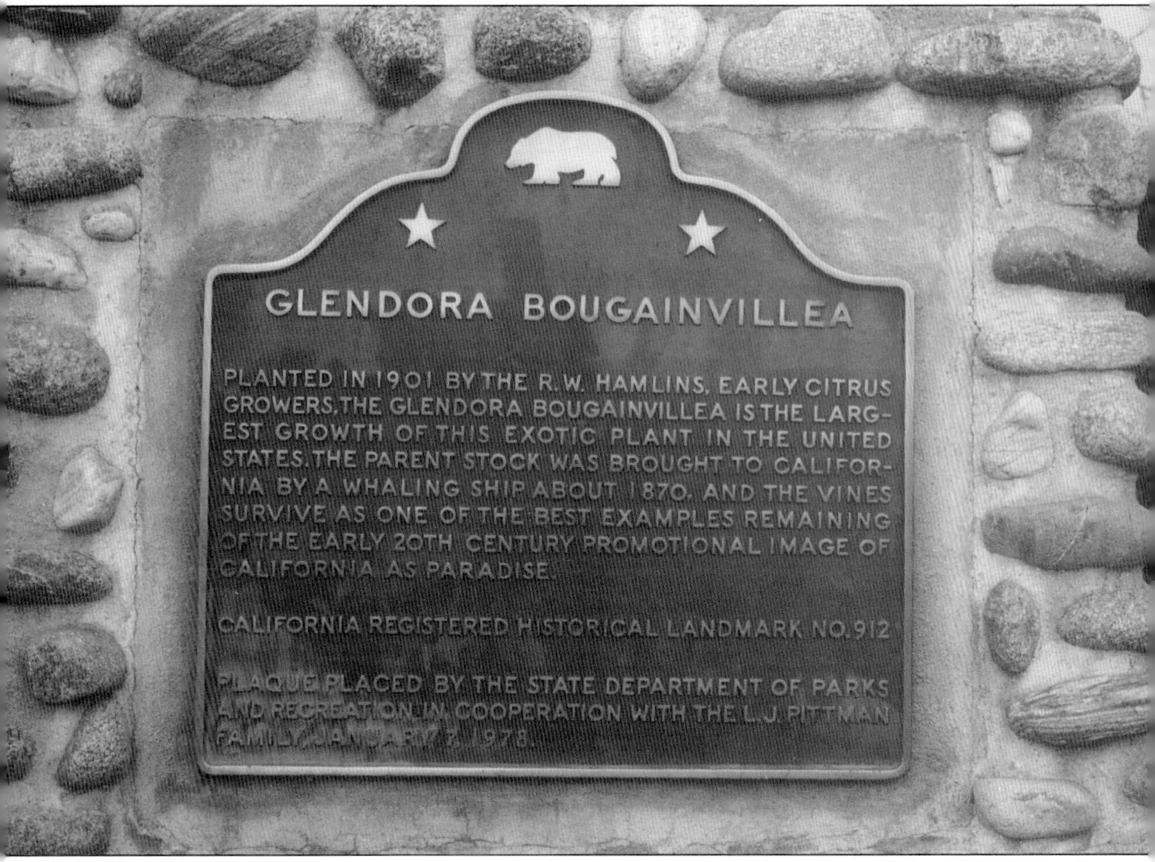

These bougainvillaea are reported to be the largest growth of this exotic plant in the United States. The parent stalk was brought to California by a whaling ship in the 1870s and remains one of the best examples of the early-20th-century promotional image of California as paradise. (J. Landers.)

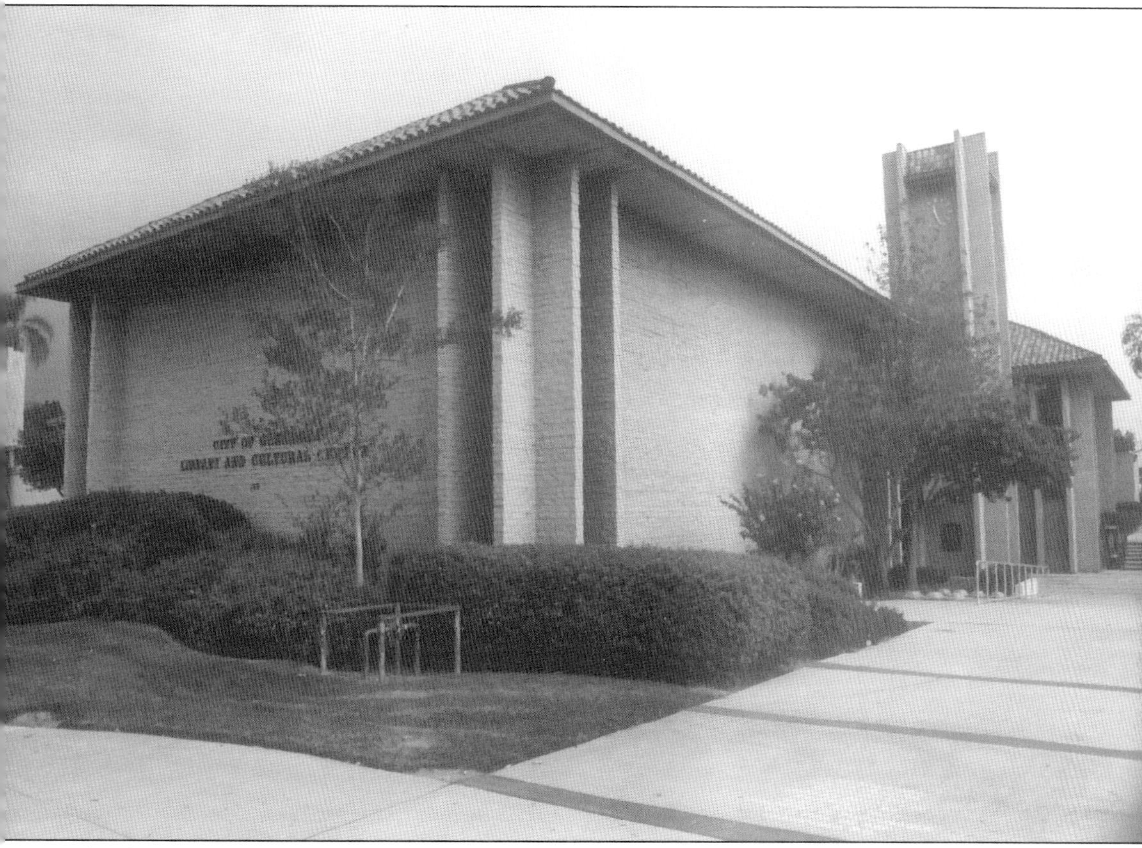

Glendora wanted to give its residents a new cultural center for public meetings and for scholarly study. They built the Glendora Library and Cultural Center just south of city hall. (J. Landers.)

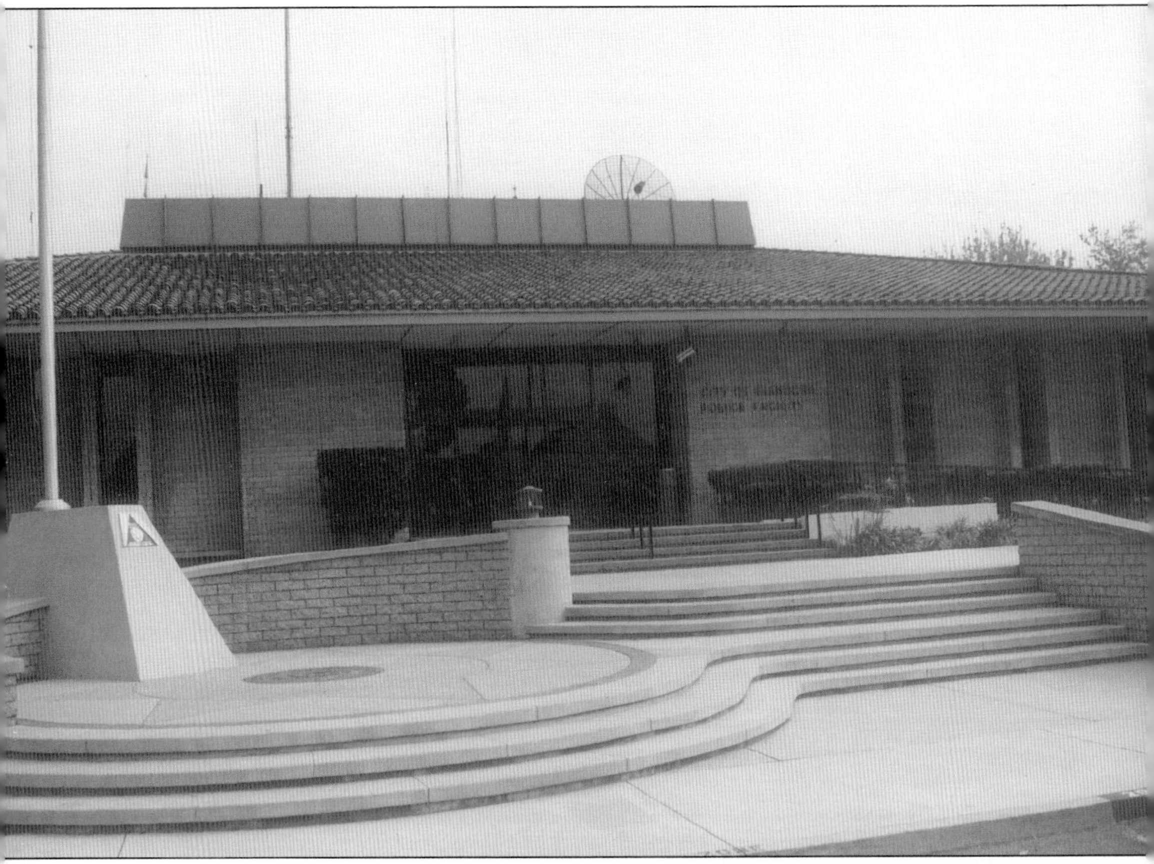

The days of the fire station, jail (holding cell), and city hall being located in one building have long gone. Glendora has built a modern police station and jail that incorporates all of the new technology and tactics of a modern police force. It has also joined the ranks of cities who have had to honor those law enforcement officers who have given their lives in the line of duty. The Louis Pompei Memorial and eternal flame can be seen in the foreground. (J. Landers.)

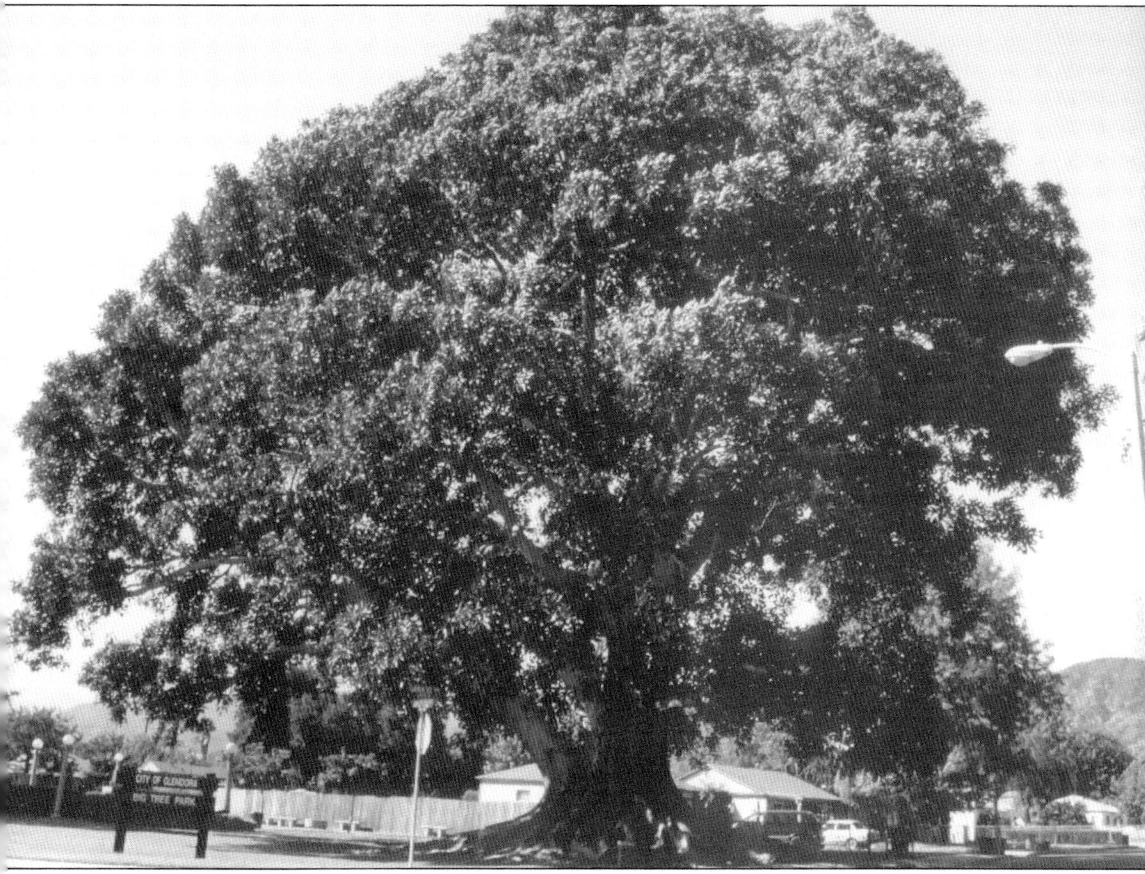

"Big Tree" Park is seen here as it appears today. This is the largest Morton Bay fig tree in the state of California. Planted by Edgar J. Owens, the tree is 90 feet high and has a branch spread of 110 feet. The trunk measures 30 feet in circumference, and the root system covers 1200 square feet of land. (Catherine Starkey.)

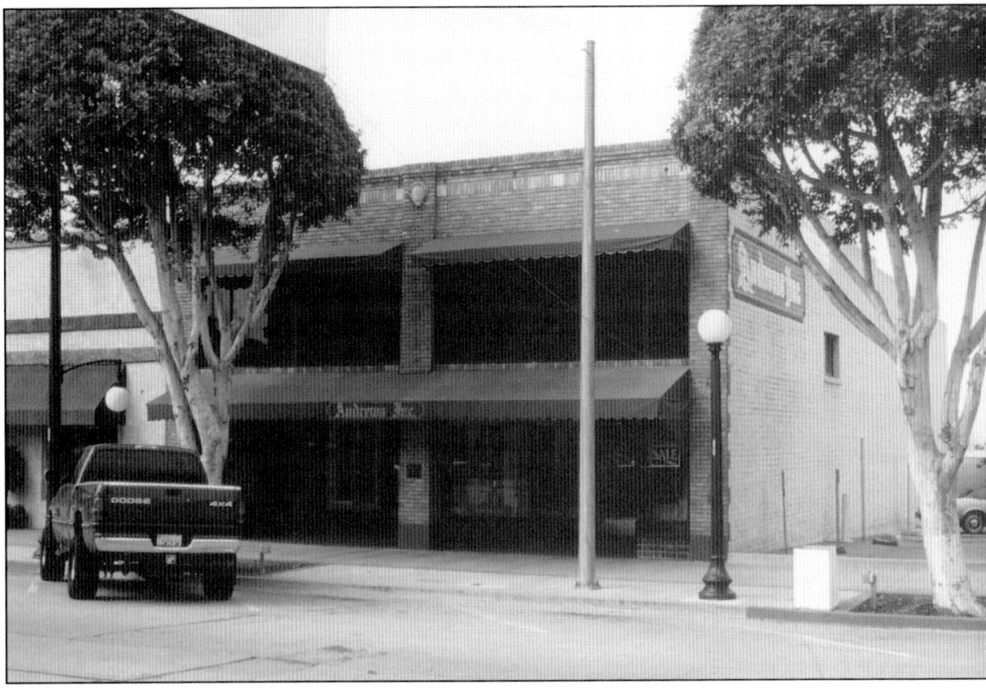

Anderson's store is still in use today as a haberdashery. (Glendora Historical Society.)

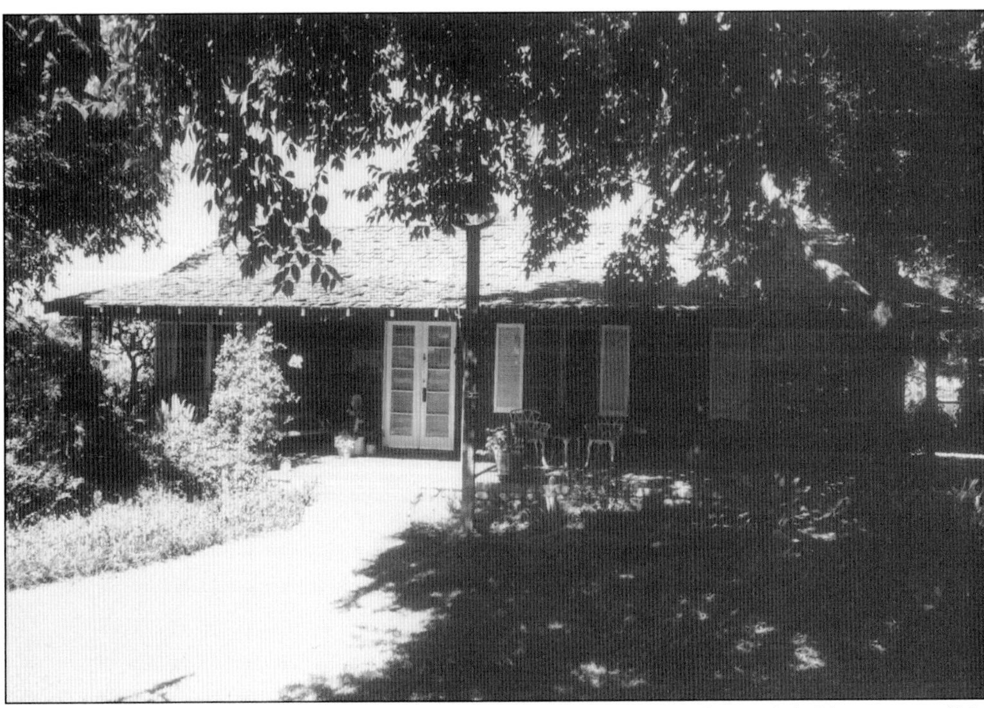

The original schoolhouse is now a personal residence, but the laughter of children can still be heard from local schoolchildren on field trips. (J. Landers.)

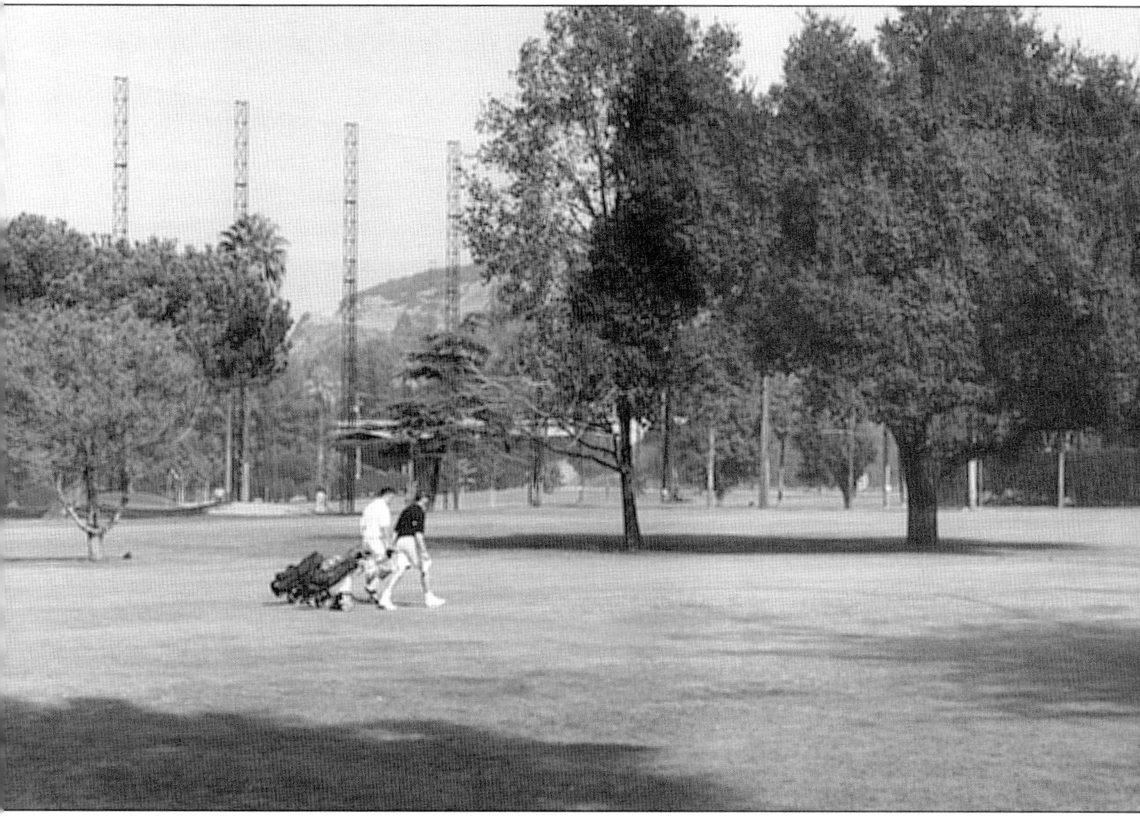

Glendora is dotted with California oaks and incorporates them in many of its parks and streets. The Glen Oaks Golf Course allows golfers to enjoy the oaks and the great outdoors. (Catharine Starkey.)

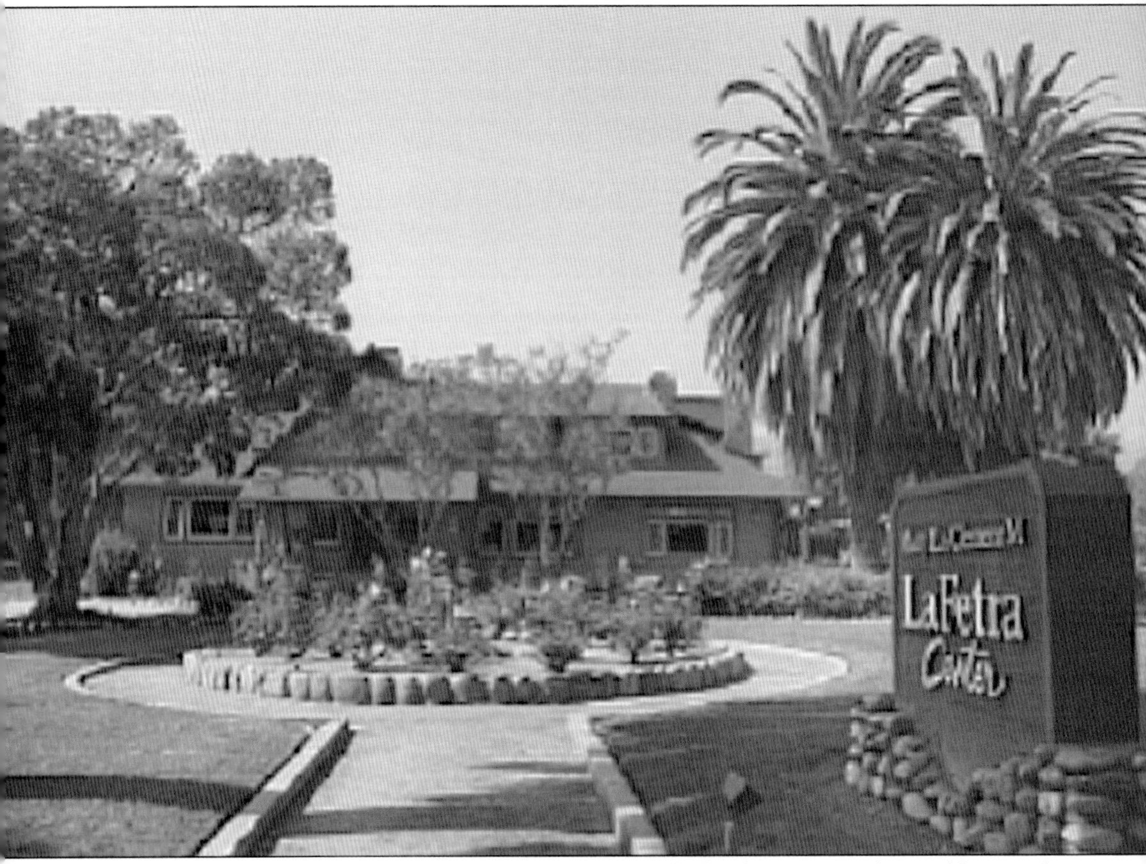

Today the LaFetra House is used as the senior center of Glendora. It was donated by members of the LaFetra family for the use by the citizens of Glendora. (Catharine Starkey.)

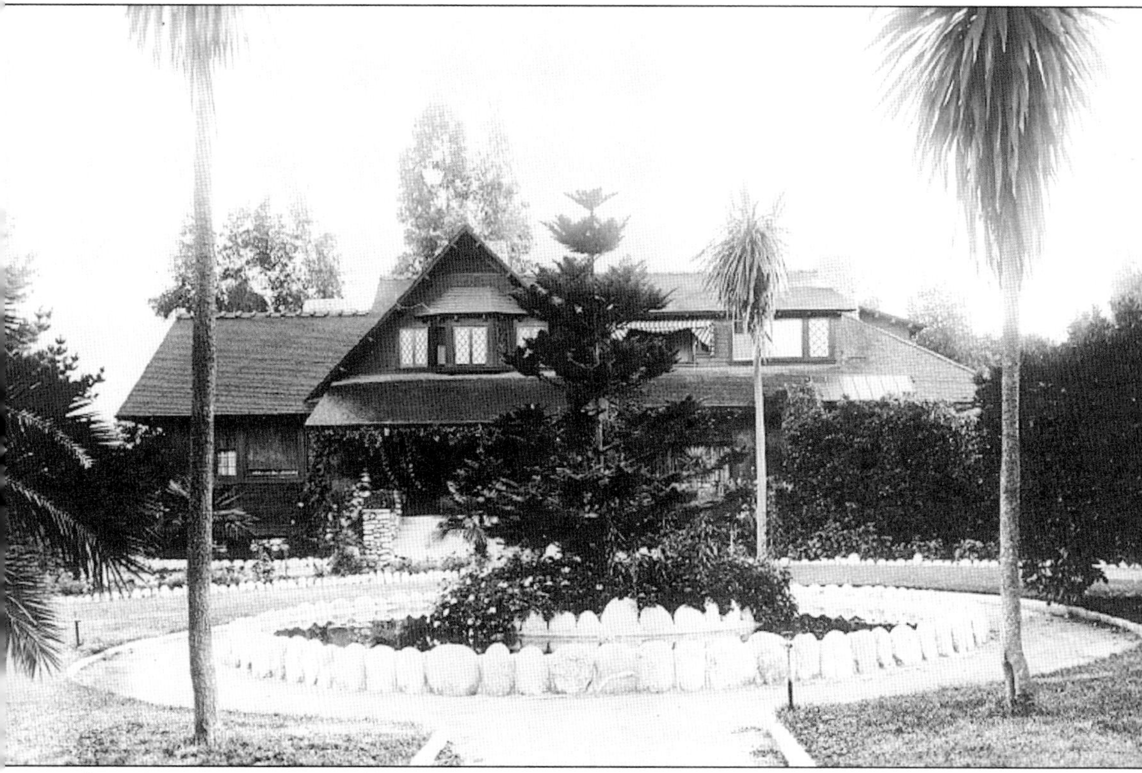

The LaFetra House, pictured here in 1910, is a classic example of a Craftsman-style home that was built in the early part of the 20th century. (Glendora Historical Society.)

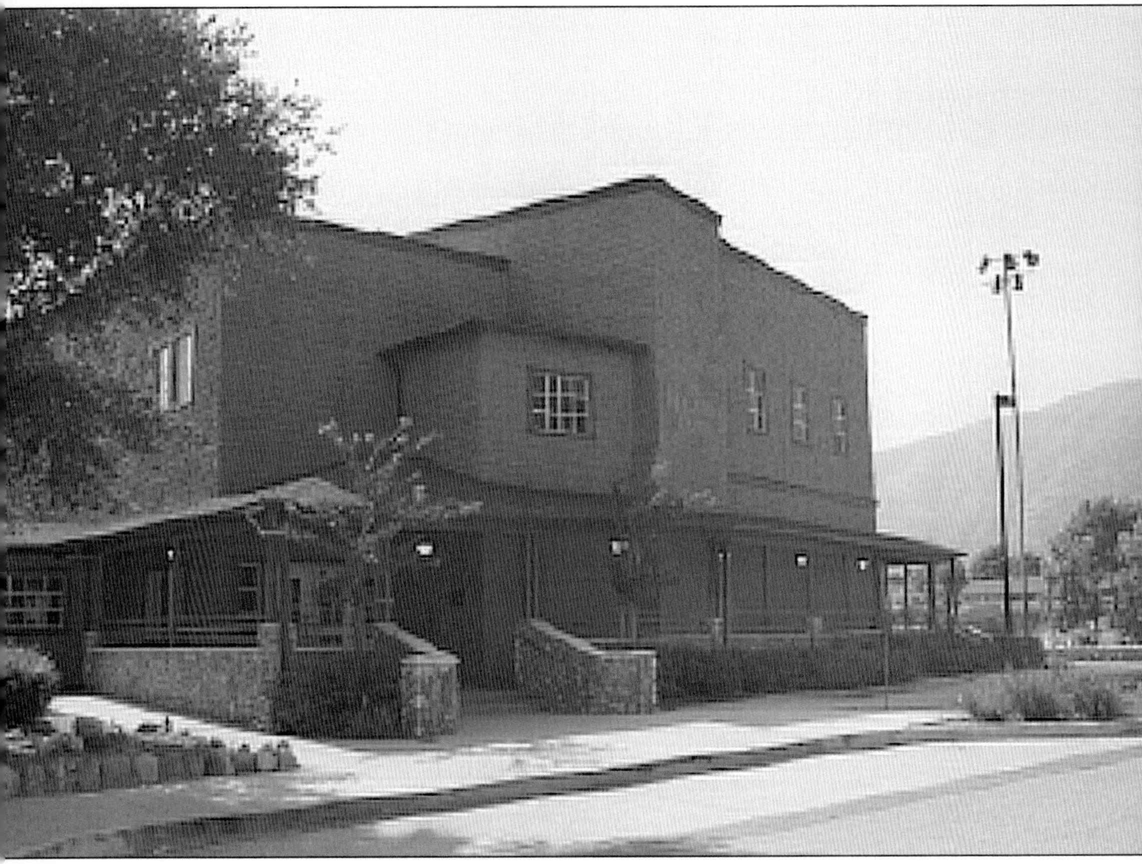

In the 1990s the LaFetra Senior Center was added to the original house. (Catherine Starkey.)

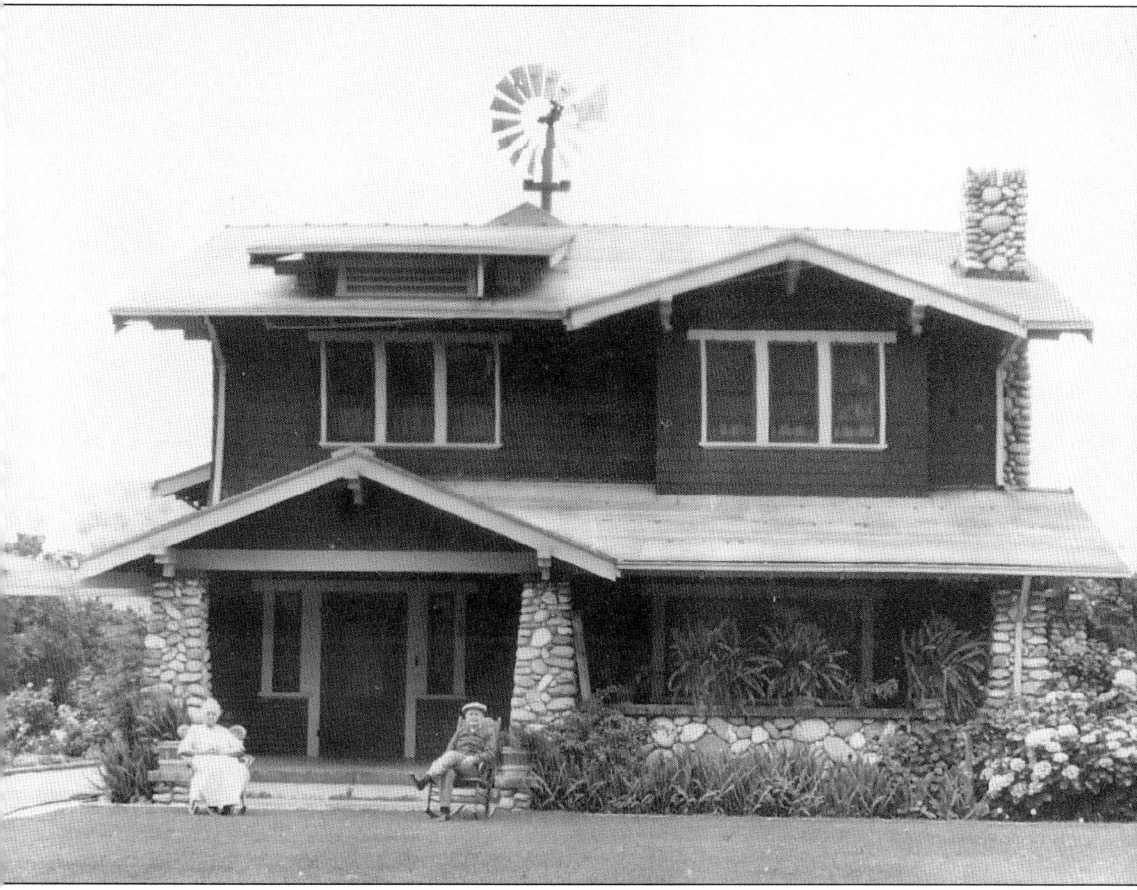

The Ragan House is another example of Glendora's architectural history and why the Historic District was created to preserve it. (Glendora Historical Society.)

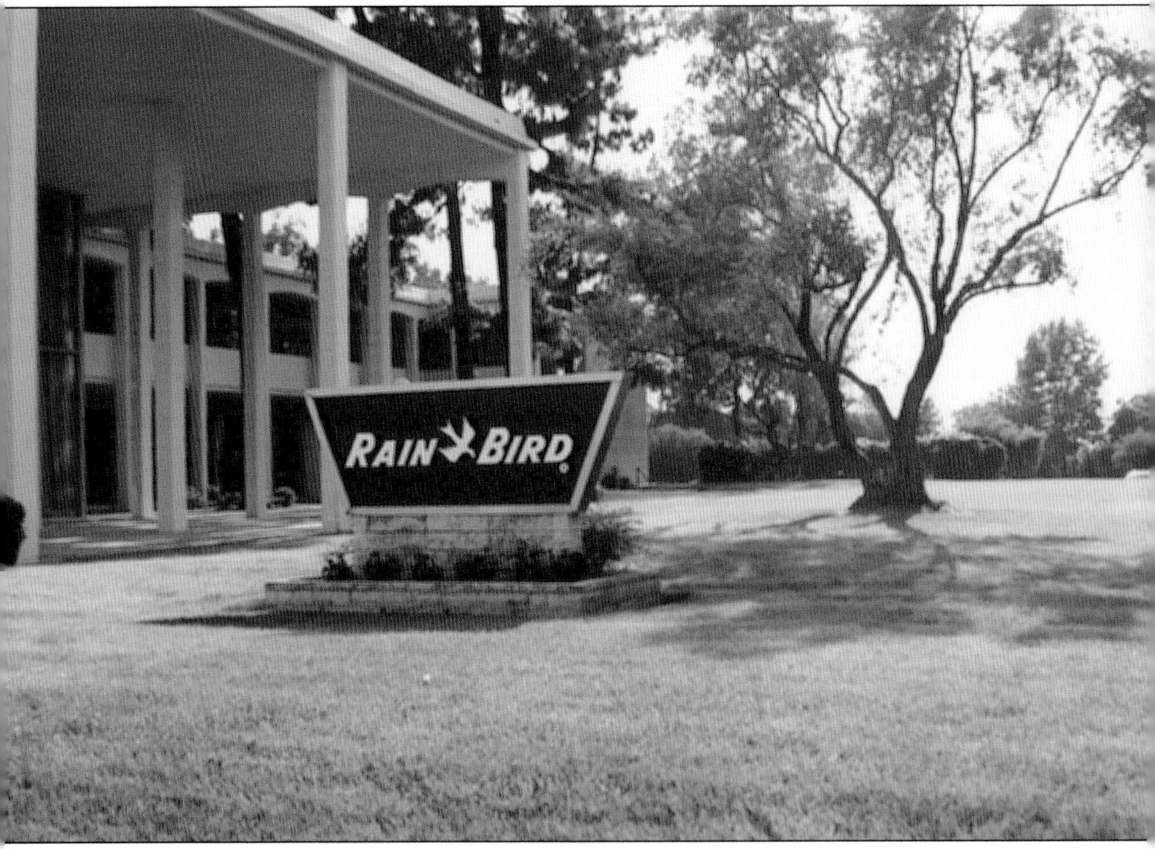

The Rain Bird Company has grown up in Glendora, and its modern office deals with a global market. (Catherine Starkey.)

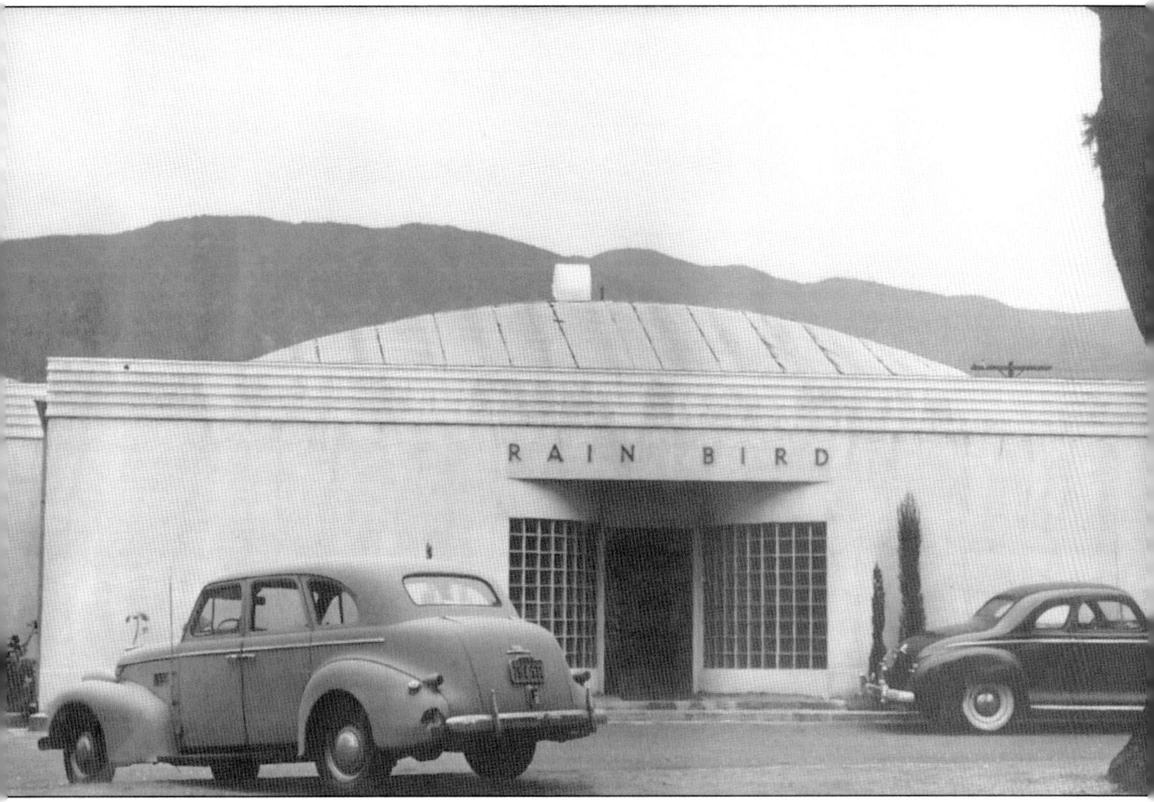

Pictured is the original Rain Bird Plant Building on Foothill Blvd. (J. Landers.)

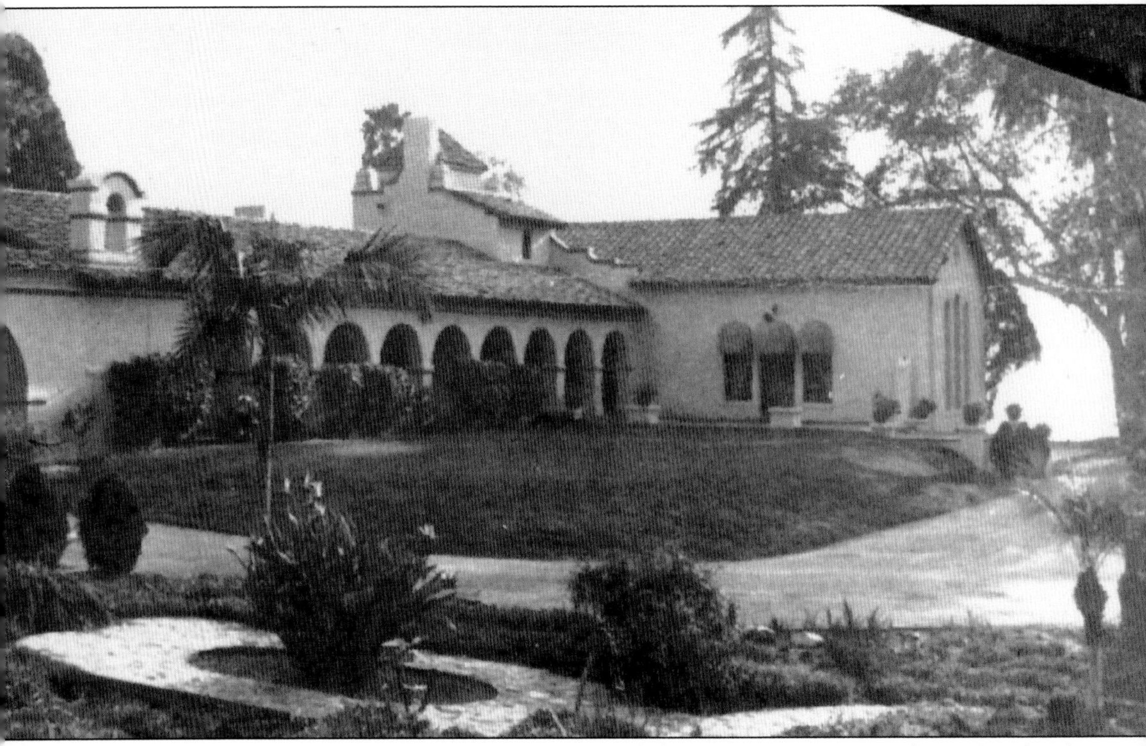

Pictured here is the Singer Mansion. Members of the Singer Sewing Machine Co. family bought this mansion in the early part of the 1900s. (Catherine Starkey.)

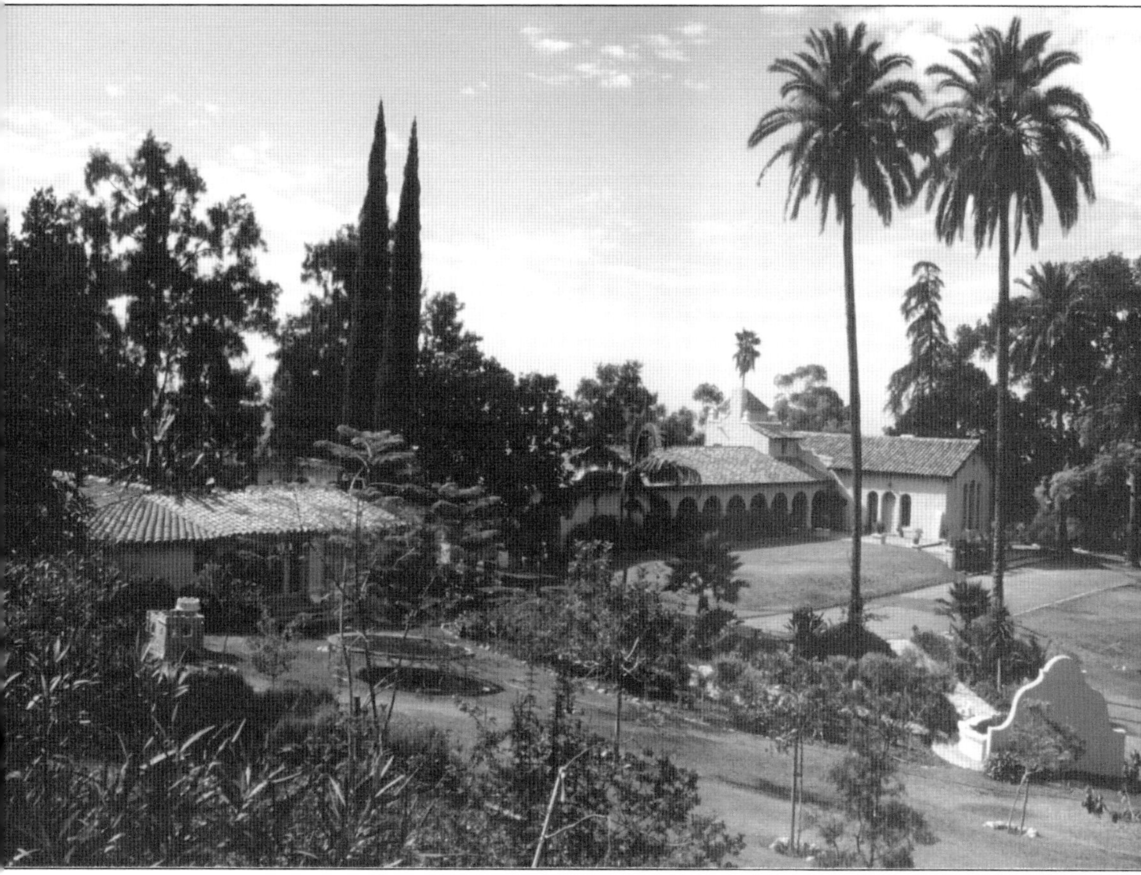

Here is the Singer Mansion as it appears today. (Catherine Starkey.)

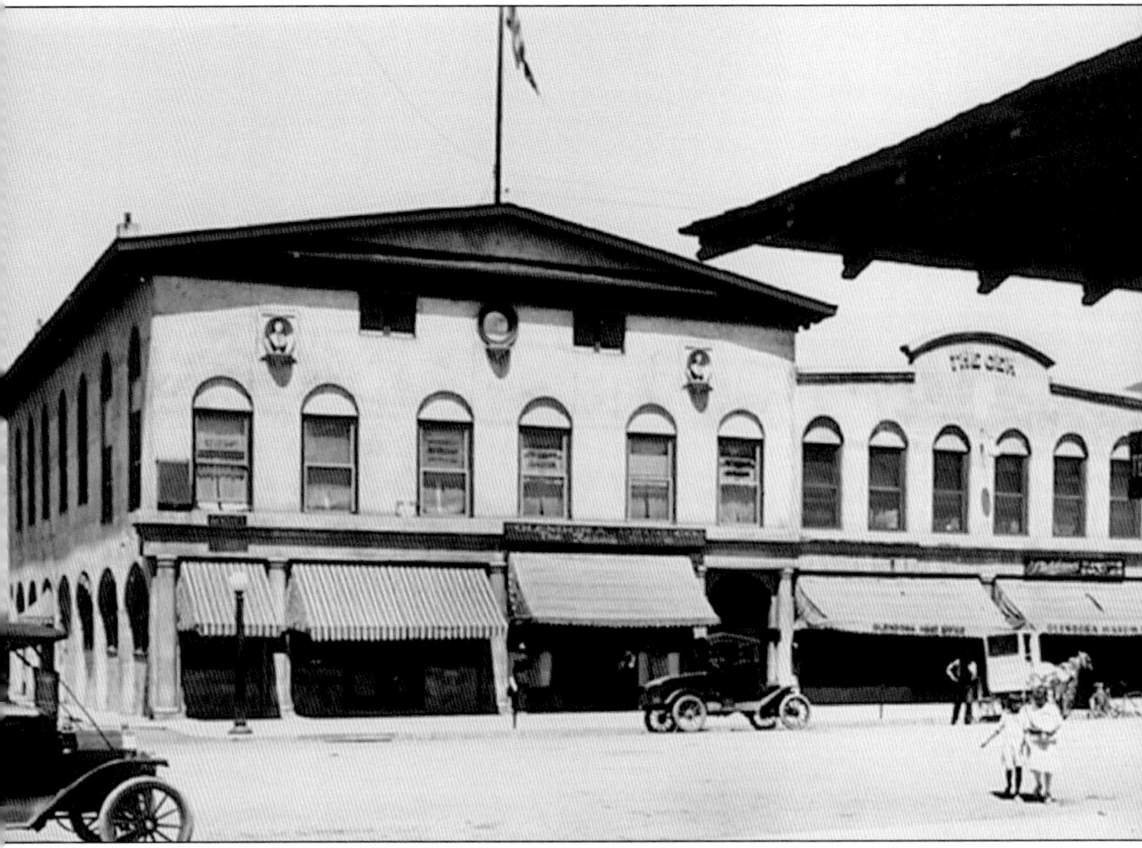

The Opera House and the Gem buildings are pictured here as they appeared in 1920. (Glendora Historical Society.)

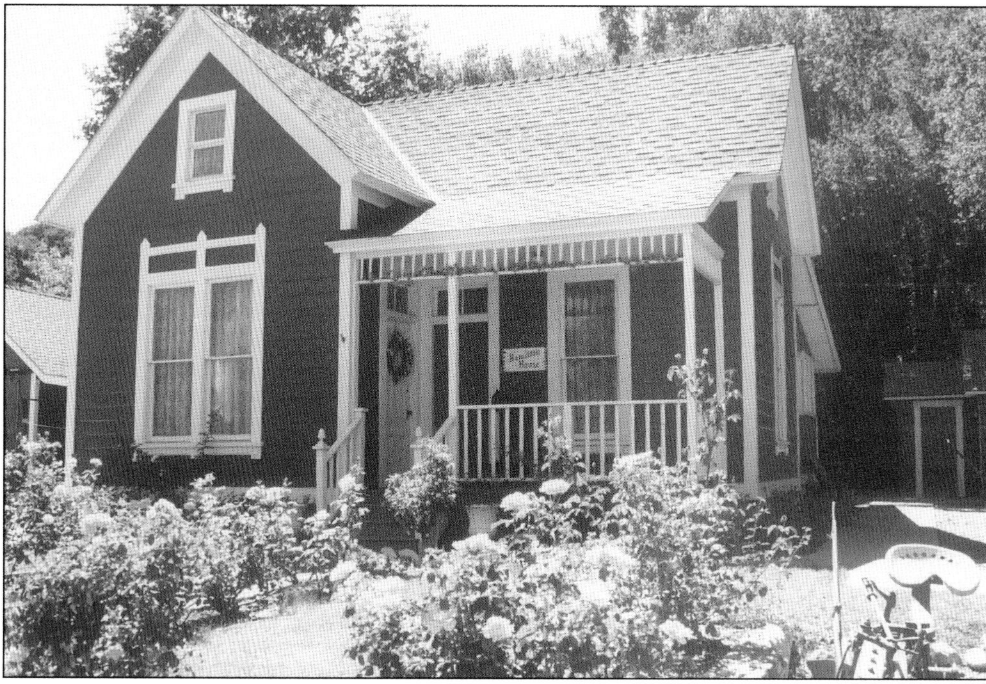

Hamilton House was the first land office in Glendora. It is now at the Centennial Heritage Park. School field-trips allow children and adults to visit and learn about Glendora's citrus history. (J. Landers.)

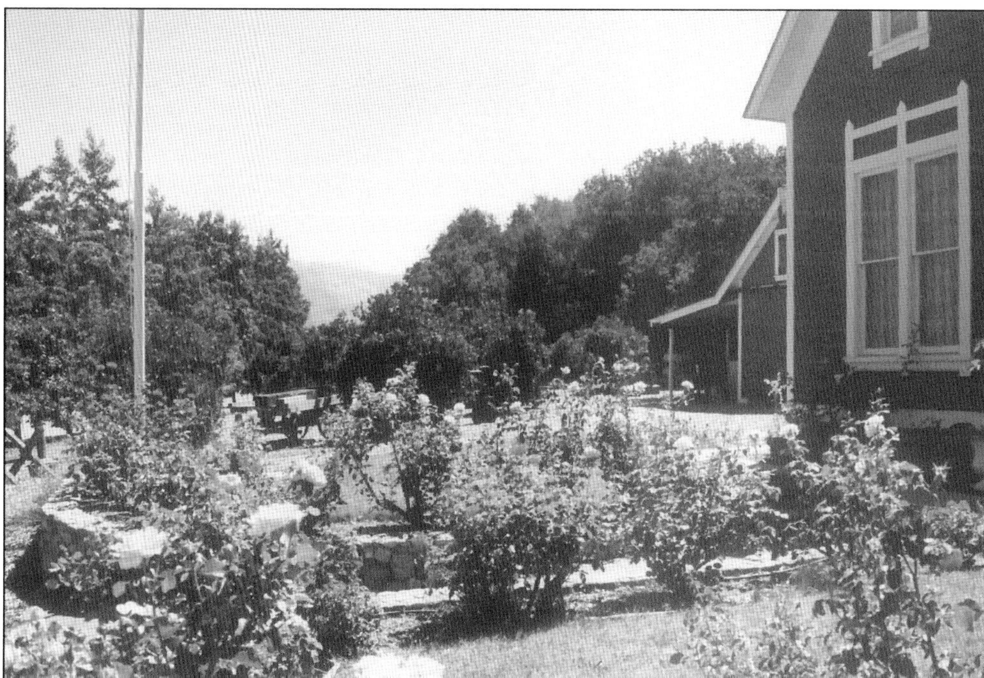

Pictured is the Hamilton House with a rose garden leading out into the last remaining orchard in the area. (J. Landers.)

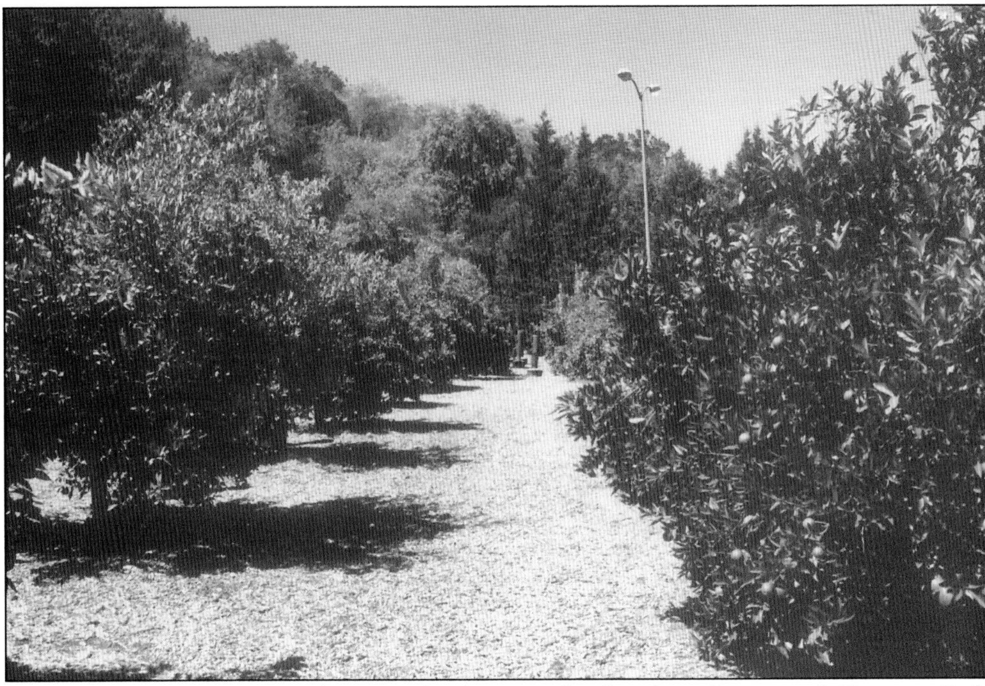

The only large citrus grove left in Glendora can be found at Centennial Heritage Park. Schoolchildren can walk along the orchards and visit the educational center to learn how the citrus industry was a dominant part of Glendora's past. (J. Landers.)

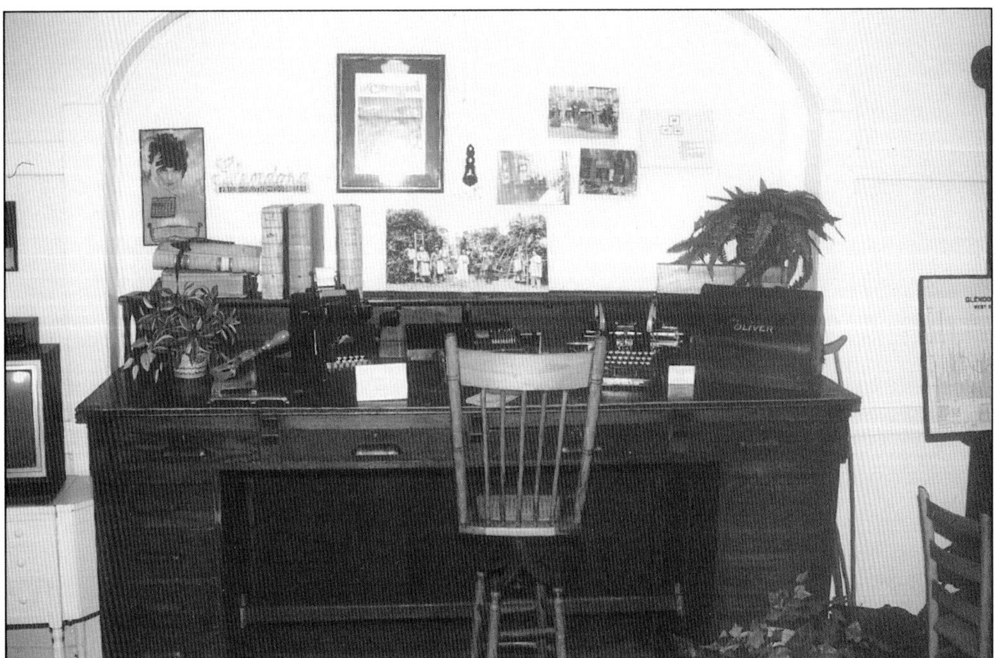

The original land office desk is in the Glendora Historical Museum as a reminder to the young that not all business was done on a computer. (J. Landers.)

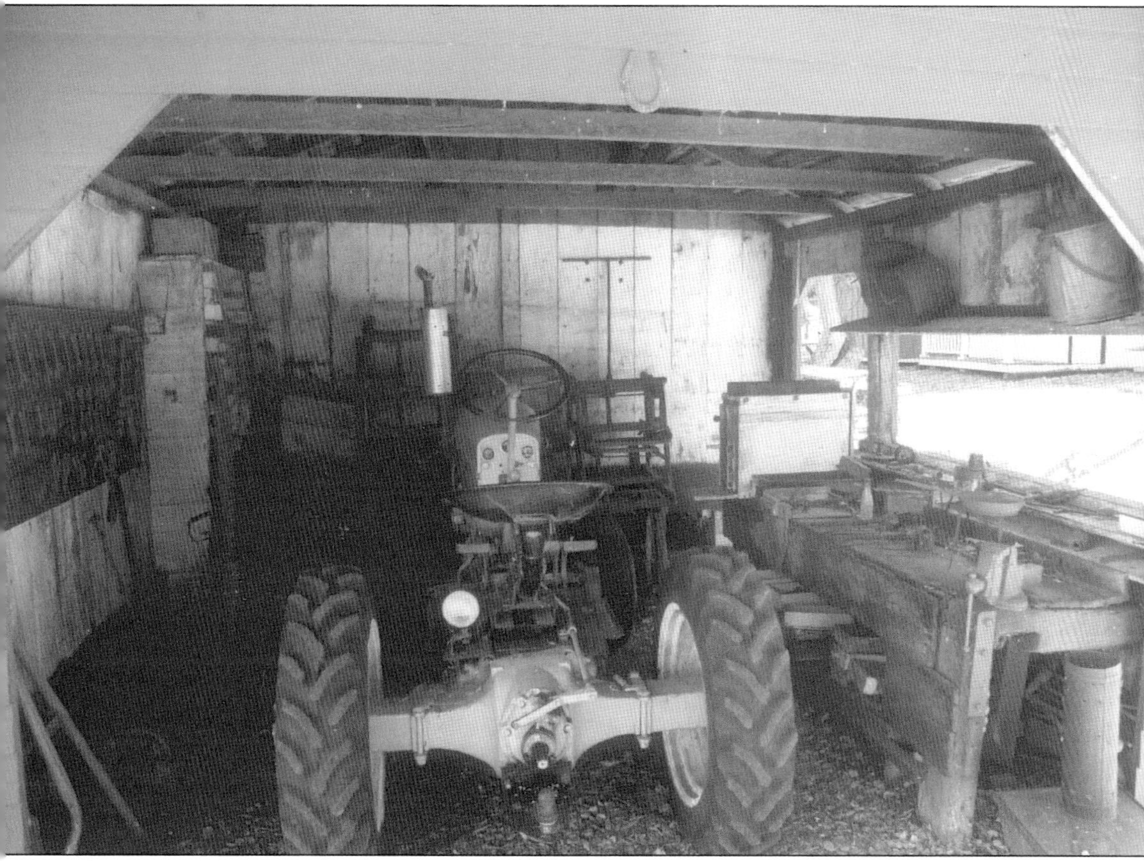

The original barn of Clement and Mary LaFetra in which Orton Englehart invented the impact drive sprinkler can also be seen at Heritage Park. On December 18, 1933, Mr. Englehart received a patent for his novel watering device, the "spring activated horizontal impact arm driven sprinkler." (J. Landers.)

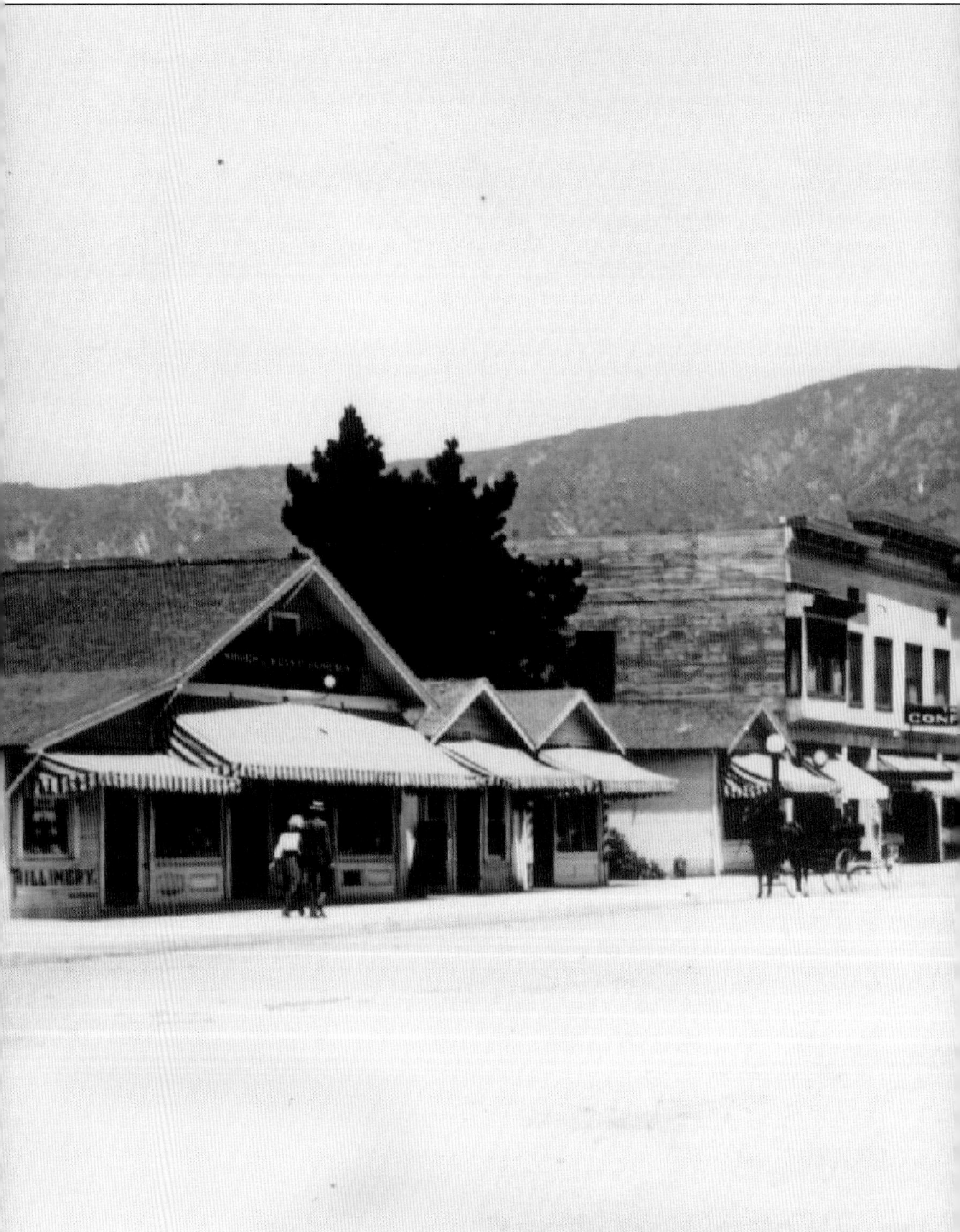

Pictured is a panoramic view of Foothill Blvd. in the early 1940s After World War II things once again began to change for Glendora. The citrus industry was declining and slowly disappearing.

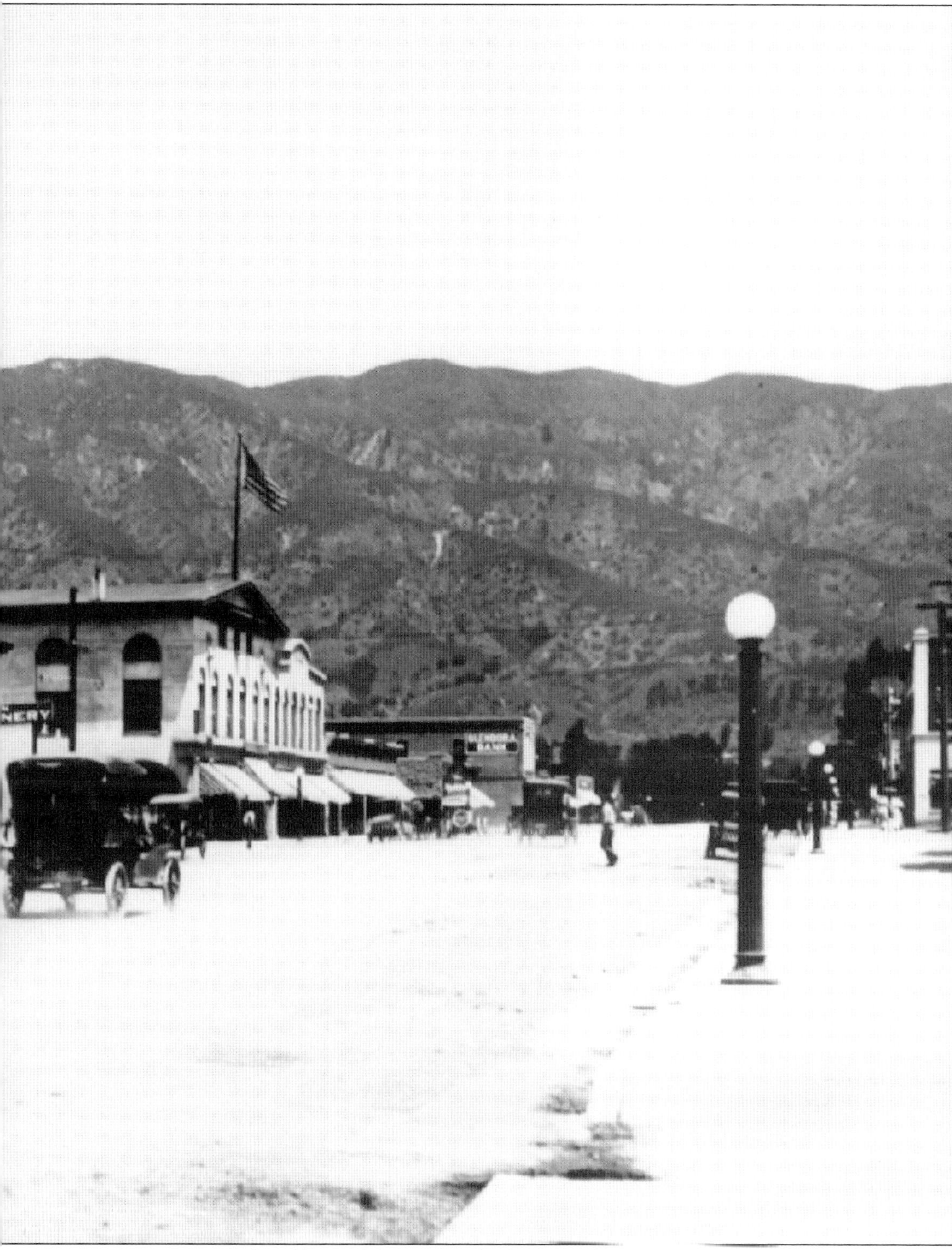

Citrus Groves were replaced by track housing and urban growth, making Glendora one of many Los Angeles suburbs. (Glendora Historical Society.)

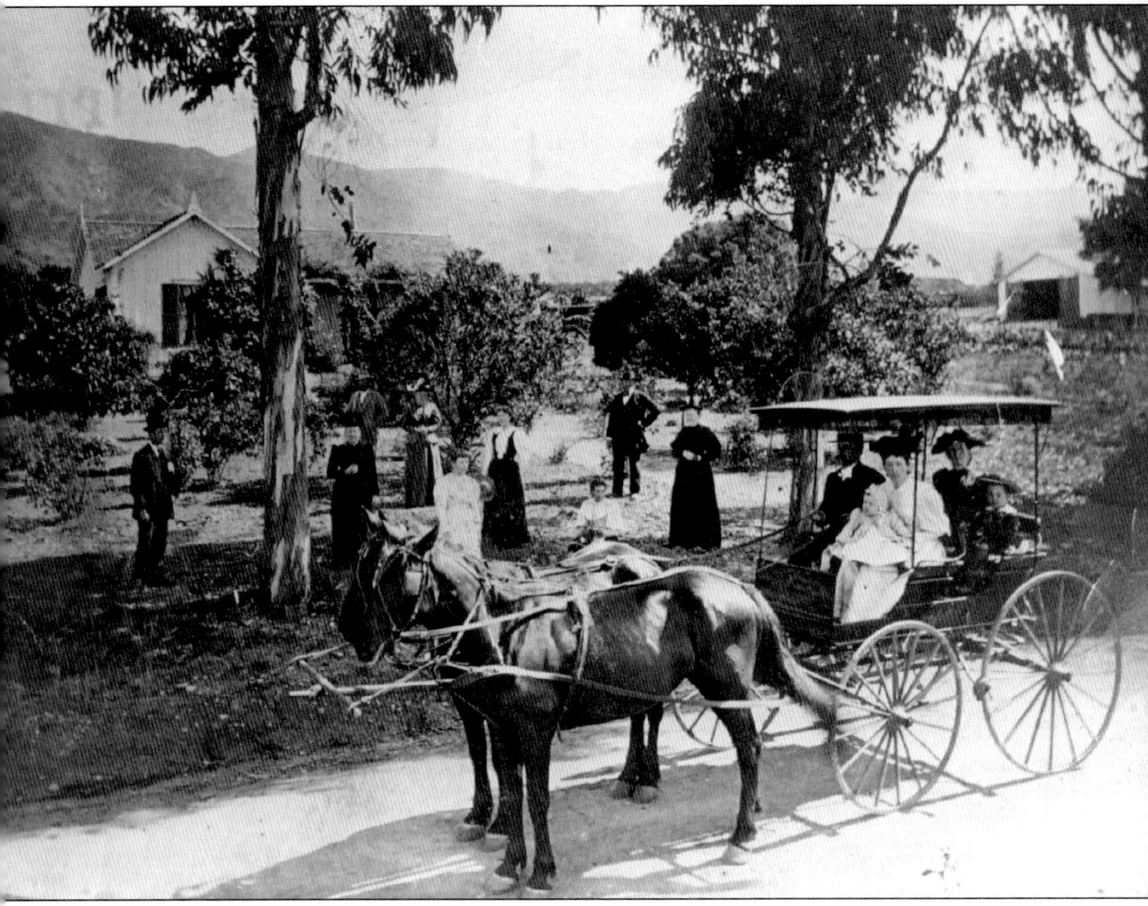

Like the early pioneers who came and settled the Azusa-Glendora area in the late 1800s the people of Glendora today have a pioneering spirit that allows them to hold on to traditional values while planning for the future.

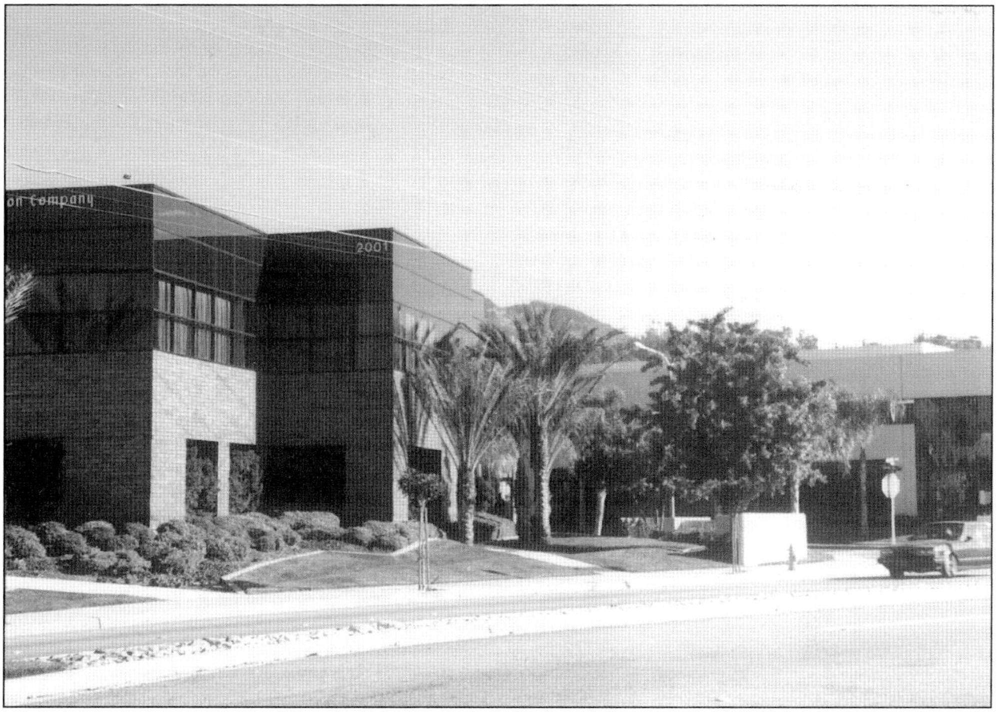

Modern high-tech companies now dot the landscape where citrus groves once stood. (J. Landers.)

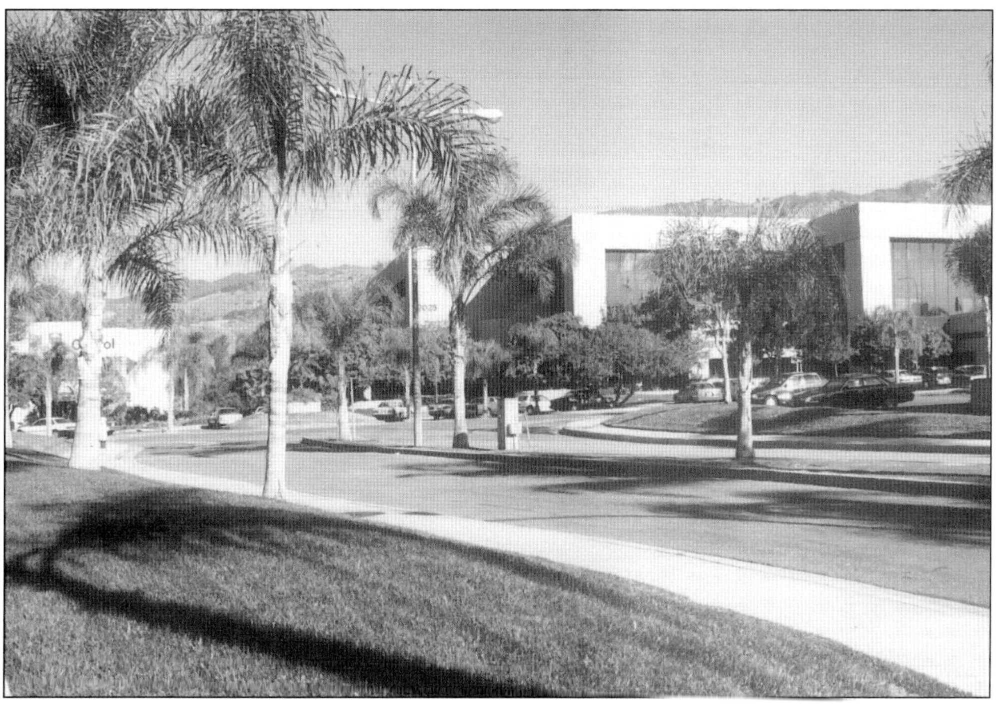
Small town doctors are gone, and in their place are modern medical buildings with state-of-the-art equipment. (Catherine Starkey.)

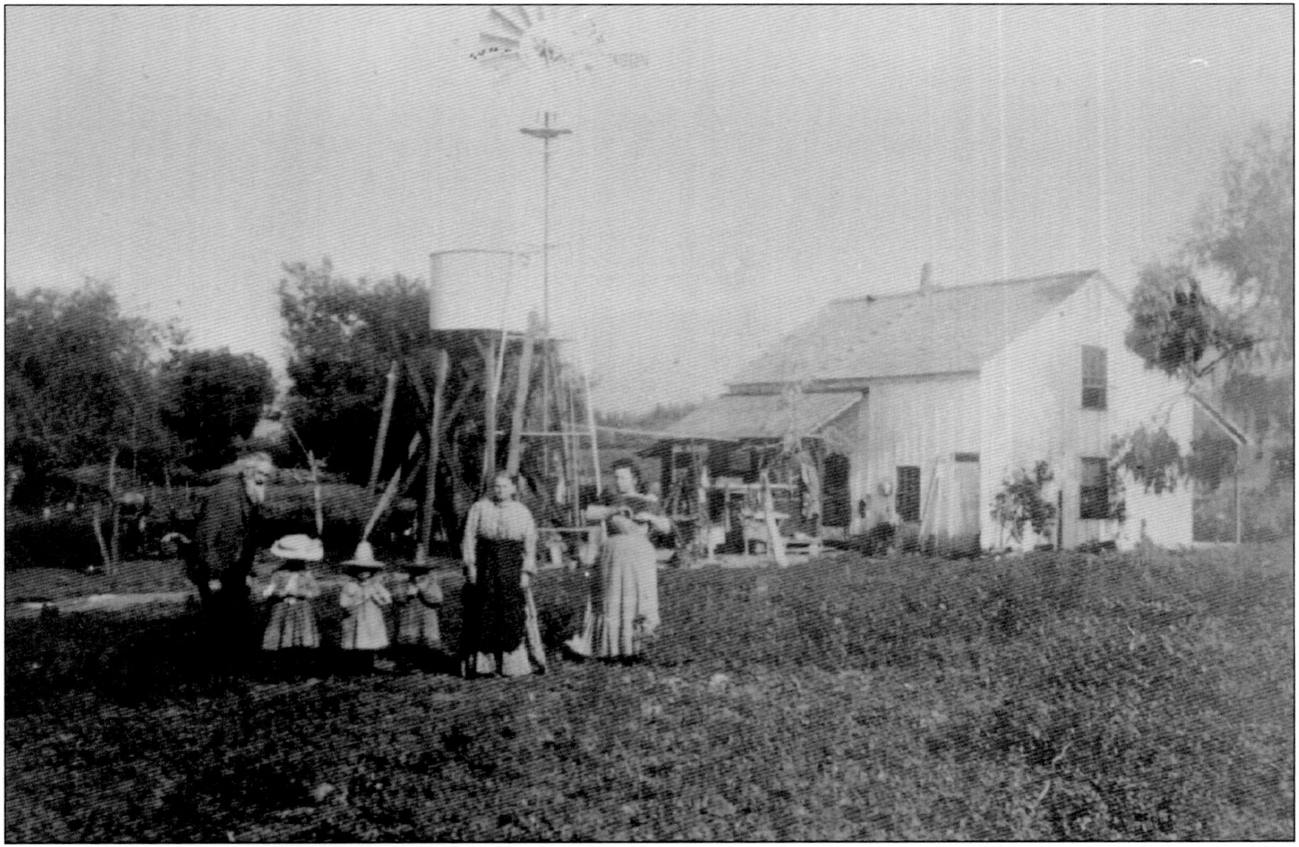

The original founders of Glendora cleared the land and built a legacy of hard work and self-determination, showing the best that the American spirit can achieve. (Glendora Historical Society.)

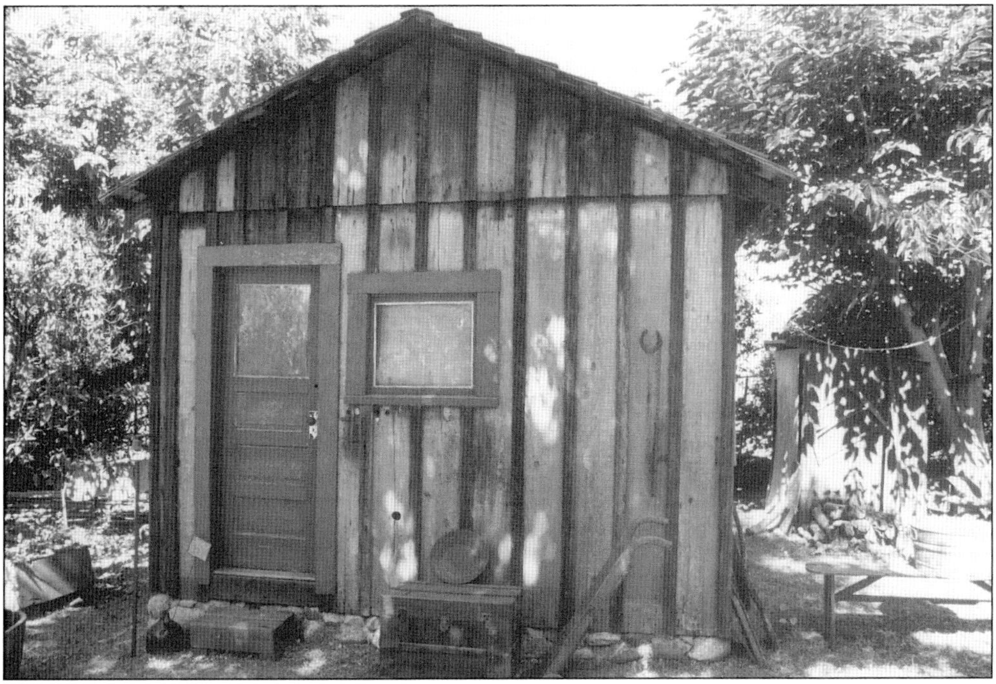

When John Bender came and settled in the Glendora area, he dreamed of building a life that would lead to prosperity. From this one-room squatter's shack he purchased, he did go on to build a life that was prosperous, and he made a difference in the life of Glendora. (J. Landers.)

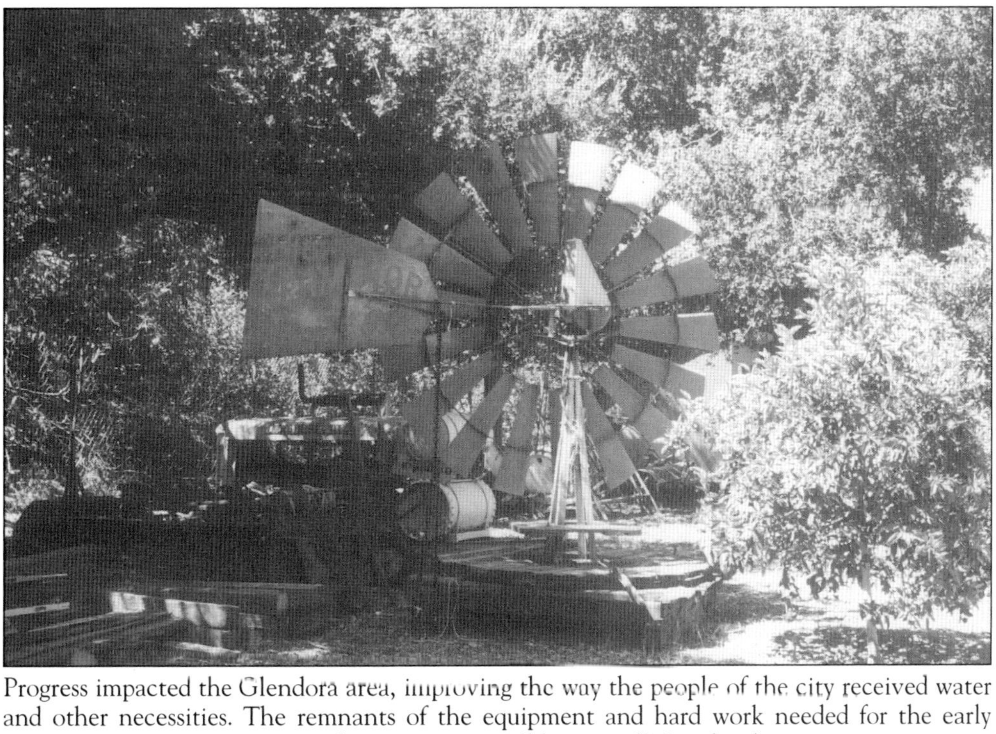

Progress impacted the Glendora area, improving the way the people of the city received water and other necessities. The remnants of the equipment and hard work needed for the early citizens to get water to irrigate their crops can still be seen. (J. Landers.)

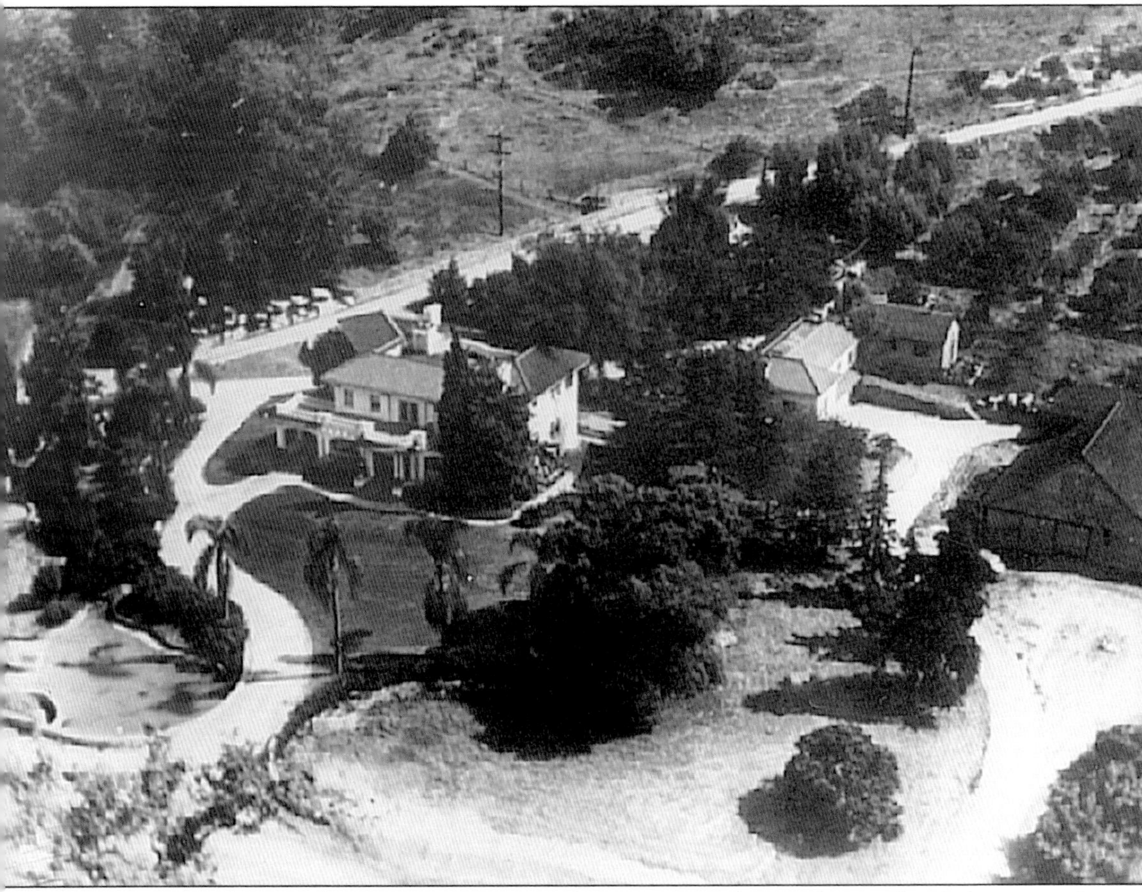

Many of the homes of prominent citizens no longer serve as homes for one family but instead have been donated or converted into buildings for public use. The Warren Estate, for example, is no longer the home of a single family but has been turned into the Glendora Country Club. (Glendora Historical Society.)

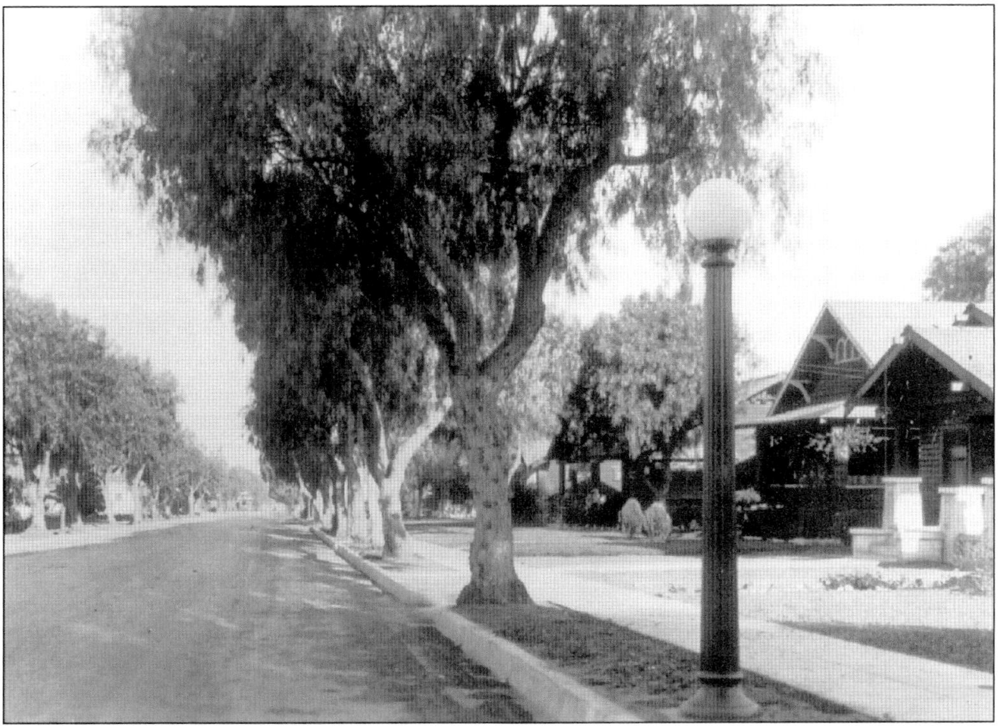

Many of the streets in Glendora have changed from this scene from 1940, but if one walks down some of the older streets, one feels as if he/she has traveled back in time to the historic beginnings of Glendora. (Glendora Historical Society.)

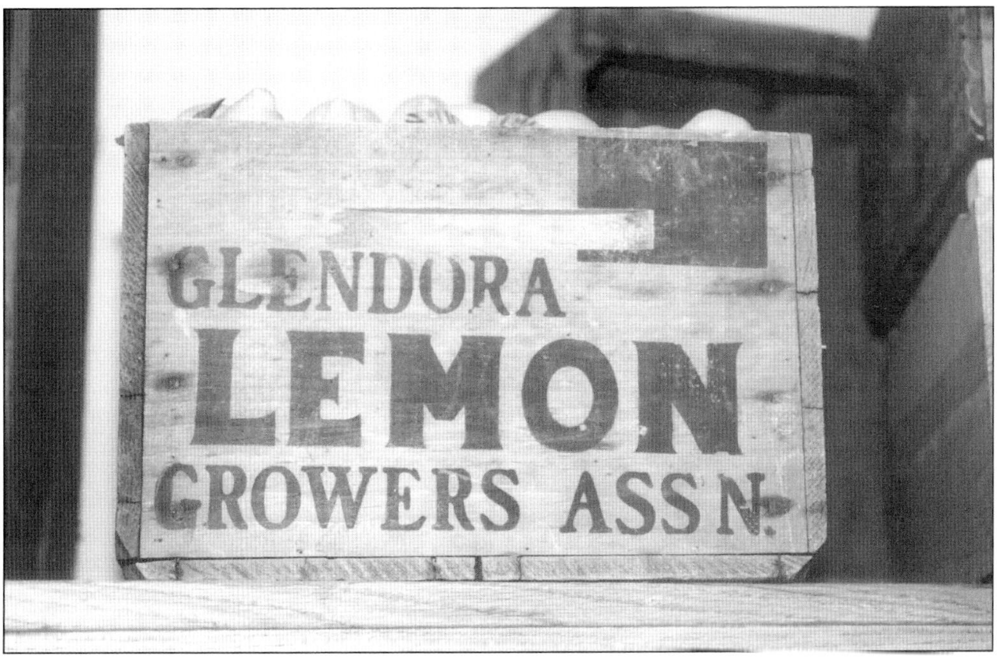

Today the only crates of citrus bearing the Glendora name are in the Glendora Historical Museum. (J. Landers.) Pictured is a citrus end-label *c.* 1940. (Huntington Museum.)

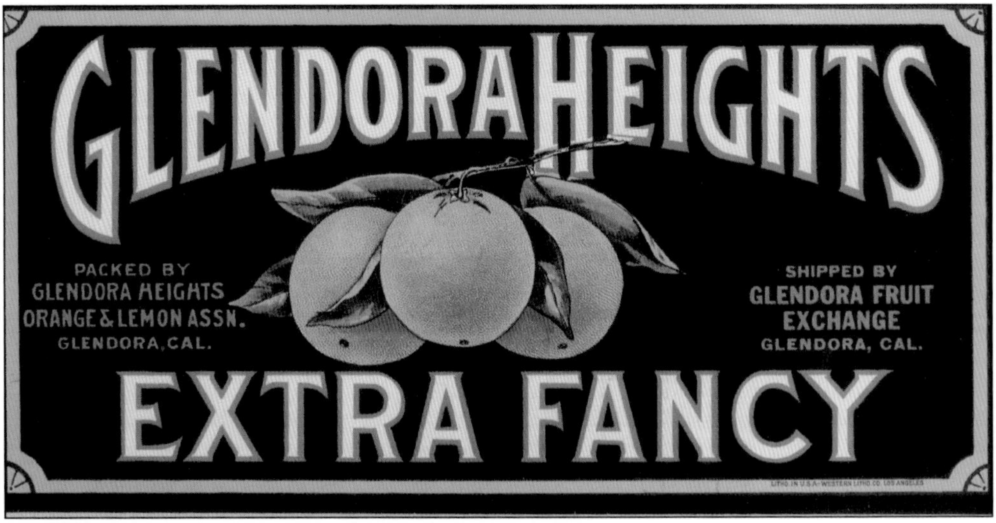

Pictured is a citrus end-label *c.* 1940. (Huntington Museum.)

BIBLIOGRAPHY

Glendora Gleaner. 1909–1940, 1911–1932.

Jackson, Sheldon. *Beautiful Glendora, Its People and History*. Azusa Pacific University Press, Azusa, CA 1982

Jackson, Sheldon. *A British Ranchero in Old California: The life and times of Henry Dalton and The Rancho Azusa*. Glendale: the Arthur H. Clark Company, 1977

Pflueger, Donald H. *Covina*. Claremont, Calif: Saunders Press, 1967